THE GOSPEL OF JOHN
AS LITERATURE

NEW TESTAMENT TOOLS
AND STUDIES

EDITED BY

BRUCE M. METZGER, Ph.D., D.D., L.H.D., D. Theol., D. Litt.
Professor of New Testament Language and Literature, Emeritus
Princeton Theological Seminary
and
Corresponding Fellow of the British Academy

AND

BART D. EHRMAN, Ph.D.
Assistant Professor, Department of Religious Studies
University of North Carolina at Chapel Hill

VOLUME XVII

THE GOSPEL OF JOHN
AS LITERATURE

An Anthology of Twentieth-Century Perspectives

SELECTED AND INTRODUCED BY

MARK W.G. STIBBE

E.J. BRILL

LEIDEN · NEW YORK · KÖLN

1993

The paper in this book meets the guidelines for permanence and durability of the Committee on Production Guidelines for Book Longevity of the Council on Library Resources.

Library of Congress Cataloging-in-Publication Data

BS
2615.2
.G65
1993

The Gospel of John as literature : an anthology of twentieth-century perspectives / selected and introduced by Mark W.G. Stibbe.
    p.   cm. — (New Testament tools and studies, ISSN 0077-8842 ; v. 17)
    Includes bibliographical references.
    Contents: Is the fourth gospel a drama? / F.R.M. Hitchcock — John's narrative style / H. Windisch — Literary form in the fourth gospel / J. Muilenburg — The structure of the fourth gospel / D. Deeks — Theology and irony in the fourth gospel / G. MacRae — John 9, a literary-critical analysis / J. Resseguie — Women in the fourth gospel / S.M. Schneiders — It is written / J.D. Crossan — The wooing of the woman at the well / L. Eslinger — John 4:16a / J.E. Botha — John 5:1-18 / R. Alan Culpepper — The birth of a beginning / W. Kelber — The elusive Christ / M.W.G. Stibbe.
    ISBN 9004098488 (alk. paper)
    1. Bible. N.T. John—Criticism, interpretation, etc. 2. Bible as literature. I. Stibbe, Mark W.G. II. Series.
BS2615.2.G65   1993
226.5'066—dc20
                                                            93-24705
                                                            CIP

Die Deutsche Bibliothek - CIP-Einheitsaufnahme

The gospel of John as literature : an anthology of twentieth-century perspectives / selected and introd. by Mark W.G. Stibbe. – Leiden ; New York ; Köln : Brill, 1993
    (New Testament tools and studies ; Vol. 17)
    ISBN 90–04–09848–8
NE: Stibbe, Mark W.G. [Hrsg.]; GT

ISSN   0077-8842
ISBN   90 04 09848 8 (bound)
ISBN   90 04 09932 8 (paperback)

CONTENTS

PREFACE

In preparing this collection of essays for publication, some editorial work has been necessary in order to create a uniform style throughout the book. Where essays originally had endnotes we have placed them at the foot of each page. Where essays originally had bibliographies, we have maintained them. These have not been incorporated into the main bibliography because the latter is restricted to works which examine the Gospel of John as literature. Many of the works in the bibliographies at the end of the essays, however, are non-literary in character.

The Gospel of John as Literature is the third book that I have put together on John's Gospel. The first was published in 1992, under the title *John as Storyteller: Narrative Criticism and the Fourth Gospel* (Cambridge). The second has just been published under the title, *John: A Readings Commentary* (1993, Sheffield).

I regard these works in a sense as a trilogy. All three share the same aim which is to highlight the aesthetic qualities of the Fourth Gospel. In fulfilling this aim, *John as Storyteller* provided the hermeneutical foundations, *John: A Readings Commentary* provided the exegesis, while *The Gospel of John as Literature* provides the historical, interpretative background. My prayer is that these works will help people to rediscover a passion for the Gospel of Eternal Life.

"I have come that you may have life, and life in all its fulness."

ACKNOWLEDGEMENTS

I would like to thank those who have helped this book to come into being. I am grateful to David Orton, senior editor of E.J. Brill, for accepting the proposal for this volume, and for being so supportive in its preparation and production. I also want to thank Professor Bruce Metzger, editor of the New Testament Tools and Studies series, for his enthusiastic support for this volume, and for accepting it into his series.

I want to thank Linda Russell-Ward for typing the many letters that were sent asking for permission to reproduce the chapters of this book.

Thanks is due to the following for permission to use previously published material: The Society of Biblical Literature for J. Muilenburg's "Literary Form in the Fourth Gospel" (*Journal of Biblical Literature* 51, 1932);

Cambridge University Press for D. Deeks' "The Structure of the Fourth Gospel" (*New Testament Studies* 15, 1968);

Richard J. Clifford of Weston School of Theology for George MacRae's "Theology and Irony in the Fourth Gospel" (the Weston Press no longer exists);

Abingdon Press for J.L. Resseguie's "John 9: A Literary-Critical Analysis" (*Literary Interpretations of Biblical Narratives*, ed. K. Gros Louis, Volume II). Copyright ©1982 Abingdon Press;

Biblical Theological Bulletin for Sandra Schneiders' "Women in the Fourth Gospel" (*BTB* 12, 1982);

John Dominic Crossan and *Semeia* for "It is Written: A Structuralist Analysis of John 6" (*Semeia* 26, 1983);

Oxford University Press for Lyle Eslinger's "The Wooing of the Woman at the Well" (*Literature and Theology,* Volume 1 Number 2, pp. 167-183). Copyright © Oxford University Press, 1987;

Jean-Daniel Kaestli for R. Alan Culpepper's "John 5.1-18: A Sample of Narrative-Critical Commentary", a translation of "Un exemple de commentaire fondé sur la critique narrative: Jean 5,1-18", in *La communauté johannique et son histoire,* ed. J.-D. Kaestli, J.M. Poffet & J. Zumstein, Geneva, Labor et Fides, 1990, pp. 135-151;

Bruce Lategan of *Scriptura* for J.E. Botha's article, "John 4.16: A Difficult Text Speech Act Theoretically Revisited" (*Scriptura* 35, 1990);

W. Kelber and *Semeia* for Kelber's article, "The Birth of a Beginning: John 1.1-18" (*Semeia* 52, 1990);

and finally *Journal for the Study of the New Testament* (Vol. 44, 1991) for my article, "The Elusive Christ: A New Reading of the Fourth Gospel".

I am extremely grateful to all of the above for their kind cooperation. I am also grateful to David Orton for translating the article by Hans Windisch (from the German).

Last, and most importantly, I want to thank Chris Lee, a former undergraduate in Biblical Studies here at Sheffield University, a member of my church at St.Thomas', and a friend. Chris transferred all the articles onto Apple Mac™ computer both swiftly and efficiently. There is no way that this book would ever have come about without him. I want therefore to thank him most sincerely.

Mark Stibbe

St. Thomas' Church, Crookes, Sheffield. December 1992.

INTRODUCTION

1. THE CONCEPTION OF THIS VOLUME

The writer of Ecclesiastes once remarked, "What has been will be again, what has been done will be done again; there is nothing new under the sun" (Ecc 1.9). If this wise and melancholy writer had been a Johannine scholar today, he might have rephrased this warning as follows: "What has been in Fourth Gospel research will be again; what has been done by scholars will be done again. There is really nothing new under the sun". Indeed, he might have gone on to warn all publishers of Johannine scholarship that "Of the making of many books there is no end. So watch what you publish!"

So why produce an anthology of selected twentieth-century perspectives on the literary qualities of the Fourth Gospel?

I have two principal aims. The first is to give contemporary scholars an account of the history of literary interpretation of John's gospel. Most contemporary scholars who are interested in John's aesthetic qualities betray what Gadamer has called "a loss of historical consciousness". They may have corrected his other lament, "the loss of an aesthetic consciousness", but they have not corrected the former.

There is a twofold sense in which current literary critics of John have lost their "historical consciousness".

First of all, and most obviously, they have rejected historical criticism. Nearly all the books which study the final form of John's Gospel begin with at least some brief and iconoclastic rejection of former, more historical methods, such as source and redaction criticism. Indeed, this kind of comment has become something of a cliché in John studies.

Secondly, nearly all the scholars working in this field are guilty of a covert modernism—the philosophy which says that only the modern is valuable, that only the contemporary is innovative. Even in Alan Culpepper's excellent book, *Anatomy of the Fourth Gospel. A Study in Literary Design* (1983), the author fails to provide any historical survey of previous studies of John's literary design. There are no references to the forefathers of Johannine literary interpretation in the nineteenth and twentieth centuries. Even the bibliography is devoid of the books and articles which exemplified this approach in the periods 1900-1939, and 1970-1980.

During the early 1980's, I found an old, rather dusty book which immediately exposed the fallacy of this presumption. On a shelf in an academic library I discovered a copy of F.R.M. Hitchcock's *A Fresh Study of the Fourth Gospel,* published in 1911. Hitchcock, an Anglican clergyman and Donellan lecturer, wrote this book to combat the celebrated "partition theory" which was so popular in Germany at the turn of the twentieth century. H.H. Wendt was perhaps the most famous proponent of this school of thought.[1] He argued that the Fourth Gospel is by no means an organic, literary unity but rather a theological interpretation of the notes which the Apostle John made on the discourses of Jesus. These notes—which Wendt called *die Quelle,* the Source—were greatly elaborated and set in an historical frame by a member of the Asiatic community, working in the first quarter of the second century.

The reason why Wendt's work was known as "the partition theory" was simply because he proposed dual authorship of the Fourth Gospel. On one side of the partition are the discourses of Jesus, which were taken down in note form by the Apostle John. On the other side (the later part) are the narrative portions which Wendt attributes to the second century writer. He saw the discourses as historical, and most of the narratives (the settings for the discourses) as fictional.

Hitchcock praises Wendt's scholarship, not least because (unlike many theories) it provides such a positive perspective on the historical value of the discourse material. However, it quickly becomes clear that Hitchcock is also opposed to the partition theory. Indeed, in the gathering storm before the first world war, Hitchcock rather undiplomatically describes these prophets of the theory as his "opponents".[2] He refers to them as "the Germans"[3] and criticises their source-critical tendencies and their rationalistic, sceptical hermeneutic on questions related to the supernatural (i.e. the divinity of Jesus and his miracles).

Hitchcock proposes a different approach. Instead of stratifying the gospel into early sources and late redaction, Hitchcock argues for a literary interpretation. He writes,

> A different method of study would be to approach these documents without any presuppositions whatever, and to apply to them the same historical and literary canons of exegesis which would be employed in the case of classical literature. This method would be fairer to the

---

[1] Chapter three of Hitchock's *Fresh Study* engages with Wendt's partition theory (in *Das Johannesevangelium:* Eng. trans., *St. John,* ET, Edinburgh, 1902).
[2] Hitchcock, ibid., p. 74.
[3] Ibid., p. 74.

writers and their work, and would not be hampered by having to find
facts to support given hypotheses.[1]

Hitchcock's aim is therefore to start from the organic unity and the
literary integrity of the Fourth Gospel. He sets his sights to focus upon
"the structure of the Gospel", on "the internal evidences of mind and art",
"the consistency of character drawing" (what we would now call
'characterisation') and "the dramatic development of the narrative".[2] Thus
Hitchcock's fourth chapter is entitled, "The Organic Unity of the Gospel",
the fifth "The Character Drawing of the Gospel", the sixth "The Dramatic
development of the Gospel", and his seventh "The Artistic Structure of
the Gospel". Throughout these chapters, Hitchcock makes various
judgements on the literary qualities of the Fourth Gospel:

> Consistent character drawing is an aesthetic mark of the organic unity
> of the Fourth Gospel.[3]

> As in the *Oedipus Tyrannus,* the masterpiece of Attic tragedy, superb
> delineation of character is here united with the highest constructive
> skill.[4]

> No Evangelist had a keener eye for a situation or a truer sense of vivid
> narrative.[5]

> ...every word and occurrence contributes to the advance of the
> drama, at every step the tragedy grows to climax. The author had
> much of that sense of proportion and harmony which was peculiarly
> Greek.[6]

Hitchcock's *Fresh Study* is something of an eye-opener for those who
believe that the recent reactions against historical criticism, and the
concomitant rise of literary and narrative critical works on John, are
themselves 'fresh studies'. Culpepper's introduction to his *Anatomy* is a
case in point. His words immediately evoke a sense of *déjà vu*. On the
very first page Culpepper criticises redaction, historical and source critics
of John (the Germans are again the opponents), and then argues for an
approach which enables us to appreciate the literary design of the gospel.
So he begins by reviewing the approach of his forebears as follows:

> In the majority of studies the gospel has been used as a source for
> evidence of the process by which it was composed, the theology of

---

[1] Ibid., p. 74.
[2] Ibid., p. 56.
[3] Ibid., p. 86.
[4] Ibid., p. 102.
[5] Ibid., p. 116.
[6] Ibid., p. 141.

the evangelist, or the character and circumstances of the Johannine community.[1]

Culpepper qualifies this with the widely publicised remark that

The model of research is that of a "tell" in which archeologists can unearth strata which derive from different historical periods.[2]

What Culpepper proposes in its place is a method which aims

to contribute to understanding the gospel as a narrative text, what it is and how it works. The emphasis will be upon analysis and interpretation rather than upon the construction of hypotheses or critique of methods. The gospel as it stands rather than its sources, historical background, or themes is the subject of this study.[3]

The last thing I want to be is too critical of Alan Culpepper. He has done more than anyone to help both the church and the academy to appreciate the literary aspects of the Fourth Gospel. I, for one, honour him and I honour his work. However, I draw attention to this *lacuna* in *Anatomy*—that is, the lack of any history of literary interpretation— simply to highlight a trend in contemporary studies of the Fourth Gospel. This trend is the widespread assumption that the literary appreciation of John is a new phenomenon, which it patently is not. For example, Culpepper's introduction to *Anatomy* in 1983 sounds very similar to the kinds of statement being made by Hitchcock in 1911, in that context against the partition theory of Wendt. In one sense, therefore, it feels as though "there is nothing new under the sun".

In what sense is the *Anatomy* new then? On the one hand Culpepper's book is not new insofar as it resurrects the literary approaches to John which, we shall see, were produced in England, Germany and America in the first 40 years of the twentieth century. On the other hand Culpepper's book *was* new, insofar as it applied to John certain literary methodologies which have grown up in the period after 1945. Principal amongst these were the New criticism, reader reception theory (especially that of Iser), and narratology (especially that of Gerard Genette). The use of these on John was, in fact, completely new, and the resultant method—which we may call 'narrative criticism'—enabled readers for the first time to understand John's use of time, plot, point of view, characterisation and so forth.

This brings me to a second major aim for this present volume: if the first is to provide a sense of the historical development of Johannine

---

[1] R.A. Culpepper, *Anatomy*, p. 3.
[2] Ibid., p. 3.
[3] Ibid., p. 5.

literary appreciation, the second is to give at least a rudimentary account of the plurality of such approaches since Culpepper's book. Culpepper's *Anatomy*, as I have indicated, was a subtle, eclectic blend of methodologies forged in post-War literature faculties. I have called it 'narrative criticism'. But since that time other approaches have been tried, with varying degrees of success. In this volume alone I have included structuralist, literary-critical, feminist, reader-response, speech-act and deconstructionist versions of the literary, synchronic paradigm. This, I hope, will put the reader in touch with both a sense of the historical development of Johannine literary appreciation, as well as the current plethora of readings on offer. In this sense I hope the present volume will be regarded as a valuable New Testament tool and study.

2. THE CRITERIA FOR THIS VOLUME

In a volume which attempts to survey works which help us to look at 'The Gospel of John as Literature' it is important to be clear about what criteria have been used in the selection of the essays included here.

The first criteria have been hermeneutical ones. Put simply, I chose only those essays which employed a literary hermeneutic. So how do we spot a literary interpretation of the Fourth Gospel? One of the easiest ways is by looking for works in which John has been treated with those interpretative strategies associated with the study of secular literature. Thus, Hitchcock's work immediately qualifies because the author overtly declares that his aim is to treat John as if it were classical literature. Indeed, his approach applauds the fourth evangelist for creating a gospel which has many of the highest stylistic qualities derived from Attic tragedy. Other essays also immediately qualify. Crossan's piece uses the method of structuralism, Schneiders' uses feminist literary interpretation, Eslinger's uses reader-response criticism, Kelber's uses deconstructionism. All of these methods are primarily associated with the study of secular literature. Like Hitchcock's essay, these studies all qualified on hermeneutical grounds.

Titles have been another clue concerning the literary nature of the essays. Muilenburg's essay is about "Literary Form in the Fourth Gospel". By "literary" Muilenburg means "aesthetic". By "form" he means "design" or "unity". This straight away marks it out as a 'literary approach' because literary appreciation focuses on the artistic qualities of the final form of a text. Resseguie's essay is similarly straightforward. His study on John 9 is a "literary-critical analysis". It exposes the structure, irony and characterisation visible on the surface of the whole narrative. George MacRae's article qualifies for the same reason. He too is interested in structure and irony, with the added bonus of comparing John's passion narrative with Greek tragedy—in this instance, the *Bacchae* of Euripides. Deeks' essay also celebrates the structure of the gospel.

This just leaves my own contribution, which is a self-conscious application of the narrative and historical methodology worked out in my book *John as Storyteller*[1], and J.E. Botha's essay, which employs a method derived from the study of speech acts. Since it is Botha's aim to look at the literary characteristics of the speech acts of characters within John's narrative world, as well as the characteristics of the dialogue between the narrator and the various readers of the gospel, his essay obviously demands attention. His methodology betrays an indebtedness to narrative and reader-response criticism, both of which emerge from the study of narrative literature.

If the first criteria for selection were hermeneutical ones, the second were historical ones. I not only wanted to choose essays which represented certain forms of literary interpretation, I also wanted to include pieces which gave a sense of historical evolution. Thus it was very important to have Hitchcock's work, not only because its qualities merit its inclusion, but also because it highlights the fact that Johannine literary interpretation was being practised 70 years before Culpepper's *Anatomy*, and indeed outside of North America. The same goes for Windisch's essay, written in the same year (1923). This piece undermines the position of anyone who chooses to accuse all twentieth-century German scholars of a lack of literary sensitivity. Both Hitchcock's and Windisch's essays, along with Muilenburg's, reveal that there were some very insightful, early twentieth-century attempts to examine the Gospel of John as Literature. All three essays function as indisputable counter-evidence to the contemporary modernist trends which I deplored at the beginning of this introduction. In this respect they had to be included.

However, it is also true that these essays are the exception rather than the rule in Johannine scholarship between 1900 and 1939. During this period of time, methodologies which we now recognise as source and form criticism were beginning to emerge and these were not so obviously compatible with literary approaches. Rudolf Bultmann's magisterial commentary was published in 1941. This work systematically rearranged most of the gospel on the grounds that an original, comprehensible order had been deconstructed by various later redactions. This kind of source criticism subsequently influenced Johannine scholarship in a way that was productive in terms of tradition historical considerations, but at the same time destructive in terms of aesthetic appreciation. How could scholars

---

[1] See, in particular, *John as Storyteller,* pp. 9-13, 67-92.

appreciate the artistry of a gospel whose final form had been so violently dislocated? How could those who were concerned with what lies *before* our eyes, function openly in a context where what now mattered was what lies *behind* the text?

Source criticism of the Fourth Gospel therefore produced a drought of Johannine literary appreciation after 1945. If the reader cares to consult the bibliography it is immediately obvious how little was published on the literary dynamics of John's gospel between 1945 and 1970. Indeed, it was not until 1970 that a *book* appeared which dared to challenge this diachronic tide in Fourth Gospel research. The book in question was David Wead's *Literary Devices in the Fourth Gospel*. This revised version of a dissertation in many ways swam against the current and presaged the deluge of literary studies which appeared subsequently—as a steady stream in the 1970's, a rising river in the 1980's, and a fierce flood now in the 1990's. In this light we can see how articles such as the one by David Deeks stand out between 1945 and 1970.

So hermeneutical and historical criteria have been employed. I also, in passing, have to confess to some entirely personal criteria. The fact is I have included these essays because I have enjoyed them. They are not only important for what they represent; they are important for what they give us—a pleasurable and indeed valuable glimpse into the multivalent delights of John's narrative art. I hope the reader will gain similar pleasure from these texts.

3. THE CONTENTS OF THIS VOLUME

A few brief comments are called for on each of the pieces included in *The Gospel of John as Literature*.

The first essay, by Hitchcock, was written in 1923. However, Hitchcock had already written on the same subject in an article in 1907 and in his 1911 book, *A Fresh Study*. His name must therefore come first in the volume even though Windisch's essay came out in the same year as Hitchcock's (1923).

The importance of Hitchcock's approach to the Fourth Gospel should not be underestimated. It set in motion a number of works devoted to the appreciation of John as drama. Lord Charnwood, R.H. Strachan, C. Bowen and Windisch himself were clearly influenced by Hitchcock in the twenty years after *A Fresh Study*. Indeed, there has been a continuous flow of works devoted to the dramatic character of the Fourth Gospel since the early years of this century: Connick (1948), Lee (1953), Pierce (1960), Martyn (1968), Smalley (1978), Flanagan (1981), Domeris (1983), Ehrman (1983), Stibbe (1992) and others have all attempted to expose John's dramatic qualities. Most of these make valuable contributions to our literary appreciation of the Fourth Gospel.

However, a certain caution also needs to be exercised. Few of these pieces distinguish between drama and the dramatic. Most argue that John's gospel is drama not narrative. This can hardly be sustained. John's gospel is obviously a story told by a narrator, not a spectacle to be performed by actors. Future work in this area needs to look at John as dramatic narrative rather than as narrative drama. It will also need to take into account the *purpose* of this dramatic dimension to the Fourth Gospel. Does this have something to do with the liturgical use of the narrative in the Johannine community?

The next essay, by Hans Windisch (1881-1935), is one of the most valuable pieces in this volume. It is rarely quoted and hardly ever included in bibliographies. It has certainly never before been translated into English and made available to a wider audience. And yet it is extremely significant. It was originally included in the Gunkel Festschrift published in 1923. Gunkel himself was interested in the literary form and style of the Old Testament literature. Windisch's essay represents an attempt to apply Gunkel's more aesthetic version of historical criticism to John's gospel. It also represents an early example of the Johannine literary appreciation that has recently become so popular.

What is regrettable about Windisch's essay on "John's Narrative Style" is its lack of impact on subsequent German scholarship. It was not long after this that the influence of scholars like Bultmann steered people away from Windisch's form of stylistic criticism. Even though Schweizer and Ruckstuhl argued for the stylistic unity of John,[1] it has only been in relatively recent days that German scholars have started, once again, to show an interest in the literary qualities in the final form of John's narrative. The work of H. Thyen in the 1980's should be noted in this regard. He now advocates that "The interpretation of the Gospel of John must begin...from its transmitted text".[2]

The next essay, by James Muilenburg, is a fine study of the rhetorical dynamics in the Baptist narratives in John 1. I have included it because it begins with some allusions to the debate about the literary qualities of the Fourth Gospel during the nineteenth century (Matthew Arnold et al.), it clearly follows on from Hitchcock and Windisch, and it provides a very early example of rudimentary, rhetorical criticism. Muilenburg himself made a massive contribution to the advance of rhetorical criticism in Old Testament Studies. This essay represents Muilenburg's rare foray into

---

[1] E. Schweizer, *Ego Eimi* (Göttingen: Vandenhoeck & Ruprecht 1939), and E. Ruckstuhl, *Die literarische Einheit des Johannesevangeliums* (Freiburg: Paulus 1951).
[2] H. Thyen, "Johannesbriefe", *TRE* 17, 1987, p. 211.

Fourth Gospel research and in some ways presages the advent of rhetorical approaches to John in the 1980's.

Foremost amongst the scholars who use this particular method—one designed to highlight the literary strategies with which the author attempts to persuade the reader—have been George Kennedy (1984) and Wilhelm Wuellner (1991). This methodology has an obvious application in John's gospel, whose author has so self-consciously employed the "art of persuasion" in order to convince the reader of his Christology (Jn 20.31). There is consequently a bright future for rhetorical criticism in our field. Indeed, in my Readings commentary I have described much of the discourse material in Jn 5-10 as "judicial rhetoric".[1]

The next piece, by David Deeks, takes us from the early 1930's to the late 1960's. I have deliberately left a large gap between these essays for two reasons: first, because there were very few literary studies on John during this period; secondly, because I wish to highlight the way in which source criticism postponed any appreciation of John's final form.

In order to understand where Deeks fits into the picture it is important to appreciate the three stages of literary theory and literary criticism during the twentieth century. Robert Morgan has written:

> The modern study of literature in Britain and North America may be divided into three periods, with boundaries around 1930 and 1960. Before the New Criticism, which originated with I.A. Richards and T.S. Eliot in the 1920's, English literature had been taught in universities since the late nineteenth century with a strongly historical and philological emphasis inherited from the educational model provided by the study of classical literature. The New Criticism won independence from that model, and integrity for the new curricula, by insisting on the autonomy of the individual work of art, which was to be judged by aesthetic norms. This successful struggle for the discipline's identity involved a reaction against the historical emphasis which lasted until the period beginning around 1960, when the new diversity of approaches included structuralism's more radical hostility to history and also a renewal of literary history.[2]

Morgan therefore proposes three phases in the development of literary criticism in the twentieth century. Between 1900 and 1930, texts are examined with reference to philological and historical questions—in a way influenced by the study of classical literature. We may call this the *Classical Stage*. The next stage, between 1930 and 1960, we may call the *New-Critical Stage*. Here the vogue was to dismiss historical questions and to examine the literary text as a self-enclosed world. What mattered now

---

[1] See, in particular, the section on John 8.12-59 in *John: A Readings Commentary*, (Sheffield: Sheffield Academic Press, 1993).

[2] R. Morgan, *Biblical Interpretation* (Oxford: Oxford University Press, 1989), p. 217.

were the aesthetic qualities intrinsic to the text. The third stage, which we may call the *Pluralistic Stage,* has extended from 1960 to 1990 (and beyond). In this phase a plethora of new methods—structuralism, feminist interpretation, Marxist criticism, psychoanalytical criticism, deconstruction, reader-response criticism, etc.—produced a bewildering pluralism. As Morgan puts it, "The third period in the recent history of secular literary criticism is a hurricane of conflicting tendencies".[1]

We can see something of these three stages reflected in the literary interpretation of the Fourth Gospel during this century. Between 1900 and 1930, the *Classical Stage,* the literary approaches to John tend to treat the gospel as classical drama. In the period between 1930 and 1960, literary interpretation of John virtually disappears while scholars prefer to use source criticism. This means that we have to wait until Deeks' essay in 1968 before we see a New-critical approach to the Fourth Gospel. We might therefore see the *New-Critical stage* in Johannine studies starting about forty years after it began in literature faculties, and lasting about a decade, between 1968 and 1978. Then, in 1979, the *Pluralistic Stage* begins with a vengeance, about twenty years after it began in the study of secular literature. It begins with Frank Kermode's application of poststructuralist literary criticism to Mark and John in *The Genesis of Secrecy.*[2] Since that time, most of the newer methods in literary criticism have been applied to the Fourth Gospel.

So Deeks' essay has an important place in this volume. It is New-Critical insofar as it embraces an exclusively text-immanent perspective. The article by George MacRae is similar. MacRae is primarily interested in the use of irony in the Fourth Gospel. Clavier (1959) and Wead (1970) had already started on this journey, but MacRae's essay is regarded by many as a classic. Indeed we may trace the subsequent interest in Johannine irony to this piece—most notably Paul Duke (1983) and Gail O'Day (1986a, 1986b). MacRae's essay is therefore of historical interest as an example of New Criticism. The same goes for Resseguie's excellent article on John 9.

The next essay by Schneiders is an example of a feminist literary interpretation of the Fourth Gospel. Not all who study the Fourth Gospel agree that John has a positive attitude towards female characters in his story. Margaret Davies has recently contended that women are always seen in a subservient relationship to men, and that the Fourth Gospel is therefore one of the last texts which a woman would find liberating.[3] However, the majority of scholars who expose John to a feminist

---

[1] Ibid., p. 217.
[2] See F. Kermode, *Genesis of Secrecy,* chapter 5 for a discussion of John's narrative.
[3] Margaret Davies, *Rhetoric and Reference in the Fourth Gospel,* p. 227.

hermeneutic disagree with Davies and follow Schneiders (e.g., Nortje, 1986; Theissen, 1990). In her essay "Women in the Fourth Gospel", Schneiders manages to highlight the different and valid perspectives that can be attained as a result of a non-patriarchal literary criticism. Indeed, her essay is a convincing argument against those who say that the New Testament excludes women from leadership in the church. As such, it has a relevance much wider than the present volume.

With Crossan's article we turn from the New-Critical to the Pluralistic stage. Crossan's piece examines John 6 from a structuralist perspective. As I have shown in *John as Storyteller,* there are essentially three forms of structuralist literary criticism. There is first of all the *binary* approach, which looks at the way in which opposites are mediated in a literary text. There is secondly the *functional* approach. This looks at a literary text as a manifestation of a transcultural grammar of narrative possibilities. There is thirdly the *actantial* approach, which reduces a work to its essential plot and then maps that against a universal narrative grid discovered by A.J. Greimas.

Crossan's structuralist analysis of John 6 is a good example of the *binary* approach. It is highly regarded for the way in which it explores the binarism of Feeder and Food. At the start of the chapter, Jesus is the one who gives bread to the masses. At this point, Feeder and Food are separate. By the end of the chapter it is Jesus himself who is the Bread from Heaven. Here the separation between Feeder and Food has been reduced to a Christological metaphor: "I am the Bread of Life". Crossan's article, first published in 1980, is therefore important. Indeed, it is the first of a number which uses structuralism in an attempt to uncover deeper literary dynamics in the Fourth Gospel. Others who have followed are Girard (1982), Patte (1983, 1990), and Stibbe (1992, 1993c).

Eslinger's piece is an example of reader response criticism. It uses the insights of former literary approaches to John 4 (notably that of Cahill in 1982) but with a new emphasis upon the reader. This again is significant. M.H. Abrams showed, in *The Mirror and the Lamp* (1958), how literary criticism has emphasised different things at different stages. First of all it emphasised the universe imitated by a text, then the author whose feelings are expressed in the text, then the aesthetic qualities intrinsic to the text, and most recently the reader's response to the text. Eslinger's essay reveals some of the promise in this latest reader-oriented approach in the development of literary criticism. Many others have experimented with this reader-approach to John: Phillips (1983), Kotzé (1985a), Staley (1986a, 1991), Reinhartz (1989a), Braun, Henaut and Botha (1990). Clearly this is a method with a long future.

The next essay by J.E. Botha is included for several reasons. First of all it highlights the burgeoning literary criticism on the Fourth Gospel in South Africa. Botha is one of a number of South African scholars in this field. Others include Kotzé, Du Rand, and Domeris.[1] Secondly, Botha's approach is an example of a text-immanent methodology which relies heavily on linguistic theory. Others who take a similar line (though not reliant upon speech act theory) are Olsson (1974), Boers (1980, 1988), Cotterell (1984, 1989), and Malina (1985). Botha has recently published a book-length study of John 4 using this speech act approach (1991).[2] Botha's essay shows that there are likely to be other methods which will be introduced in the next decade, and which will be identifiable as a branch of literary or narrative criticism.

The next essay is by Alan Culpepper. It would have been impossible not to have had a piece of work by Culpepper in a volume dedicated to the advance of Johannine literary criticism. The essay included here is the translation of a relatively unknown piece written in French. It is a fine example of Culpepper's work, and at the same time it functions as a very helpful introduction to what is the most promising recent development—narrative criticism on the Fourth Gospel. Those who have followed Culpepper (e.g., Duke, Staley, Du Rand, Giblin, Van Aarde, Stibbe, Reinhartz, Wiarde) have found Culpepper's writings invaluable in their attempt to appreciate the Gospel of John as Story. We are therefore privileged to have this recent article in our volume.

The essay by Werner Kelber on the prologue of John's gospel employs a deconstructionist approach. Stephen Moore, heavily dependent upon Kelber, has also explored the potential of this philosophy in connection with the Fourth Gospel in his book, *Literary Criticism and the Gospels*. John's gospel seems well-suited to a deconstructionist approach. If deconstructionism is partly about the dismantling of a *logocentric* world-view, then it cannot afford to neglect the Gospel of the Logos.

This leads finally to my own article. Any editor of a volume like this, who chooses to include some of his own work, will always run the risk of seeming immodest. I apologise to the reader if that impression has been given. I have included "The Elusive Christ" because I want humbly to suggest that the future of literary criticism on the Fourth Gospel must lie in some kind of integration of the older, historical-critical method, and the more recent forms of literary criticism (especially the narrative

---

[1] Other countries are also seeing a growth in literary criticism of John: Moloney (Australia), Calloud and Genuyt (France), Staley, Segovia and Duke (USA) and Thyen (Germany).

[2] See my forthcoming review of J.E. Botha's book in *Biblical Interpretation* (E.J. Brill), Vol. 1, 1993.

approach). "The Elusive Christ", like *John as Storyteller* and Meg Davies' *Rhetoric and Reference*[1] does attempt some kind of betrothal between the two. I therefore offer this article as a pointer towards the marriage of literature and history in Fourth Gospel research.

"The Elusive Christ" indicates that there are a lot of questions still left to be asked and answered. Some of these questions are urgent: "What is the relationship between literary history and literary criticism in the future of Johannine research? What effect does the literary approach to John's gospel have on its status as Holy Scripture? Does it turn John into just another book? Is John more than a great work of literature? To what extent does literary criticism rescue John from a form of scholarship which has alienated the gospel from both the church and society? Do these new forms of literary criticism contribute at all towards theological questions, such as the claim that the Bible is the revelation of God?" All these and many more remain unanswered.

---

[1] Margaret Davies, ibid., p. 7 et al.

IS THE FOURTH GOSPEL A DRAMA?*

F.R.M. HITCHCOCK

The Fourth Gospel appears to be cast in a dramatic form. There are critical periods called "hours" which mark the dramatic development of the work.[1] Its dramatic unity is also proved by the nexus and naturalness of the scenes from the pictures of the waiting Baptist to Thomas's crowning confession of faith. No evangelist has a keener conception of a situation, or of dialogue or characterisation. The vividness, variety and progress of the scenes, together with the number, individuality, and distinctness of the characters; the play of question and retort; the pointed and allusive manner of the Master's sayings; the reality of His surroundings; and the growing interest of the narrative, give dramatic force and movement to the work. Clearly the writer had the dramatic sense by nature, which may have been improved by experience and association with men of artistic tastes. We shall see how closely he follows the canons of Aristotle, but while we may not draw any conclusion regarding indebtedness, we are free to point out that adherence to the then recognised canons of the drama would establish the dramatic character and unity of this Gospel, whose writer, while attending to his characters, did not neglect the structure of his plot, which according to Aristotle (*Poetics*, vi. 9,15) is "the soul of a tragedy"—i.e., that in which the dramatic conflict is unfolded. In *Poetics* (vii. 1) he says:

> Tragedy is the representation of an action which is complete and one whole. By whole I mean that which has a beginning, a middle, and an end. A beginning is that which does not follow anything by causal necessity, but after which something naturally is, or comes to be. An end, on the other hand, is that which is naturally preceded by some other thing, either by necessity or as a rule, but which nothing follows of necessity. A middle is that which is preceded and is followed by something else. Those who would construct their plots properly must not begin or end where they choose, but must conform to these principles.

---

* This article first appeared in *Theology* 7 (1923), pp. 307-17.
[1] See *A Fresh Study of the Fourth Gospel* (London: SPCK), vi; also *Expositor*, September, 1907, "The Dramatic Development of the Fourth Gospel", by the present writer.

Poetics (xviii. 1) explains more fully the structure of the plot.

> Every tragedy has two parts, complication (δέσις) and unravelling or
> dénoument (λύσις). Complication I call all that extends from the
> beginning up to the time where there is the turning-point. The
> unravelling is that which extends from the beginning of that change
> to the end. Accordingly, in an ideal tragedy we look for a true
> beginning (which is only to be found conditionally in every tragedy
> we know), a true central point, and a true consummation or end.
> Towards the central point the whole action must ascend in orderly
> sequence, and from it descend in an equally ordered sequence to the
> end.

Accordingly, as Horace observed, there must be no more and no less than
five acts in a tragedy (*Ars Poetica, 189f.*). There is the beginning, the
development towards the central point, the central point, the development
towards the end, the end. The true beginning is "that which does not
follow anything by causal necessity."

In the Fourth Gospel we have the ideal beginning—the Word who was
in the beginning and from whom all things follow by causal necessity (δι᾽
αὐτοῦ). In the raising of Lazarus (ch. 11) we have practically the
mathematical centre of the work which is its moral centre also. It is a true
centre, for it is at once highest point and turning point, *apex* and *vertex*.
The greatest act performed by the Lord, it set in motion forces that led to
His betrayal, trial, and crucifixion. Towards it the Christ-drama rises,
from it the Christ-drama falls, until it reaches its end. But the end is only
apparent. The true consummation is the Resurrection and the
pronouncement of Thomas. Further and higher than that human faith
cannot go. It is the Epilogue that makes one realise that the apparent end
is but a new beginning.

The Gospel has five divisions with prologue and epilogue. The
prologue is appropriately conceived and constructed. The drama has a
true beginning in the eternities. The evidence of the Baptist, as an
interlude of human music in the Divine anthem of the Word, is a link in
the great chain of reasoning that is gradually let down from the heights of
existence and light, which no man can approach unto, to the levels of
human thought and being, until the Word, who made the world and giveth
light, stands revealed as an historical figure upon the stage of life. And
the subsequent appearance of the Baptist, his dramatic reply, gesture, and
record, form a fit prelude to the selection of the disciples, which is
described with delicate and graphic touches that make the figures live and
speak before us. Aristotle's direction that the poet, when constructing his
plot, should regard himself as much as possible as a spectator, is faithfully
followed (albeit unconsciously) here and all through the drama.

(1) The time of Jn 1.19-2.12 is evidently spring. The visit of Jesus to the Baptist may have synchronised with the preparations for the Passover. On His return from the wilderness with the marks of His recent struggle and fasting, like all the indications of His sufferings in the Gospel, suggested rather than described, He is pointed out with the remark: "Behold the Lamb of God," which has a true Passover ring. The time of Passover would also account for the presence of so many Galileans in Judea, while the very air of these early scenes is spring, the budding life of the year, in the buoyant sunshine when mens' hearts are most ready and eager for a change of life. The interview with Nathanael is spontaneous and suggestive of the problems to be met and solved in this drama. All this might have happened a month before the Passover. The next scene, that of the wedding in Cana, is still within the Saviour's circle, and is vividly depicted. The details are related as by an eye-witness, who succeeds in conveying a distinct impression of aloofness and meditation in the Lord's manner, that prepares one for His subsequent appearance and action in the Temple. "Mine hour is not yet come." That hour does not mean here the time for the "sign" is clear from the use in this Gospel of "hour" "to denote some momentous epoch."[1] While meditating upon a course of action which might open the eyes of the Jews, His train of thought was disturbed for a moment, to be resumed after the help suggested had been rendered. No decisive action followed immediately, but His restlessness may be read in the words: "And they remained there *not many days*" (2.12). His soul is now filled with its great purpose, now that the consciousness of His mission has been stirred within Him, and He follows the crowd of pilgrims to the city, where He is determined to assert in public the power and authority of which He has so far given evidence only in the private circle of friends and disciples. The "hour" has come in the Temple, but His vigorous actions, vividly described, failed to produce the desired effect. The protest of the Jews is followed by the prophecy of Jesus. "Destroy this shrine, and in three days I will raise it up." The end, still remote, is seen in the hour of failure, but in the light of the Resurrection. He is repelled by the hostile attitude of the Jews, and is thrown back upon Himself. An assumed aloofness conceals His feelings, which are seldom betrayed in these pages. "He would not trust Himself to them." Nicodemus, unable to break down that barrier of reserve in public, came to Him privately by night. An alteration in His method of self-revelation, and a more cautious manner, are the results of an episode which Professor Wendt described as "unrelated and without consequence." A discussion on purification calls forth the noble tribute of

---

[1] E.g., 7.30; 8.20; 12.23, 27; 13.1.

the Baptist, but reveals a latent jealousy of Jesus, who felt compelled by the growing publicity of His mission to leave Judea. The monotony of the return journey is relieved by the interview at the well. The circumstances and the words that passed were noted by one who may have been seated near. The setting of the scene, the mountain, the well and field, are as historical as the speakers are real. The eagerness of the woman and the returning hopefulness of the Master which found expression in His remark about the whitening fields, and the Samaritans' statement of faith, are a contrast to the happenings in the city and the unsympathetic attitude of the Jews, and prepare us for the second miracle in Cana in answer to the request of an anxious parent, which may be regarded as the close of the first episode or act in this drama.

(2) The conflict presently begins between the Messiah and His people on His return to the city. A crowd of infirm folk are lying in the shade of the Bethesda porches on the Sabbath, among them a chronic and helpless invalid. In pity Jesus bids him take up his pallet and walk. The Jews protest against this profanation and demand the name of the healer. The man found by Jesus again in the Temple informs against Him. His act of mercy becomes fraught with disastrous consequences. Henceforth, He is a marked man. From that time the Jews meditated hostile action (ἐδίωκον) (v. 16). The reference to the Baptist in v. 35 as "a lamp that used to shine" is a note of Time. The conclusion of the chapter (5) reveals the fact that His enemies are determined to *accuse* Him before the Sanhedrin—a threat which He answered in His own way: "Do not think that *I will accuse you*" (v. 45). In the meantime they are maturing their plans and keeping a watch upon His words and actions. The next scene, by the Sea of Galilee, shows how far-reaching their organisation is, and how astute their policy. It is just before the Jewish festival, when multitudes follow Jesus, as in Mt 5. The scene is graphically depicted. We almost hear the people exclaiming: "This is the prophet that cometh," and almost see the movement of some instigated by His foes to seize Him and make Him a king thwarted by His withdrawal to the mountain. Arrived at the other side, He discerns among the crowd hostile faces from the city (Mt 15.1), and rebukes them and others for seeking Him for a wrong motive. They demand a sign, and then cavil openly at his discourse regarding the Bread of Life, and persuade many to desert Him. The band of disciples, with one exception, is unaffected, and the Lord's challenge, "Will ye also go away?" is answered with the same spontaneity as in Mt 16.16, where St. Peter's confession is made after a like conflict with a deputation from the city. The prediction of the Betrayal at this point intensifies the dramatic interest of the passage, which shows all through an observant eye and mind. The Master reveals His discovery of the character of Judas

doubtless in recent transactions with the deputation (6.70). "The leaven of the Pharisees and Sadducees" (Mt 16.11) is beginning to work. The conflict has commenced. The toils are being drawn slowly but surely round the Master's feet. The presence of a malignant spirit becomes a new force in the tragedy, blighting His happiness and work. This is the conclusion of the second act or division of the drama.

(3) At the beginning of the third act He is actively employed in Galilee (περιπάτει 7.1). Judea has become a zone of danger to Him, and He does not wish to expose Himself yet to the active hostility of the Jews. The approaching Feast of Tabernacles gives Him another opportunity. The taunts of the brethren, the search made for Him in the city, and the murmurings of the people as they incline now this way and anon that, are vividly portrayed. But in the midst of the Feast He arrives and speaks boldly. The three parties, the crowd of pilgrims (ὁ ὄχλος), the hierarchical and nationalist factions, and the residents, are vividly described (verse 12). Their arguments and movements lend animation to the scene. Some even attempted to seize Him (verse 30). A diversion was also caused by some men sent by the Sanhedrin to arrest Him, but who instead listened to His teaching. The next day there was again a commotion when He taught, and one party said He was a prophet; others challenged that statement, and though some would have seized Him, no one ventured to touch him (verse 44). Sidelights upon the issue are given by the meeting of the Sanhedrin to receive the report of their officials, at which Nicodemus makes his protest, and by the scene (if genuine) with the adulteress and her accusers, who brought her to Jesus in order to show that the Teacher who appealed to the Law of Moses against them was Himself working in opposition to that Law. Jn 8.5 looks like an answer to 7.19. This scene reveals the subtlety of the Jewish enemies to the calm self-control of the Master.

In the next scene a stage of advance is registered. The exasperation of the Pharisees is more marked, and their opposition is better organised. But His hour is not yet (8.20). The opportunity passes, and Jesus resumes His discourse on His departure. "I go away." "Will He kill Himself?" they asked, a question which may have sunk into the mind of Judas, whose fate is not recorded in this Gospel. There is a marked advance in the words, "Ye are from beneath; I am from above" (8.24), and in the foreshadowing of the lifting up of the Son of Man in 8.28. Many appear to be moved by His words. Their nascent faith He puts to a severe test (verse 32). While they stand silent, His enemies attempt to weaken the impression He has made by construing His words into an insult to their ancestor and their freedom. The gauntlet of innocence is then thrown down: "Which of you convicteth me of sin?" which would be amply effective if the accusers of the adulteress were present. They hurl back

His taunt with a *tu quoque*. And His answer, "Before Abraham was born, I am" (verse 58), makes them realise the greatness of His ever-advancing claim. They took up stones but when they stooped, he had passed away. The scene with the blind beggar follows. It is full of dramatic movement and its characterisation is life-like. It arises naturally and logically from the circumstances of the previous scene, and shows the now fixed determination of the Jewish party to crush Jesus and molest His followers. Then Jesus gave privately to the outcast a special and spontaneous revelation of Himself, and the man, whose rugged and steadfast nature is a pleasant contrast to the weakness and insincerity of others, *worshipped* Him. In itself this act of worship is a climax, not only of this scene, but also of the whole course and progress of the drama up to this point. The restoring of the blind man's sight made a diversion in our Lord's favour (10.20f.). Some time after, as He walked in the stoa of Solomon, He is challenged to make His claims clear, and He in answer describes His relation to the Father as higher than that claimed for the New Messiah. "I and my Father are one" (10.30). This was the climax of His self-revelation to the Jews, and provoked another hostile movement, but he passed away from their uplifted hands, and withdrew beyond Jordan.

We have now reached the centre of the plot—the Raising of Lazarus—which is vividly described as if from the life, and is in perfect harmony with all that has preceded and all that is to follow in this gospel. When He received the message, He perceived the significance of the sickness occurring at the time in connection with His own life and fortunes. The secrecy with which Martha acts shows the consistency of the scene with the preceding. The sisters' movements, the remarks of their friends, and the details that follow are naturally drawn, and seem beyond the power of invention. The scene is not due to an attempt to give literary or dramatic expression to the belief in Jesus as "the Resurrection and the Life" (11.25). It is evident that it was intended to lead up to the Resurrection scene of 20.1-18, and so has a place in the drama and a bearing upon its development, apart from the relation of the raising of Lazarus to the tragedy of the Christ. The latter is made apparent in the following scene in the council chamber, where the authorities make it the concern of their political life to accomplish His death, and the remark of Caiaphas makes the work of Jesus assume a national significance. So His execution becomes a measure of State policy deliberately planned and relentlessly carried out by the principal men of the nation. From that day they determined to do what they had hitherto desired (5.16, 18; 7.32; 10.39; 11.53).

This is the crisis of the drama, and so the *apex* of our Lord's work becomes the *vertex* or turning-point of His earthly career. The Lazarus scene contained the material that led to His death, and so may be regarded as the centre of the drama. But to avoid precipitating matters, Jesus withdrew to the wild district of Ephraim. He appears, however, to have been under surveillance all the time of His absence from the city, as the council gave orders for information of His movements (11.57). This prepares one for the Betrayal, and concludes the third division or act of the drama. Henceforth there is an inevitable though gradual descent towards death.

(4) Six days before the Passover, Lazarus entertains at Bethany the Lord, and others who have come to see Him for His own sake. The traitor who is to bring about the catastrophe criticised the extravagance of Mary's action. "Let her keep it for the day of My *entombment*" (12.8) said the Betrayed. This incident, trivial as it seems, reveals the shadow of the tragedy, and heightens its pathos. The drama is progressing slowly but surely.

A short scene intervenes between this and the entry. It is the council chamber, where reports of the supper of Lazarus have been brought; and the members resolve upon the death of Lazarus also. From the standpoint of the believer, the blunt obduracy of the Jews stands revealed in all its diabolical malignity, and constitutes a tragedy in itself. Their grim determination to leave nothing undone to accomplish the ruin of their victim prepares us for the subtly planned and carefully arranged steps in the arrest and trials of Jesus which are described in this Gospel. These scenes must have come from a Jewish source, probably Nicodemus. Their place in the drama is significant and important from the light they throw upon its development. The importance of the raising of Lazarus is also shown by the statement that "the crowd went out from the city to meet him because they had heard of this sign" (12.18). The account of this "sign" therefore, may not be removed without injury to the structure of the Gospel and the plot. The visit of the Greeks, a scene full of natural colour, follows. Contemplating His own death, to which He alluded in His analogy of the seed-corn, He exclaims: "Now is My soul troubled, and what shall I say? 'Father, save Me from this hour!' But for this cause came I unto this hour." This momentary hesitation in a life of which every step hitherto seems prearranged gives another touch of reality to the passage. It is but momentary, and ends in a resolution of self-abnegation confirmed by the divine assurance that His death would glorify God. The impressions of the people are recorded. The spiritual atmosphere is tense and suitable for the supreme crowning revelation of Himself—"If so be that I be lifted up I shall draw all men unto Myself" (12.32)—reached in an hour of intense spiritual strain and suppressed feeling, and related logically and naturally to the visit of the Greeks. The importance of the moment is also indicated by the grave warning given about following the Light just as "the Light" was departing (12.36). The public mission is ended. The mixed result is given by the writer in the words of Isaiah 6.10. The scenes that follow are concerned with Jesus' own disciples and His doctrine. But as if for the last time He comes forward as a solitary figure upon the stage and sums up in a few pregnant words the purpose and result of His public mission (12.44-50).

The scene of the feet-washing is dramatically conceived and evidently reported by an eye-witness. The Master's preparations and actions, and St. Peter's remonstrance and subsequent recantation, are drawn from the life. The words "Ye are clean, but not all," are an omen of the storm that is to break upon them. The Master's evident distress (verse 21) and yet more definite statement regarding His betrayal add to the tension of the situation. The gestures and requests of the disciples and the abrupt departure of Judas into the night after our Lord's words, "What thou doest, do quickly," make the scene intensely real.

The discourse in the Upper Room consists largely of questions and answers such as might be made or given by men sitting at or after a meal. The general nature of the conversation, the variety of the topics, and the sententious manner of the answers are in keeping with the environment of the Upper Room, and in striking contrast with the continuous discourse (15-16) which may have been uttered on the way to the Garden. A feature of these discourses is their connection and development of thought.[1] Here it suffices to call attention to the solemn awe which hangs round the little circle. The silence and solitude of the midnight hour and the vivid stillness of that midnight walk can be almost felt as the mysteries of the Godhead are revealed. The thanksgiving prayer fitly crowns the discourses by gathering up into one sublime summary their thoughts and themes. Uttered in the presence of the disciples it relieves the tension. Its dominant note is glory, the glory of consummation and victory after defeat, sorrow, trial. The scene in the Garden brings one back to the field of action. Full of movement, it marks what Aristotle would have called the dénoument (λύσις) of the drama. The traitor, the soldiers and temple officials with lanterns, torches and weapons, disturb His vigil and intimidate all but Him. Prepared for His flight or resistance, the men are confused and move backwards, tripping over one another. Some indescribable feeling bewildered them in that weird hour. The discovery of recognition (ἀναγνώρισις) which was frequently employed in the Greek drama in connection with a reversal of fortunes (περιπέτεια) is used with great effect in this and later scenes. Here we have the discovery

---

[1] *A Fresh Study of the Fourth Gospel* viii-ix, by the writer.

attempted by the soldiers, in the eighteenth chapter that is attempted by Pilate, and in ch. 20 those made by Mary and Thomas. Our Lord recalls the soldiers to their duty in His desire to save His followers. But one will not be saved, and his rash action is instantly rebuked in words that recall Mt 20.22, 26.39. Bound and led away to Annas, he is followed by St. Peter and "another disciple known to the high priest." The latter enters with his Master, but St. Peter stands at the door until the other returns and obtains admission for him. But the maid accosts Peter as he enters, and the other hears the lying response as he hurries on to hear the examination before Annas, Peter remaining in the court, fearful of entering the audience chamber lest he should provoke another challenge. Sent by Annas before the tribunal of Caiaphas, Jesus is hurried through the court followed by the other disciple. And they hear Peter's denials. The writer of the Gospel writes from the standpoint of the other disciple, and shows that he could have overheard the three denials.

The next scene is in front of the Praetorium. Pilate stands on the steps confronting the priests, who from motives of ceremonial purity refused to enter, although others did, including "the other disciple", who overhears the ensuing dialogue between Pilate and Jesus, which is cast in a more dramatic form than in the Synoptists. Finally, convinced that Jesus is not a malefactor, but a philosopher, Pilate leaves Him without waiting for an answer to his last question, and informs the Jews that he finds no guilt in Him, and reminds them of their Passover custom. Their rejection of Jesus in favour of Barabbas marks the *peripeteia* of the tragedy. Then follows the mock coronation scene, and Jesus is led forth in regal attire, and Pilate, who had an eye for a dramatic situation, says, "Behold the Man." The chief priests cry "Crucify!" and declare His crime against their law, which causes Pilate to renew his conversation with Jesus and his efforts to procure His release, but he is silenced by their references to "Caesar's friend." For the last time he withdraws and orders Jesus to be led forth into the Paved Hall, called Gabbatha, probably in full view of the people, or into which their law might allow them to enter (the Hebrew name suggests the latter possibility), and says, as he takes his seat as judge, "Behold your King." Justin's reading, ἐκάθισαν αὐτόν, would not be suitable. Our Lord would not have been so well seen sitting as standing. In these scenes we note that the proprieties—what Aristotle called τὰ ἁρμόττοντα[1]—of the different parties are maintained. The writer also observes consistency (τὸ ὁμαλόν[2]), Aristotle's fourth requisite in character drawing. The crowd not only behave as a crowd, but as a

---

[1] *Poetics*, II. xv.
[2] *Ibid.*

Jewish crowd of the time; Pilate not only as a Roman judge, but as a judge convinced of the prisoner's innocence; our Lord as he has been depicted all through, regal in His serenity. Pilate yields to clamour, and the scene is over. Now follows the *pathos*, the third part of the drama according to Aristotle,[1] "which consists of destructive or painful actions, the public display of death, bodily anguish and wounds."

The writer does not, however, linger over the harrowing account of the crucifixion, but, as usual, selects certain minute details which add considerably to the effect of the situation, and give point and pathos to the Passion.

The concluding scenes, as evidences of the Resurrection, are skilfully depicted, the recognition scene in the Garden being one of the most pathetic and realistic in all literature. It is a transcript from the life, an idyll inimitable and touching, described with the self-restraint and simplicity of a master. In the epilogue the writer permits himself more freedom. Its contents are, as Aristotle would say, "outside the tragedy." Artistically, it was not needed, for St. Thomas's confession is the real end of the drama; but morally it was required to exemplify the principle, "On the earth the broken arcs; in the heaven a perfect round." Throughout the drama the *ars celandi artem* is displayed. Every detail has point. The scenes are constructed and marshalled by one whose eye for the dramatic enabled him to sort his materials, to compose the settings of his scenes, and to arrange and use his *dramatis personae* with effect. His genius for characterisation and dramatisation, not in the sense of creating scenes or inventing characters, but in the sense of representing the men he had known in all their strength and weakness, of delineating human character in all its complexity and depth, and of seizing just those episodes in the Master's life which were the real turning-points of the tragedy of the Cross, making this Gospel a tragedy, real, intense, progressive. Every occurrence contributes to the advance of the drama; at every step the tragedy grows to climax. The writer had something of that sense of proportion and harmony which was essentially Greek. The outline of his picture was presented with Greek distinctness. It is filled in with Greek naïveté, directness and self-restraint, and the whole is rounded off with that symmetrical and pure type of workmanship which is rarely met outside the drama of Sophocles. Such is the form in which this work is presented. Judged by such internal evidence of mind and art, structure and character, the organic unity of the Gospel may be said to be established.

---

[1] *Ibid.*, II. ix

JOHN'S NARRATIVE STYLE*

HANS WINDISCH

To date, investigations of style that have been devoted to the Gospels, under the influence particularly of Hermann Gunkel, have chiefly illuminated the literary and stylistic features of the synoptic Gospels. To my knowledge, as far as the Gospel of John is concerned there is only the excellent, if not yet complete study by E. Stange (1914)[1] of the character of the Johannine product, which, however, confines its discussion to the style of the discourses. Of course important observations have long been made about John's narrative style.[2] But there is still no thorough study which evaluates the results of the investigations of the style of the synoptics. In what follows there is no attempt at exhaustiveness either. The aim is only to bring together some important observations and draw some points of reference for assessing the individual character of John's narrative style and of the composition of the Fourth Gospel that is conditioned by it.

The most important result of the investigations into the style of the synoptic Gospels is in the matter of the pericope-type character of the individual passages. The synoptic narratives are all *pericopes*, i.e. individual narratives which were formed separately, are self-contained and were originally circulated in isolation; and the synoptic Gospels are pericope-works; the evangelists collected the individual stories and created a more or less continuous historical report by loosely juxtaposing and grouping the stories together. The originator of this pericope-composition is Mark. The connection between the individual anecdotes in the tradition is restricted to short introductory and concluding remarks, which in their totality represent the framework of the Gospel story.

---

* This article first appeared as "Der Johanneische Erzählungsstil", in *Eucharisterion: Studien zur Religion und Literatur des Alten und Neuen Testaments, Festschrift für H. Gunkel*, Vol.II. (Göttingen: Vandenhoeck, 1923), pp. 174-213.
Translated from the German by David E. Orton.
[1] On this, see Bultmann, *TLZ* (1916), cols. 532ff.
[2] I would mention particularly F.R. Montgomery Hitchcock, *A Fresh Study of the Fourth Gospel* (1911) with its chapters concerning "The Dramatic Development of the Gospel" and "The Artistic Structure of the Gospel", which I have consulted since preparing this article.

A comparison of Mark with Matthew and Luke makes the character of this pericope-system particularly clear. Both evangelists changed Mark's order of pericopes at many points, without the context suffering damage as a result: they changed the order of the pericopes, moved them around and made connections between them according to different aspects; they removed individual pericopes and inserted new pieces of tradition which were unknown to Mark, into the Markan sequence. It is natural that the pericopes should have lent themselves to arrangement in various sequences.[1]

The Gospel of John is quite different. Though it does not completely resemble the seamless garment of his Christ, in comparison to the synoptics it presents a much more unified composition. Certainly, John too has pericopes of synoptic brevity (the marriage in Cana, the cleansing of the temple, the healing of the official's son, the anointing in Bethany, the entry into Jerusalem, some of the Easter stories; later, the added story of the woman taken in adultery); but these do not represent what is characteristic of the Johannine narrative—they disappear in the otherwise quite different construction of the whole, and their presence almost in fact creates something of a problem. The strange thing about John is rather that he does not, like the synoptics, present a colourful mosaic of innumerable vignettes but a small number (in comparison to the synoptics) of mainly fully elaborated narratives, discussions and dispute scenes.

John did not (as was the concern of the synoptics) collect everything available to him in the tradition that seemed credible, but made a particular choice and then presented the stories and scenes he had chosen generally with considerable detail. His choice shows evidence of an authorial plan as far as the execution and sequence are concerned—in brief: the progressive self-revelation of Jesus, the contrasting rising opposition of the Jews, the catastrophe, which ends with the victory of Jesus and the confirmation of faith over against unbelief. John is concerned to present all this in his Gospel. To this extent, the Fourth Gospel is thus an organic whole and a literary work of art as it attempts to illustrate these fundamental ideas by means of its narratives and its discourses.

---

[1] See recently K.L. Schmidt, *Der Rahmen der Geschichte Jesu* (1919); M. Dibelius, *Die Formgeschichte des Evangeliums* (1919); R. Bultmann, *Die Geschichte der synoptischen Tradition* (in "Forschungen zur Religion und Literatur des Alten und Neuen Testaments", new series, 12; 1921); M. Albertz, *Die synoptischen Streitgespräche* (1921); C. Bouma, "De literarische vorm der Evangeliën" (Diss., 1921)—this is the only work to include a study of John, in which, however, as in the work as a whole, more attention is given to the content than to the literary form.

The elements of the Gospel that are characteristic of John are therefore not the small pericopes, which moreover are in the main properly integrated in the organism (see section 7, below), but (1) the broadly elaborated, dramatically presented narratives, (2) a connection between narrative and dispute discourse, and (3) the sequence of individual scenes that belong together.

1

Four narratives belong to group 1 mentioned above: the conversation with the Samaritan woman, the healing of the man born blind, the raising of Lazarus and the appearance of the risen one at Lake Galilee in John's addendum. All four stories are characterised by a much more strongly developed dramatic impulse than is found in the synoptic Gospels, which is evident in the greater expansion of conversation as well as in the division between various scenes. The dramatic character of the synoptic narratives is—as is well known—extremely simple. The action generally takes place in a single scene, and the conversation is a dialogue which runs in one movement. The synoptics do, however, show knowledge of a somewhat more developed technique. In the story of the Canaanite woman a dramatic tension is created by means of Jesus' initial refusal of her petition; a conversation in various parts thus develops of its own accord. In Matthew there is also the interference of the disciples, speaking, which leads to Jesus' mouth being opened and gets the conversation going. In the conflict stories in particular Jesus' words are directed alternately to two different addressees, the object of his healing (usually a sick person) and the opponent or the opposing group; but a conversation between three parties never arises: the needy person generally remains silent, such as the paralysed man, the sinful woman, even Mary (next to Martha, who does the speaking). Peter's denial falls into three short scenes; each time Peter turns to one person, or one group.[1]

Healing stories are usually arranged so that the healing is preceded by a conversation. The most detailed example is represented by the story of the epileptic boy, where the nature of the illness and the condition for the healing fill the conversation. The Zacchaeus pericope is an attractive two-scene story (Scene 1 in the street, Scene 2 in the house); quite similarly 'the call of Levi and the meal in his home', but here two pericopes have evidently been pushed together. The event which the account of the end of the Baptist presupposes is particularly rich in scenes (Introductory part: the Baptist's announcement concerning Herodias and the arrest; Main

---

[1] Cf. Bultmann, p. 186.

part: the banquet, the dance; conversation between the daughter and her mother; the posing of the request in the hall; the decapitation; the presentation of the head). But Matthew avoids mentioning a word of this and Mark has inserted words only in the middle scenes. None of the evangelists felt moved to provide richer dramatic detail though the material suggests it.

The most common form of scene change is the scheme—used also in the Talmud—of appended discussion with disciples: Scene 1 takes place in public; Jesus speaks or acts with an opponent or sick person, while the disciples are silent witnesses. Scene 2 takes place "in the house" or after the external characters have been dismissed, such as what follows in the circle of the disciples after the healing of the epileptic boy in Mark and Matthew (deleted by Luke), after the conversation about pure and impure in Mark and Matthew, and after the encounter with the rich disciple. The most extensive composition of this type is the conversation with the sons of Zebedee with the attached teaching for all disciples. This scheme of course has its own *Sitz im Leben*, but has been artificially applied by the evangelist with the purpose of associating freely circulating utterances of Jesus with the narrative. The synoptic healing story with the most scenes is the Jairus narrative: in Scene 1 Jesus is fetched by the father in the street; Scene 2 is an extraneous pericope which the tradition has introduced, which in this context represents an intermediate act and explains the change in the situation which is assumed by Scene 3, in which the father is informed about the death of the girl which has occurred in the meantime; it is only in Scene 4 that Jesus completes the miracle.

The way in which a significant action is prepared for by special measures is peculiar to the synoptics. There is then a sequence of three scenes: Jesus' commission to the disciples, the performance and the action itself; this is the case with the entry into Jerusalem and the last supper. Characteristically, Scene 2 is the shortest in each case: the main thing is the commission and Jesus' prediction.

The Passion narrative presented a chance for a richer elaboration of the story: Jesus' struggle in prayer in two settings, the arrest with the three parties (Jesus, the prosecutor and the disciples), the cross-examination before the high court and before Pilate, the crucifixion with five parties (Jesus, the Jews, the soldiers, the captain, the two men crucified with Jesus). But here too the composition is the simplest that could be conceived: Jesus usually remains silent, and the various characters and groups have a chance to speak one after another.

The most elevated narrative art to be found in the synoptic tradition occurs in the parables—here, however, the word is given not to the nameless tradition but to a master of the word, who shapes the tradition according to his own concerns. The most technically elaborate parables are, from a literary point of view, short, multi-scene novellas, their course extended over several hours, days or even months and years; thus, the parable of the unforgiving servant, the wicked husbandmen, the labourers in the vineyard, the talents, the ten virgins, and the prodigal son (the latter can also be classed as an example narrative), and the example narratives of the good Samaritan and the poor man Lazarus. The law of the greatest possible simplicity applies here too, however: the characters are restricted to the minimum necessary, and even indispensable figures remain silent. The conversations are dialogues: only the "lord" is generally introduced speaking.[1]

Even by comparison with these parables of Jesus, the three Johannine narratives mentioned represent a technical advance. These are real dramatic sketches. In a recent article ("An Experiment in Translation", *Expositor* 8/xvi [1918], pp. 117-25), J.M. Thompson has graphically shown, from the story of the man born blind (as also from the narrative of the trial before Pilate), how easily the Johannine narrative is able to be poured into the dramatic form that is familiar to us. Such an "experiment" is made possible by the frequent changes of scene, and by the lively sequence of conversation in these narrative sections. I can show the same thing in the case of the story of the Samaritan woman. A translation of this in the dramatic style will provide the most graphic way of looking at the Johannine narrative art.

Jesus' Conversation with a Samaritan Woman

Setting (except for Scenes 4 and 7): Jacob's Well, near Sychar in Samaria.

Scene 1

Jesus comes to the well with his disciples. The disciples go on into the city to buy food.[2] Jesus sits down at the well, tired.

Scene 2

A Samaritan woman comes to draw water.
Jesus: Give me something to drink.
The Samaritan woman: What brings you, a Jew, to ask me, a Samaritan woman, for water?[3]

---

[1] Cf. most recently Bultmann, *op. cit.*, pp. 111ff.
[2] Only v. 8 is added by the evangelist.
[3] Verse 9b is an ancient gloss.

Jesus: If you recognised the gift of God, and him who says to you, 'Give me something to drink', you would have asked him and he would have given you living water.

The Samaritan woman: Lord, you have no container for drawing, and the well is deep. Where then can you get the living water? Are you perhaps greater than our father Jacob, who gave us the well, and who drank from it himself, together with his sons and his cattle?

Jesus: Everyone who drinks of this water will get thirsty again. But whoever drinks from the water which I give him, will never get thirsty again for all eternity, but the water which I can give him will become in him a spring of water which will bubble up into eternal life.

The Samaritan woman: Lord, give me this water, then I will not be thirsty any longer and will not need to come here to draw water.

Jesus: Go, call your husband, and come back here (with him).

The Samaritan woman: I have no husband.

Jesus: You were right to say, 'I have no husband'. For you have had five husbands; and the one you have now is not your husband. You spoke the truth there.

The Samaritan woman: Lord, I observe you are a prophet. Our fathers have (always) prayed on that[1] mountain; and you (Jews) say that the place where one must pray is in Jerusalem.

Jesus: Believe me, woman, the hour is coming, when you will pray to the Father neither on that mountain nor in Jerusalem. You pray to what you do not know; we (Jews) pray to what we know; for salvation comes from the Jews. But the hour is coming, and is already here, when the true worshippers will worship the Father in spirit and truth. For the Father too requires such worshippers for himself. God is spirit; and those who worship him must worship him in spirit and truth.

The Samaritan woman: I know the Messiah is coming;[2] when he comes, he will explain everything to us.

Jesus: That's me, who is speaking to you.

Scene 3

The disciples return. They are clearly astonished because Jesus is in conversation with a woman. No one expresses his astonishment in words. The woman leaves the pitcher standing and goes into the city.

---

[1] She indicates Gerizim with her finger. The evangelist omits this remark; a modern playwright would also have omitted it as superfluous.

[2] "Who is called Christ" is a gloss by the Greek evangelist.

Scene 4

Setting: (a street) in the city. The woman comes up (running); people gather round her.

The Samaritan woman: Come and see a man who (from his own knowledge) told me everything that I have done. Perhaps this could even be the Christ.

The people go with her willingly.[1]

Scene 5

The action occurs during the absence of the woman from the well.[2] *The disciples place the food they have brought in front of Jesus.*[3]

The disciples: Rabbi, do eat.

Jesus: I have food to eat which you do not know.

The disciples (among themselves): Has someone (else) brought him something to eat?

Jesus:(who has been listening):[4] My food consists in my doing the will of him who sent me, and completing his work. Isn't it a saying of yours, 'In four months the harvest will come'? Look, I tell you: Lift up your eyes and look at the lands, they are white (and ripe) for harvest. The reaper is already receiving (his) pay and collecting fruit—for eternal life, so that the sower and the reaper have their joy at the same time. For the saying is appropriate in that the one is the sower, the other the reaper. I have sent you to reap a harvest, for which you have not worked. Others have had the work, and you have the benefit of their work.

Scene 6[5]

The Samaritans have come to the well. Jesus has spoken to them.[6]

The Samaritans: Please stay with us.

Jesus goes into the city with them.[7]

Scene 7

Setting: a street in the city (perhaps in front of the woman's house); two days later. Many Samaritans are gathered around the woman.

---

[1] Cf. v. 39.

[2] Cf. "meanwhile", v. 31.

[3] This is not expressly stated by the evangelist; a modern playwright would probably not have omitted the remark.

[4] Not expressly mentioned by the evangelist; not strictly necessary.

[5] Verse 39 can be used dramatically only in the way indicated above.

[6] The evangelist hurries towards the end and only gives the characteristic conclusion of a longer-lasting scene.

[7] John: "and he stayed there two days".

The Samaritans:[1] We do not (any longer) believe because of your account. For (now) we have heard (it) ourselves, and know that this man really is the saviour of the world.

Our experiment has shown, above all, how well suited the Johannine narrative is for translation into dramatic form. The narrative is almost exclusively conversation in lively exchange; the speaking characters come and go. The jumps in the sequence of thought become understandable. Only in the middle (Scene 4 and the end) does the narrator content himself with brief indications: a purely dramatic representation would have given more colour here too.

There is no synoptic conversation that runs in such detail, that displays so much pastoral skill on Jesus' part, or so well depicts the character of the person facing Jesus and deals with so many religious topics. The appearance of the disciples is also without parallel. In the synoptic stories the disciples are either absent or present as silent witnesses who only speak at the end, if they do so at all. Quite exceptionally, they interfere in the conversation: cf. Mk 5.31=Lk 8.45; Mt 15.23. Here Jesus is at first alone with the woman; but the temporary absence of the disciples is expressly explained, and after the conversation with the woman has reached its second climax, they reappear and give Jesus cause to make a profound, far-seeing declaration. The content of Jesus' witness, too, is richer in content than a synoptic conversation ever is. Three subjects are dealt with: the water of eternal life, true worship and the messiahship of Jesus. Each subject grows quite naturally out of the course of the conversation. In the synoptics this would correspond to three different pericopes. Admittedly, conversations that climax with a confession of Jesus as messiah that is voluntary, if prompted by the conversation partner, are entirely absent from the synoptics (except for the trial before Pilate).

Nor do the synoptics know of an individual conversion as a preparatory stage in a mass conversion. The possibility of this is alluded to only once in the commission that Jesus gives the healed Gadarene man in Mk 5.19f.=Lk 8.39. John has the Samaritan announce her experience to her fellow citizens on her own initiative, and he indicates the success of this, though he does emphasise that the faith of most Samaritans came about without the mediation of the woman's testimony.

---

[1] Presented by the evangelist in an indirect version.

The Healing of the Man Born Blind

Even richer than in the conversation with the Samaritan is the change of scenes in the story of the man born blind (John 9).[1] Scene 1 comprises the encounter with the blind man, the conversation about him and the intention of the cure (vv. 1-7). A synoptic blind-healing story would have confined itself to this (cf. Mk 8.22-26). Scene 2 (vv. 8-12) is a lively exchange of words between the neighbours concerning the healed man, and between them and him. In Scenes 3-5 the Pharisees discuss the case, with the healed man (vv. 13-17), with his parents (vv. 18-21), and again with the healed man (vv. 24-34), though here the way the healed man honours Jesus and the anger of the Pharisees represent an intensification. Scene 6 is a second encounter with Jesus, which climaxes in the self-revelation of Jesus (vv. 35-38), and Scene 7 is Jesus' witness concerning his mission, with symbolic use of the blind man's healing and with the way the Pharisees who are so ill disposed towards him are dealt with (vv. 39-41).

Without doubt the narrative has been carried out with the greatest dramatic artistry at this point. How anyone can speak of merely "paper realism" here, I cannot understand. If one translates the report into dramatic form, one is bound to be struck by the naturalness and engaging graphic detail of the narrative. Of course the narrator did not introduce the further scenes, unparalleled in the synoptics, simply out of the enjoyment of telling stories; pragmatic, apologetic and theological motives led him to do this. He wanted to bear witness to the factuality of the miracle, for one thing, hence the conversations concerning the identification of the healed man with the man born blind; he wanted, moreover, to show theological proof that a man who opened the eyes of the man born blind could only have been sent by God; hence the Pharisees' deliberations, who seek in vain to avoid this conclusion, and the description of how the healed man is led to make his full confession.

And finally, he wanted to illustrate the unbridgable opposition between Jesus and the Pharisees and pillory them and their feeble machinations. The narrative is therefore borne along and inspired by particular tendencies. But it is dramatic skill that has been able to put these tendencies to use. While others would use simple testimony, logical proofs or proof from prophecy in order to realise the motifs cited, here the evangelist has made use of the much more effective means of dramatic scene-setting.

---

[1] Cf. Thompson, *op. cit.*, pp. 119-23.

As has been mentioned, the motifs featured in Scenes 2-7 are not common in the synoptic tradition. The synoptics never have relatives and neighbours of the healed person appear—except for the father or the mother who brings the sick person to Jesus. In the synoptics it is frequently described how a healing provokes a conflict with the spiritual leaders of the people; but in general the conflict occurs in a short scene before the conclusion; at the end of the conflict the opponent is disarmed (cf. Lk 13.17; 14.6); and if there is some resistance by the opponent, the synoptic style is to be content with a brief remark (cf. Mk 3.6). Only in the Lukan account of the healing of the crippled woman does the dispute follow the healing (critical words from the ruler of the synagogue to the people; Jesus' reply, Lk 13.14ff.); but the scene is not changed there either. Discussions with the healed person, and the threat to him, are scenes which have no counterpart anywhere in the synoptics, nor any subsequent clash between the enemies and Jesus. The motif of a repeated encounter between the healed man and Jesus, elaborated so movingly in Scene 6, is used again in John's story of the paralysed man (cf. 5.14f.) but in the synoptics only in the Lukan story of the ten leprosy sufferers, which has thereby become a composition from two scenes of equal value (Lk 17.15-19); but here the 'second encounter' has another character than in John, since it is combined with the numerical motif, "only one of ten".

The scenes that follow the healing stand in complete contrast to the synoptic motif of secrecy as regards Jesus' miraculous power and his messianic dignity. The miracle is the talk of the day, and the Pharisees have to come to terms with it; if they do not draw the right conclusions, they reveal their blindness and their guilt. The healing of the blind man in John is an epiphany in the grand style: in front of everyone Jesus' miraculous power is displayed. It is typical of the synoptics, in contrast, that in the healing of the blind man in Mk 8.22-26 the healing takes place outside the village and the healed man is expressly forbidden to go back into the village. The narrator of John 9 has managed, by means of the dramatic skill that he has developed, to make his account much more natural to the reader than those of the synoptics.

The Raising of Lazarus

The third dramatically structured piece of narrative is the resurrection of Lazarus. The synoptics have two resurrection stories. The simpler one is the Lukan narrative of the youth at Nain, consisting of a single, admittedly graphically presented scene in which only Jesus speaks, in two short words. Then there is the story of Jairus, presented, as mentioned above, in four scenes (Scene 1, the first request from the father; Scene 2, the stop on the way; Scene 3, the receipt of the news of the death; Scene 4, the resurrection in the house). The whole thing is narrated more in the style of the novella than developed dramatically; in particular there is no real conversation. By contrast, the Johannine resurrection story displays the same ability to give dramatic shape to the narrative as does the healing of the blind man. Unlike the latter, and similarly to the Jairus narrative, the concluding scene is formed by the miracle itself, which is followed by a sequel in another setting. The first two scenes take place a long way from the place of resurrection. Jesus receives a messenger from the sisters and speaks apparently reassuringly about the condition of the sick man (11.3-4). Scene 2, which takes place two days later, presents us with a conversation with the disciples (vv. 9-16).

Jesus: Let us go back to Judaea.

The disciples: Rabbi, the Jews have just been trying to stone you, and you want to go back there again?

Jesus: Are there not twelve hours in the day? If someone goes by day he does not stumble, because he sees the light of this world; he only stumbles if he goes by night, because the light is not in him.[1]

Pause.

Jesus: Lazarus, our friend, has fallen asleep. But I will go to him, to wake him up.

The disciples: Lord, if he has fallen asleep, he will get well.[2]

Jesus: Lazarus has died, and I am glad for your sake that I was not there, so that you might believe.

But we must now go to him.

Thomas (to his fellow disciples): Let us go too, so that we may die with him.

Scene 3 (vv. 20-27) probably takes place at the entrance to Bethany: Martha comes to meet Jesus, and the beautiful conversation develops, which climaxes both in Jesus' testimony concerning the resurrection power that is in him and in every believer, and in the woman's confession of faith. Then there is a short Scene 4 in the house of rest: Mary in the house, with many Jews around her comforting her. Martha comes and whispers to her sister, "The Master is here and is calling you". Mary gets up quickly and goes out (vv. 28f.). The Jews leave the house and follow her; they can be heard saying, "She is going to the grave, to weep there".

---

[1] It is possible that this first half of the conversation was not originally part of the Lazarus story (so, Faure, *ZNW* 21, p. 114). But the insertion is not a clumsy one.

[2] Verse 13, a note by the evangelist; similar to an editor's note in an "annotated edition".

Scene 5

Setting as for Scene 3. Mary comes to Jesus. The Jews following her come in too. Mary sees Jesus and falls at his feet.

Mary: Lord, if only you had been here, my brother would not have died.

She weeps. The Jews accompanying her also weep.

Jesus shows great emotion and looks disdainfully at the mourners. Then he speaks: Where have you laid him?

The Jews: Come and see.

Jesus now bursts into tears.

The Jews: Look how much he loved him.

Others: Couldn't he who opened the eyes of the blind man prevent this man from dying?

Jesus shows emotion once again, and goes on to the grave.

Scene 6

At the grave, a cave with a stone in front of the entrance. Jesus (and his disciples), Martha (and Mary), the Jews.

Jesus: Push the stone away.

(A putrid smell becomes noticeable.)

Martha: Lord, he already smells bad; he has been lying in the grave four days already.

Jesus (to Martha): Didn't I tell you that if you believed you would see the glory of God?

The stone is pushed aside.

Jesus (his face lifted towards heaven): Father, I thank you for hearing me. I well knew that you always hear me. But for the sake of the people standing around, so that they might believe that you have sent me:

(Then in a loud voice) Lazarus, come out!

The deceased appears, bandages wrapped around his feet and hands, his face covered with a cloth.

Jesus: Untie him and let him go.

Many Jews show evidence of their faith. Some show unfriendly expressions and leave the spot.

Scene 7 (vv. 47-53) marks the conclusion, a council meeting between the high priests and the Pharisees, in which the situation following this miracle is discussed and Caiaphas gives his prophetic advice, a dramatic performance of the bald announcement in Mk 3.6 par., whereby the great deed is pragmatically inserted in the course of the catastrophe.

The narrative is of course to be regarded primarily as an *epiphany story*. With this grandiose example the evangelist shows the power over death that belongs to the Son of God. The scenes that precede the deed have the purpose of confirming the miracle by providing proof, in the most graphic and clear manner, that the man has really died: Jesus hesitates to come; so of course the sick man dies in the meantime. In Bethany everything is under the cloud of the sad death; Jesus is reproached for coming too late. The smell makes it clear that the buried man is already putrifying. But the evidence is not presented with the usual motifs associated with a miracle narrative, but brought out in a dramatic way in a lively sequence of scenes, encounters, conversations and expressions of emotion. From the point of view of style, the story is a dramatically formed *family novella:* three siblings—two sisters, the brother terminally ill; they send for the family friend, the miracle doctor; he comes too late. The sisters receive him individually with a reproach. He tries to move them to believe in his ability. And he actually calls the deceased brother out of the grave alive. It is a family novella, full of moving human features, like the story of the prodigal son, or even better the Tobit narrative: just as in Tobit the son is protected by a companion who is in reality an angel, so here the family has a friend who is a wonder-worker and who on this occasion even proves himself to be lord over life and death.

The dramatic shape of the conclusion leaves something to be desired from our point of view: there is no description of the immediate impression the resurrection makes, especially the greeting between brother and sisters, a corresponding gesture, or a word from Jesus along the lines of Lk 7.15's "he gave him back to his mother", the touching conclusion to the family novella. The scene is broken off prematurely; the creative touch goes lame, or rather the joy of narrating is extinguished after the fact of the miracle has been demonstrated, which has been sufficiently prepared for in what precedes it. This narrator wishes only to depict the 'legal sequel' in order to show how the mighty deed provided the last push towards the tragic outcome of the earthly story of Jesus.[1]

It is possible that our story has received various additions at the hands of a reviser (cf. e.g. Wellhausen, *Das Evangelium Johannes*, pp. 50ff.); however, the story as a whole in its present form gives the effect of a

---

[1] There is a remarkable similarity here to the Asclepius myth: Zeus kills Asclepius by means of a flash of lightning, either because he dares even to raise the dead, and he, Zeus, fears that people might be able to protect themselves from death with the remedy used by Asclepius, or because Pluto complains that Hades would no longer receive new arrivals (cf. the motivations in Apollod. III. 10.4 and Diodor. IV 71). The Jews decide on the death of Jesus because he has raised a dead man and they fear a general defection to him.

(relatively) unified composition—the more so if one elects for the rendering in the form of drama.

We shall deal with the fourth example, the appearance on Lake Galilee, in the context of our treatment of the other Easter stories.

The novella with a dramatic plot is thus a narrative form that characterises John's distinctive narrative style. It owes its existence and composition to the evangelist's undeniable joy in narrating and to his interest in the most impressive possible demonstration of the effectiveness of Christ's power and revelation for faith. The evangelist has taken up and developed three examples of this stylistic form, a pastoral discussion and two miracles; common to all three stories are the frequent changes of scene in them, and the fact that they show how people who see Christ come to faith in him; the two healing stories also depict the effect that the manifestations of divine power evoke in the enemies of Christ.

While the synoptics only have affinities with this stylistic form, a full parallel can be found in the Acts of the Apostles. Its author was able to allow himself more authorial freedom in the second volume of his work than in the first, where he was bound to an already relatively fixed and commonly known tradition. So alongside the numerous pericopes in the synoptic style we find there a number of more broadly conceived pictures, more rich in scenes, such as the conversion of Cornelius and the arrest and release of Peter (ch. 12).

The pastoral conversation or conversion dialogue is represented in two further examples in John, the conversation with Nicodemus at night, and the approach of the Greeks. Strangely enough, in both stories the dramatic form is limited to the beginning, and the poor presentation in these pieces has given rise above all to critical judgment and has brought upon John the reproach of artistic ineptitude and deficient interest in the historical as such.[1] Such criticism, as our analysis thus far has shown, is one-sided and inappropriate. In the three narratives we have discussed John shows an enjoyment in graphic storytelling and a mastery of technique that none of the synoptic evangelists was able to achieve. But what, then, of the two apparently unsuccessful essays?

The scene with Nicodemus begins with the indication of the time, which is at least sufficient to make it 'paintable'—he came to him by night—and with a dialogue which after the third utterance by Nicodemus leads into a religious speech by Christ which leaves no further opportunity for Nicodemus to speak and also dispenses with any

---

[1] Cf. e.g. Overbeck, *Johannes*, p. 303.

concluding statement to round off the narrative. The exposition is only the cue for the insertion of a sermon by the evangelist into the Gospel story. It ends with the last thought expressed by the preacher, just like a section in the First Epistle of John. Here, then, the preacher has pushed the dramatic shape to one side; the joy of narrating has been smothered by the compulsion to preach and bear witness. A synoptic analogy would be the eschatological chapter: there too we find a lucid exposition with the description of the setting (the slopes of the Mount of Olives) and a question of the disciples (Mk 13.3f. par.) and attached to it the apocalyptic discourse, without any further thought being given at the end to the situation and the hearers. There too the graphic historical insertion is only made in order to give the discourse a 'setting' in the 'story of Jesus'; the apocalypse could just as easily, like the Revelation of John, have been poured into the mould of a revelatory discourse by the elevated Son of Man.

Richer and more promising is the dramatic exposition of the pericope concerning the Greeks. Scene 1 has the Greeks come to Philip; Scene 2 adds Andrew to their number; in Scene 3 Jesus receives the deputation from the two disciples. In what he says one can recognise symbolic connections with the approach of the Greeks; but there is no continuation to the 'narrative of the Greeks'. There is no lack of dramatic impulses, but they no longer have anything to do with the Greeks. The scene develops into a testimony for the Jews and a dispute with them (12.29-36). For the sake of this continuation the evangelist has dropped the narrative of the Greeks and has therefore missed out not only on an exciting moment in the story, Jesus' encounter with the Greeks who desired to see him, like Zacchaeus, but also a dramatically effective contrast between the Greeks, who sought contact with Jesus, and the Jews, who have it but do not know what to make of it; such a contrast is depicted so vividly in the synoptic pericope of the Roman centurion in Capernaum. In view of this one cannot say here, either, that John has no interest in the historical course of affairs or that he lacks the gift of carrying through a dramatic scene. It is only this one story that he does not carry through, and this is because, for one thing, he loses his way in another narrative and another stylistic form, but also because he cannot, for the sake of his overall view, bring the Greeks together with Jesus in the flesh and he can only regard their approach as a prophecy of the time of the glorified Christ, as the sign of approaching crisis, which would lead through death to his glorification and to the universal extension of the Christian proclamation.

There is also a stylistic relationship between the Nicodemus conversation and the last testimony of the Baptist (3.22-36). The concrete exposition is especially rich here; it leads into a question which his disciples ask him (v. 26) and which then gives the cue for a longer testimony (vv. 27-36). Here too there is no narrative to round it off at the end; but here the omission of any comment on the effect of the message that is given is nowhere near as disturbing as in the Nicodemus pericope.

2

The second form of narrative we listed as being specifically Johannine is the connection between narrative and testimony- and dispute-discourse. There are only weak parallels in the synoptics, such as the message of the Baptist with the attached testimony of Jesus concerning him and himself, the defence against the Beelzebub slander in the Matthaean version, where there is a preceding succinct healing story (Mt 12.22ff.), and the question of authority in Mk 11.27ff. par.—if it can be included with the story of the cleansing of the temple. The synoptics did not, then, bring this type to full development. John has two extensive examples of it: the healing of a paralysed man and the miracle of the loaves. Both chapters are composed of "narrative" and attached 'speech'.

The story of the paralysed man (5.1-16 or 18) is again a dramatic novella, though considerably shorter than the main essays. In content and form it bears a close resemblance to the story of the man born blind. It runs to five scenes: Scene 1, the healing, a 'synoptic' pericope, but with particularly rich local colouring; Scene 2, deliberation between the healed man and the Jews, who reproach him for carrying his bed on the sabbath (cf. Lk 13.14) and want to know who has healed him on the sabbath; Scene 3, a further encounter between the healed man and Jesus (v. 14, cf. 9.35-38); Scene 4 (only sketched), the healed man informs the Jews that Jesus was his doctor (vv. 15f.); Scene 5, the Jews meet with Jesus (the situation can only be surmised) and raise their objection (v. 16); Jesus justifies himself with brief reference to his Father, which the Jews see as a new sin (vv. 17f.).

The Johannine sketch could have ended here; we would have a dramatic sketch of a healing which has aroused the displeasure of the Jews and would give one an inkling of the fate to come. But the evangelist again lets Jesus have the word and indeed the opportunity for a discourse that is approximately twice as long as the narrative, the first part a testimony concerning the relationship between the Son and the Father and the authority given to him (vv. 19-30), which with slight changes could just as easily have been inserted in the Johannine Epistles, and the second part an apostrophisation of the Jews, a judgment and punishment discourse in the style of the discourses that follow in chs. 7 and 8, but here without any interrupting and tension-building interjections by the Jews. The connection with the contrast that is so vividly made in the narrative is a loose one. The discourse is scarcely inspired by the narrative in particular. The combination is thus artificial and is borne along only by the dual interest in giving a concrete historical occasion for the tesimony- and dispute-discourse and in supplementing and expounding the narrative by means of a sermon. While the synoptics either have Jesus act or preach,[1] the Fourth Evangelist attempts to put the actions and preaching of Jesus together in a large pericope.

In the other example (John 6), the narrative that precedes the sermon concerns a completely synoptic subject, the miracle of the loaves with the subsequent walking on the water. A comparison shows that John indeed had the synoptic accounts in front of him, but that he offers an independent presentation as a whole, which—and this is again absolutely Johannine—is marked by a rather richer dramatic shape. True, he makes no mention of the preaching mentioned in Mark and Luke, because he has an extensive sermon following. On the other hand he gives the preparation of the miracle a more concrete colouring by having Jesus turn specifically to Philip (vv. 6f.) and placing the news of the available supplies on the lips of Andrew. At the end, from the information about the collection of the left-overs he forms a corresponding commission from Jesus (v. 12). Finally he adds a new, exciting scene: the call to the astonished crowd and their attempt to make the miracle-worker king (vv. 14f.). All these changes indicate an intensification of the dramatic impulses of the novella.

On the other hand John has simplified rather than dramatically intensified the following scene on the lake; in fact he omits any indication of the effect which the new revelation of power has on the disciples. While Mark and Matthew only add a new mob following, calling for healing, John reports the return of the people who were astonished at the disappearance of Jesus (vv. 22-24), in order to make a transition to a new meeting with Jesus, which—as is only mentioned later (v. 50)—takes place in the synagogue in Capernaum. The 'sermon' which now follows differs from that in ch. 5, etc., in a number of respects. First, it shows a much closer connection with the main preceding miracle—it is an exposition of the feeding miracle for the Christian community. Secondly, the discourse is continually interrupted by questions and objections from the Jews and reacts more or less exactly to them, thereby running a truly dramatic course. Finally, it emanates in two dramatic concluding scenes,

---

[1] Cf. on the one hand Jesus in the synagogue in Capernaum, where it is only stated that he taught, not what he taught, but the healing is depicted in artistic detail, and on the other hand the Sermon on the Mount.

first a short dispute with the majority of the audience who have become impatient and are inclined towards unbelief (vv. 60-65), and then, later on, a discussion with the loyal disciples. The latter takes its motifs from two different synoptic 'pericopes', Peter's confession in Caesarea Philippi and the unmasking of the traitor; John has therefore taken quite a number of synoptic 'pericopes', or at least their main motifs,[1] together with a testimony- and dispute-discourse in the synagogue, which he has composed, and combined them into a dramatic, organic whole. Chapter 6 is a short drama in two acts: feeding with return and the disputes in Capernaum; each act is constructed in various scenes; in the first act the deed-epiphanies predominate, while the second represents an epiphany of the witnessing Christ with the subsequent division of the audience into unbelievers and believers.

Of the evangelists, only John has developed the stylistic form of the miracle story with a following sermon that is prompted by it. This corresponds with his penchant, evident throughout the Gospel as a whole, for large compositions. In the New Testament its only analogy would be with the book of Acts: compare the Pentecost miracle and the Pentecost sermon; the healing of the lame and the temple sermon in Jerusalem; healing of the lame, homage and (short) sermon in Lystra. The book of Acts is a missionary book, which stands under similar literary conditions to John. The miracle stories and mission testimonies are the essential elements of the historical report there also, and the combination of both stylistic forms would have been a natural step for this writer too. Even if the connection should make a secondary impression as far as the sources and materials used by the evangelist are concerned,[2] it is a characteristic feature of the stylistic form used by the genuine author himself.

3

John's third stylistic form is the liberal sequence of individual scenes or individual pericopes that belong together temporally. The simplest and clearest example of this stands at the beginning of the Gospel narrative: the witness of the Baptist and the conversion of the first disciples. John has chosen to use this form, then, in order to illustrate very impressively and colourfully the introduction and opening of the great manifestation of the Son of God. Two acts can be distinguished: the witness of the Baptist (1.19-34) and the winning over of the first disciples (1.35-51). Act I consists of three scenes: two discussions and one witness discourse. Act II,

---

[1] The synoptic pericope of the "demand for a sign" has also been taken into the beginning of the dispute (v. 30).

[2] Cf. the judgment of most source analysts.

however, consists of quite short conversations which are linked organically together. Presentation in the form of a dramatic performance is again the best evidence for the special nature of this form of narrative.

ACT I

Setting: Bethany beyond the Jordan.

Scene 1

John the Baptist; flocking around him a deputation from Jerusalem, priests and Levites.

The envoys: Who are you?

John: I am not the Christ.

The envoys: Who (are you) then? Are you Elijah?

John: That is not who I am.

The envoys: Are you the Prophet?

John: No.

The envoys: Who are you? We have to give a report to those who sent us. What do you say about yourself?

John: I am 'the voice of one crying in the wilderness': Prepare the way for the Lord, as Isaiah the prophet proclaimed.[1]

Scene 2

The same, with envoys of the Pharisees.

The Pharisees: Why do you baptise, then, if you are not the Christ, nor Elijah, nor the Prophet?

John: I baptise with water. Among you stands one whom you do not know, who comes after me, the straps of whose sandals I am not worthy to loosen.

Scene 3

One day later. John sees Jesus approaching.

John: Look, there (comes) the lamb of God, which takes away the sin of the world. It is he that I spoke of: after me comes a man, who was (already) there before me, for he was prior to me. And I did not know him; but so that he might be revealed to Israel, that is why I came as a baptiser in water.

With a new introduction a continuation of the testimony follows in vv. 32-34.

---

[1] It is not said that these envoys departed. Interest in the precise fixing of the scene disappears when the testimony has been given.

Critics have incisively pointed out the inconsistencies in the presentation. The relationship between Scene 1 and Scene 2 seems to present the greatest difficulty: the second envoy simply continues the interview with the first, without there being any indication that they were present for the first conversation. This does indeed remain unclear. There is no need, however, to attach much importance to this. The main thing is that in two discussion scenes, with a few strokes, the atmosphere which John aroused is described, and that the testimony he gave concerning himself and concerning the one to come, grows out of a lively conversation.[1] One might compare the parallel synoptic tradition. Mark renders the logion with the simplest conceivable introduction (1.7); Matthew juxtaposes it with a woe discourse, which he introduces rather more graphically: "when he saw many of the Pharisees and Sadducees coming to baptism' (3.7). Only Luke has given the witness a context of its own, 'when the people were expectant and they were all pondering about John in their hearts, whether he might be the Christ, John explained to all of them" (3.15f.) Where such silent considerations are found, the Fourth Evangelist has now placed loud questions and thus created something that possesses real literary, artistic value.

Scene 3 crowns the whole thing, and despite its simple construction is of considerable dramatic weight: the appearance of the person who was just spoken of, whom everyone is now anxious to see, in the circle of the precursor and witness, who now has the opportunity to complete his testimony. That a master like Grünewald has been inspired by these simple words to create one of the most tremendous paintings in Christian art, is evidence that some of the highest artistic intuition has played a role in the creation of this scene. It should not be forgotten that vv. 29f. should be taken together with the preceding verses; this is no independent pericope, it is 'Scene 3'.

ACT II

Scene 1

Same setting. One day later; it is four in the afternoon. John is standing together with two of his disciples. He sees Jesus moving nearby.

John: Look, the lamb of God.

The two disciples hear this and go after Jesus. Jesus turns round and sees that they are following him.

Jesus: What are you looking for?

---

[1] At this point I am only concerned to describe the artistic effect of the text before us; it is greater than the source-investigations and division-hypotheses suggest or allow for.

The two disciples: Rabbi, where do you live?
Jesus: Come and see.
They go together.

Scene 2

Another setting. Andrew, one of the two disciples of John, finds his brother, Simon Peter.
    Andrew: We have found the Messiah!
    They go off together.[1]

Scene 3

Setting: the home of Jesus. Andrew comes up to Jesus with Peter.
    Jesus (looking at Simon): You are Simon, the son of John; you will be called Rock-man.

Scene 4

Setting as in Scene 3. One day later. Jesus is about to leave. He meets Philip.
    Jesus (to Philip): Follow me!
    (Philip joins Jesus.)[2]

Scene 5

Setting: a region of Galilee. Philip meets with Nathanael.
    Philip: The one Moses wrote of in the law, and the prophets, (him) we have found, Jesus the son of Joseph from Nazareth!
    Nathanael: Can anything good come out of Nazareth?
    Philip: Come and see.

Scene 6

Jesus' home in Galilee. Nathanael comes up to Jesus.
    Jesus: Look, a true Israelite, without guile.
    Nathanael: How do you know me?
    Jesus: Before Philip called you, when you were under the fig-tree, I saw you.
    Nathanael: Rabbi, you are the Son of God, you are the King of Israel!
    Jesus: You believe because I told you that I saw you under the fig-tree? You will see (still) greater things than these.[3]

---

[1] Indicated in v. 42a, "he brought him to Jesus".
[2] The evangelist has not explicitly mentioned this. The stage directions of the editor of these dramatic scenes are no longer expressly mentioned.
[3] Verse 52 is a logion, suitably added in the synoptic manner—cf. the new introduction, "and he says to him".

Only a few words need to be added. First of all, it is clear that vv. 35ff.
introduce a second act. Seen critically, vv. 35f. do, it is true, form a
doublet with v. 29. However, the stylistic judgment sees the repetition of
the Baptist's testimony as the indispensable and effective transition to the
new act, in which the new disciples of the Greater One appear, whom the
witness and precursor leads to the latter. There now follows, like another
bead on a chain, the next scene concerning the others. None of them has
validity on its own, they belong to one another, they maintain one
another. Everything is indicated only briefly and still the few strokes are
sufficient to make clear pictures lively. That here too an artistic spirit is
at work, can be learnt by anyone who glances at Daniel Greiner's
woodcuts on the Gospel of John (folio 3). These are simply vignettes,
short encounters, but the consequences for time and eternity are palpably
clear, and one encounter engenders another.

A comparison with the synoptics once again demonstrates the
distinctive form of the Johannine style. The synoptic call stories (Peter
and Andrew, the sons of Zebedee, Levi) are certainly more graphic and
more concrete as individual stories. But they are pericopes. The scenery
on the beach allowed two scenes, and only one repetition; the call at the
seat of custom could only be narrated as a single event. The sequence of
six scenes in which each has its own individual character, and no scheme
is particularly dominant, and one thing follows from another, was not
possible with the synoptic stylistic material.

There is, indeed, one synoptic pericope which comes close to the
Johannine scene sequence, Jesus' conversations with three different
followers in Luke (9.57-62)—in Matthew it is just two (8.19-22). But
these are only encounters of a similar kind, which have no inner
connection but are put together by the evangelist because of their close
relationship. The Johannine section is no artificial, added compilation of
small units found in the tradition, but the finished conception of an
artistically creative writer, even if the material is in part taken from
tradition.

Chapter 1 is the only example of a completely self-contained, freely
created sequence of scenes. But the possibility of similar creations was
available to the evangelist at three other places, in the appearances at the
Jerusalem festival, in the Passion story, and in the reports of the
resurrection appearances.

4

There is no mistaking a certain organic plan in the description of the dispute scenes in Jerusalem. Chapters 7f. are by no means a loose juxtaposition of small individual anecdotes as in the Jerusalem section in the synoptics, but an attempt to give a coherent description of a visit to a festival, though the composition is either not finished off in the middle and at the conclusion, or has been corrupted by later rearrangements and insertions.

The Introduction is a splendid success, a conversation with the brothers about a visit to the festival (7.1-9), then Jesus' journey (7.10) and the brief description of the atmosphere, which is reminiscent of the listing of the disciples which precedes Peter's confession in Mk 8.28 par., but is more impressive in its Johannine form (the evangelist's report on the atmosphere). Great things are expected. There then follow two scenes, one which takes place in the middle of the festival (7.14-36), the other in the last days (7.37-52). The change is immense. We soon hear Jesus teaching and defending himself against misunderstandings and attacks from the Jews, and soon again we see how the Jews argue about Jesus among themselves (cf. 7.15; 7.25-27; 7.31; 7.40-44); the last of these passages is a particularly dramatic dispute scene, without comparison in the synoptics. In addition we then have, inlaid in a thoroughly credible manner, the high priests' and Pharisees' plan to seize him, first in Scene 1, where the narrative, however, gets bogged down at the beginning (7.32), then following Scene 2, where in a sequel a quarrel in the high court (again not found in the synoptics) is presented extremely vividly: dispute with the servants who return with their mission unaccomplished, and the rebuttal of an objection from Nicodemus (7.45-52).

Just as in ch. 7 the execution of the controversy leads to numerous inconsistencies, in ch. 8 too the context leaves more and more to be desired. Three controversy scenes are loosely juxtaposed (8.12-20; 8.21-30; 8.31-59). A clearly evident context and progression is lacking. It is as if the evangelist had conceived new individual scenes one after another and had placed them together according to external criteria. The pieces are held together only by the tone of the speech, the style and the subject; these Johannine creations are not pericopes in the synoptic style either. The section does, though, have a conclusion of sorts: Jesus announces his preeminence over Abraham and can only escape the stones of the Jews by fleeing (8.58f.).

Here follows the story of the man born blind, which in its context gives the impression of a huge pericope, though it fits in with the whole to the extent that it dramatically portrays the resistance of the opponents, which is increased as a result of Jesus' continued public activity. Appended to the last scene, without any new historical scene-setting, is the allegory of the shepherd. It is only at the conclusion that the attempt is made to make it fit with the dramatic composition as a whole, by means of the representation of the effect of the speech by a lively difference of opinion among the Jews (10.19-21).

A new chapter is added, the appearance at the temple-consecration festival, a unique scene, rich in effective dramatic moments. The Jews passionately demand an open statement from Jesus as to whether he is the Christ—a parallel to the envoys in ch. 1—, think they can recognise blasphemy in Jesus' answer, want to stone him, listen to Jesus' defence, until he repeats the alleged blasphemy, then attempt to arrest him, but he is able to escape from them. The only possible comparisons with synoptic parallels are the message of the Baptist in Mt 11.2ff. par., the pericope of the question of authority and the cross-examination by Caiaphas; despite a number of unevennesses, the richer creative ability of John is evident here too. In addition, this Johannine composition is also conceived as a link in a chain.

The great Lazarus pericope brings in a new change—it seems intentional that the two stylistically linked pericopes are separated by a sequence of testimony speeches and controversy scenes. In the framework of the whole it gives a motive for Jesus' return to the outskirts of Jerusalem and—in its last scene, for the high court's solemn and formal decision to put Jesus to death. A transitional scene (11.54-57) depicts the situation of the approaching third festival, the Passover.

Chapter 12 describes Jesus' last stay in the city. The report starts off with two synoptic pericopes, the anointing and the entry, which, however, are firmly integrated in the continuing narrative by means of added remarks and pieces of information. For one thing, Lazarus is thought of in both accounts: he is a witness of the anointing; it is on his account that the people come in droves to Bethany; and it is on account of his resurrection that such a crowd comes out to meet Jesus when he enters Jerusalem (12.2, 9f., 17f.).[1] On the other hand these events strengthen the resolve of the high court to suppress with violence the increasing influence that Jesus is gaining, even if the Pharisees remark pessimistically that they are powerless to do anything about this enthusiasm (12.10f., 19). Nor, then, are these two sections arbitrarily inserted pericopes that can easily be removed, adhering only weakly to their surroundings.

---

[1] This is of course the Johannine reworking of the pericopes taken from his sources.

The narrative of the Greeks fits very nicely with the story of the entry; the testimony of Jesus, which it leads into, is dominated completely by thoughts of death. Originally it would probably have been thought of as the 'last word' to the public. This impression is destroyed not so much by a contemplation by the evangelist set in the narrative (12.37-43) as by a following, completely frameless discourse section (12.44-50) which has certainly entered later at this point.

In chs. 7–12 at any rate, we have the grand attempt to describe in a dramatically effective manner, in a coherent but varied presentation, Jesus' appearance in Jerusalem, his witness and his dispute with the Jews, his great miracles and the animosity of the Jews that is aroused by all this. A self-contained composition of the whole text can be demonstrated. Most sections, including the synoptic material, are well integrated into it. But occasionally the framework leaves something to be desired, and there is no shortage of passages which have either been inserted later, or which the evangelist was not able to rework.

Only one further stylistic form needs to be remarked upon at this point, which the evangelist uses particularly frequently in this large section, namely the controversy dialogue. The synoptics have numerous pericopes which are preserved in this stylistic form, and M. Albertz in particular has provided an excellent style-critical analysis of these synoptic controversy dialogues. If we should briefly characterise the Johannine controversy dialogues by contrast, we would observe the following. First, in contrast to the synoptic examples, they lack the pericope-type character almost completely. Individual conversations can indeed be cut out, but in the text they are mainly firmly inserted in the continuing narrative. Two types, then, can be distinguished: scenes in which the question in dispute is brought up by the Jews, and those in which something Jesus says creates the bone of contention. Only the first type corresponds to the synoptic material.[1] It is true that in John it is represented only on one occasion: the Jews' question concerning the Messiah (10.22ff.). But this one piece also shows the great difference in stylistic execution between John and the synoptics. In the latter, the course of the conversation is usually very simple: the opponents are either dismissed with a single word from Jesus, or a question and answer exchange is inserted before the dismissal. The Johannine controversy dialogue would have conformed to this schema if it could have been content with the first declaration which it puts on the lips of Jesus (vv. 25f.). It is characteristically Johannine (1) how the Fourth Evangelist lets

---

[1] Cf. Bultmann, pp. 10ff. Exceptions would be the second debate on the sabbath and the discussion about the son of David.

the testimony spin on (vv. 27-29), and has Jesus close with a saying, which raises the greatest indignation (v. 30); (2) how the reaction to Jesus' answer is an attack on his life—the Jews are much more irate in the gentle principal Gospel than in the synoptics; (3) how the Johannine Christ reacts by defending himself spiritually, asks the Jews about the grounds for their fury and refutes the reproach of blasphemy with a relatively broad argumentation by citing an argument from Scripture and repeating and expounding his first testimony. The composition is thus richer, with more theological content than the typical synoptic composition; it is a creation of the evangelist. While in the synoptic controversy dialogues the fight is against the historical Jesus (cf. Albertz, p. 93), here it is against the Christ of the church's faith. Here it is not Jesus' struggle with the religion of his contemporaries (Albertz, p. 64) but the conflict between the Jews and the positions of the post-apostolic, hellenistic church. As far as the weapons used by the Johannine Christ are concerned, we do admittedly encounter here the almost constant argument from Scripture found in the synoptic controversy accounts; but in John this is quite a rarity.[1] What the Johannine Christ actually uses as weapons are the testimony concerning the eminence of the Son, his works, and concerning the blessedness of believers and the fate of unbelievers—above all, then, the preaching motifs of (Pauline-) Johannine Christianity. And so it comes about that in the Johannine controversy dialogue we do not find the closely cut personality of the messianic prophet Jesus of Nazareth as depicted in the synoptic tradition to be especially in evidence but the heavenly Son of God, who is elevated above all human characteristics.

On the whole the characteristics of this one controversy dialogue that is prompted by the opponents are true also of the bulk of the controversy scenes caused by the testimony of Jesus. The pericope-like dressing is almost completely lost here. The whole thing is a sermon, a witness discourse, interwoven with controversy motifs, in which the witness and preacher is interrupted by objections and questions, or in which in a pause made by the speaker, misgivings and misunderstandings are expressed which then give rise to the resumption of the witness and the refutation of the misunderstandings. A specially favourite technique used by the Fourth Evangelist but uncommon among the synoptics is that of the misunder-standing. As is well known, in practice this does not always come off entirely successfully, since (1) the misunderstanding is often expressed in very rough external terms and—for our taste at least—is not very well chosen, and since (2) the answer does not always represent a real

---

[1] On the citations from Scripture in John cf. now the recent article by A. Faure, "Die alttestamentlichen Zitate im 4. Evangelium und die Quellenscheidungshypothese", *ZNW* 21, pp. 99-121.

refutation of the misunderstanding. As far as the technique is concerned, it should be noted that when he gives the word to the opponents, the evangelist likes to have them quote a single word of Christ (more or less exactly).

John's generous composition entails also the fact that whereas the synoptic controversy dialogue is regularly concerned with a dispute about a single question, in John new points of contention arise again and again in the course of a discourse (cf. 6.41ff., 52ff.; 8.13ff., 18ff.; 8.21-30, 32-59). In chs. 6 and 8, we thus see greatly extended discussions with repeated interruptions from the hearers. The testimony of Christ, however, always dominates. With few exceptions (cf. 7.52f.) the objections are restricted to short sentences and questions, while Christ answers with longer expositions and moves on to new subjects. Mostly, though not always (cf. 7.35f.), he has the last word, as in the synoptics; in his sure sense of style, the evangelist likes to have him follow the last objection with a concluding, brief authoritative word or a clarificatory, salutary explanation of what has been said (cf. 8.58; 6.62-64).

These few and necessarily (given the external circumstances) very briefly expressed remarks, will, I hope, suffice to make clear the great differences in style that obtain between the synoptic and the Johannine controversy accounts. In the former we have folklore tradition, dependent primarily on memory, corresponding to the laws of folklore, kept precise and concise, and finely honed, using the most simple means, each conversation constituting a self-contained unit; here in John we find mainly free composition, often given real, true-to-life shape, often also artificially formed and infelicitously executed, seldom composed as a conversation pericope, generally growing out of a discourse and intertwining with it, without fixed forms, and to judge by the theological content, fully steeped in the atmosphere of the hellenistic church. In the synoptics, a rich fullness of subjects, as it presents the religious practice and the religious hope of Judaism at the time of Jesus; here a conscious concentration on the work, the dignity, the origins of Jesus, so that the enlightening, negative testimony of Jesus, in particular, is marked by rich repetition and a certain monotony.

5

The presentation of the Passion story already has a special character in the synoptics.[1] Pericopes, stories that is, which are separable and have been

---

[1] Cf. Bousset, *Kyrios Christos* (2nd edn), pp. 34ff.; K.L. Schmidt, *Der Rahmen*, pp. 303ff., *idem*, "Die literarische Eigenart der Leidensgeschichte Jesu", *Christliche Welt* 11/12 (1918); Bultmann, *op. cit.*, pp. 166ff.

inserted later, can indeed be discerned here too; but there is a basic stock of narratives here which provides a self-contained sequence of actions: the last supper, the arrest, cross-examination before the high court, trial before Pilate, and sentence, and finally the crucifixion. The connection between these scenes is, then, as in the synoptics, much closer and more natural than in the pre-Passion story. But these closely connected basic reports are also marked by a pericope-type character. Here too, in a following story little or no reference is made to the preceding one. Allusions are made to elements of earlier stories (cf. especially the mocking allusions to the temple saying at the foot of the cross). But often there is no such reference when we might expect one. More importantly, the synoptic Passion story nowhere refers back to Jesus' preceding activity. This is rather strange. So many concrete objections are raised in the conflict accounts, and it is so frequently observed that the opposition's deadly enmity was aroused, that one would be justified in expecting all these transgressions of the accepted tradition to be raised in the court. Instead, the synoptic pericope of the trial shows that the council is actually embarrassed as to how it should proceed against Jesus, and the high priest's great question which saves the situation is not particularly well prepared for in the preceding synoptic tradition. The account of the trial is just as much a 'pericope' as the other individual controversy accounts, an individual story which is conceived without consideration for the remaining pieces of tradition; and this explains the fact that the synoptic tradition gives no clear information as to how it came to the trial of Jesus, and why Jesus was convicted.

All these peculiarities of the synoptic Passion narrative are overcome in the Johannine passion story. It is simply continuous narrative throughout. 'Pericopes', 'episodes' and separable scenes are completely absent. Each new narrative rests on the previous one; the whole thing is held together by a unified style. But even in respect of the story of the public activity of Jesus, the Passion story does not adopt a particularly isolated position. The trial is the natural conclusion of the mood that appears in the various controversy scenes; in John it is perfectly clear why Jesus was taken prisoner and condemned. To crown it all, Christ himself refers to his earlier proclaimed teachings before the high priest (18.20f.), and when he gives his testimony before Pilate, his words breathe entirely the spirit of his public lectures. A unified narrative runs from Christ's first appearance, even indeed from the prologue and from the testimony of the Baptist up to the trial and the crucifixion (cf. also 19.7 with 1.18; 5.18; 10.33).

The structure of the Passion story also displays great differences in comparison with the synoptics. The narrative of the last supper before the arrest, consisting of a preparatory pericope and two (in Luke, three) short scenes (conversation about the traitor, institution of the eucharist and in Luke also the pronouncement concerning rank in the Kingdom of God), is elaborated much more fully in John. First, two things happen, the footwashing and the unmasking of the traitor, both in Johannine style, complete with dramatic impulses and didactic statements, and like most Johannine narratives, well suited to real dramatic performance. Then a sequence of farewell speeches, which are seldom interrupted by questions from the disciples—testimony speeches, therefore, of a purer type than the controversy speeches that precede them.[1] Finally, a solemn prayer by the Johannine Christ, in which the cultic-mystic character of the whole meeting reaches its climax (sacramental action—expulsion of the impure—sermon—prayer). The report of the last supper in John thus achieves greater elaboration than the Passion story.

The divine Christ's high-priestly prayer now replaces the prayer-struggle of the synoptic Jesus. The arrest, too, is reshaped fully in the spirit of the Johannine picture of Christ (cf. 18.6ff.). A striking departure from the synoptic scheme is the fact that only one cross-examination, before Annas, is narrated, while the trial proper, with the solemn sentence by the reigning high priest, Caiaphas, is missing. Peter's denial is linked to the cross-examination by Annas. The dignity with which Christ faces the high priest as if facing his servant is Johannine: the sermon on the mount (Mt 5.39) and Isaiah 53, the spirit of which blows through the synoptic passion story, do not exist for the Fourth Evangelist. The two scenes which John paints in a few strokes are formed dramatically, but they do not ensue in a result. Why John rushes so hurriedly through the trial before Caiaphas is a puzzle. The explanation that he to some degree refers to the synoptic report for elaboration is untenable, since nowhere does John refer to the synoptics—indeed he is more interested in suppressing them than elaborating them[2]—and there is no indication at all why he should have passed over such a decisive scene. Either John did not recognise the synoptic account, or his narrative is incomplete at this point, or part of it has been displaced or lost.

The account of the denial of Peter is considerably simpler and shorter in John than in the synoptics—a rare occurrence, though it is also evident in the story of the entry into Jerusalem.

There now follows the gem in the Johannine Passion story, the trial before Pilate. Its eminently dramatic character has been demonstrated

---

[1] This is not, of course, the place to discuss the matter of the composition and style of these speeches. On the style, cf. especially K. Stange, *Die Eigenart der johanneischen Produktion.*

[2] I hope to be able to give more detailed grounds for this thesis elsewhere.

already by Thompson in his skilful translation in dramatic form (*op. cit.*, pp. 123-25).[1] The narrative is divided into eight scenes. The advance over the synoptics consists in the fact that John distinguishes two settings for the action on the stage and has Pilate to-ing and fro-ing between one place and the other: a terrace in front of the palace, where he deliberates with the representatives of the council, and a room indoors where he— evidently in private—speaks with Jesus alone; at the same time we learn each time exactly where Jesus is, something which remains unclear in the synoptics. John is the first to create the moving scenes: 'Jesus before Pilate' and the Ecce homo, i.e. 'Jesus presented to the Jews by Jesus', thereby giving art the most devastating reproach scenes known to it. Equally important is the fact that John has broken with the synoptic motif of the silence or word-shyness of Jesus, inspired by Isaiah 53, and has thus created real dialogues between Jesus the Christ and the representative of the Emperor. These conversations (18.33-37; 19.9-11) fill the second and sixth scenes. Since the first conversation deals with the kingdom of Jesus, comparisons with the synoptic conversation concerning the tax coin suggest themselves. Ranke has declared the saying with which Jesus there decides the question, to be the most important and significant of all Christ's statements,[2] but this Johannine scene surely is much more deserving of such a high assessment. The Judaic antithesis, Caesar–God, is transferred into the Christian antithesis, World Empire–Kingdom of God, World ruler–Christ. One has to look to the most elevated ideas for parallels which bring out the world-historical significance of this brilliant Johannine creation. I know only two comparable scenes: the temptation story in Luke and Matthew, in particular the temptation on the mountain, and the scene that derives from Jewish apocalyptic—the conversation between the 'lion' and the 'eagle', in the course of which the eagle goes up in flames (*Apoc. Ezra* 11.36ff.; cf. 12.31ff.), and the prophecy of Baruch (ch. 40), according to which the last ruler of the fourth empire, the last emperor, to be precise, is transported in chains to Mount Zion, where the Messiah calls him to account because of all his misdemeanours and then kills him. Certainly, all temptation is far removed from the Pilate scene, but Pilate and Christ are representatives of two kingdoms and two worlds, like Christ and the devil. The Jewish analogy illuminates the contrast between Jewish messianic expectation and the story of Jesus and the Christ; the roles are distributed antithetically: Pilate calls the Christ to account, and Pilate kills the Christ! But Pilate is small, nonetheless, and

---

[1] He has a predecessor in M. Hitchcock, *A Fresh Study of the Fourth Gospel* (1911), pp. 135ff. Cf. also Heitmüller's explanation in the *Schriften des Neuen Testaments* (3rd edn), 4, pp. 170ff.
[2] *Weltgeschichte*, III, p. 161.

Christ great. The authority which Pilate possesses is given him by heaven, and the kingdom of Jesus also comes from heaven. Pilate passes away, and Christ remains. The two scenes, the former in particular, represent John's greatest and most significant dramatic creation, in cultural, world-historical and spiritual respects. The great reality-splitting contrasts are drawn in a few strokes, and at the same time a picture of the character of the man Pilate is given. Before Pilate, too, the Christ again stands by his whole teaching and by his commission and in a few words gives a description of his testimony.

The change of scene (Pilate before the people and before Jesus) illustrates in the clearest way possible the great difficulty that the procurator found himself in: with the impressions that he receives outside he goes into the house, and with the impressions that the conversation with Jesus and the sight of him make upon him, he appears before the Jews. Finally, he succumbs to the human afflictions which the Jews are able to inflict upon him. Only John presents this conflict and the necessity of its tragic solution graphically and dramatically before our eyes.

The highly dramatic character of the narrative is attained also by means of John narrating only little, and rather allowing the characters to speak (cf. e.g. the treatment of the Barabbas scene in the synoptics and in John), and by his drawing pictures with sharp contrasts, by having the Jewish opponents fight with highly political arguments (cf. 18.31; 19.7, 12, 15), to which Pilate eventually succumbs, and finally, in true Johannine style, by making Pilate the unwitting proclaimer of a higher truth, grossly misunderstood by the Jews, and not even grasped by himself, at the very moment when he, the pagan, presents the Jews with their king. This 'offering' of Jesus to the Jews by Pilate seems to be an even more shattering irony than the 'prophecy' of Caiaphas; at any rate, the tragedy of the subject of 'Jesus Christ and the Jews' nowhere finds such starkly contrasting and moving expression as in this Johannine scene.

The special attractiveness of the scenes also consists in the fact that alongside the power struggle between world-historical forces, human psychology also plays a full part. I think particularly of the conflict into which Pilate sees himself thrown, on the one hand, and the superior, clever politics of the Jews on the other. I would not hesitate to count the Johannine account of the trial before Pilate as one of the greatest dramatic creations of world literature.

To conclude, I would offer an overview of the eight scenes. Scene 1, the handing over of the accused, and the case for the prosecution (18.28-31, with gloss, v. 32); Scene 2, the first interview between the procurator and Jesus (vv. 33-37); Scene 3, the announcement to the Jews and the choice of Barabbas (v. 38-40); Scene 4, the tormenting and the mockery (only here does the action predominate; 19.1-3); Scene 5, the Ecce homo (19.4-7); Scene 6, the second interview between the judge and the accused (vv. 8-11); Scene 7, repeated deliberation with the Jews (v. 12);[1] Scene 8, repeated presentation of Jesus and his being offered to the Jews (vv. 13-16). I would note also, that some motifs are indeed repeated, but that the repetition certainly does not fall flat, since the circumstances vary.[2]

In the crucifixion scene the synoptics too have developed high dramatic artistry. The Johannine version, too, which coincides with that of the synoptics in some scenes (the dividing up of the garments and the mockery), omits significant scenes found in the synoptics and replaces them with his own moving material, thereby achieves high dramatic effect, but one cannot say that it surpasses the synoptics at this point. The scenes which John offers are: the discussion between the high priest and Pilate concerning the inscription, the Johannine words on the cross, especially the scene with Mary and the disciple, and the removal of the bodies of the crucified. By means of the evangelist's omissions and the inclusion of his own material, the death of Jesus in John loses something of the grand-tragic character given it in particular by Mark and Matthew, and gains instead something moving; only the last words, "It is finished", remind the reader of the eminence of the Johannine Christ.

The character of the passage concerning the removal from the cross is more narrative than dramatic; no words are in direct speech; the editor has given the narrative the greatest importance by means of two explanations. As regards the following pericope concerning the burial, we need remark only that John provides the synoptics' Joseph with the company of his Nicodemus, and that here too he simply makes allusions rather than developing dramatic conversations.

6

As far as the synoptic Easter stories are concerned, those worthy of mention as accomplishments of artistic value would be limited to the narrative of the discovery of the empty tomb in Mark, the manifestation of the risen one at the conclusion of Matthew (despite the sketchy framework) and then in particular Luke's Emmaus novella. John, if we take the addition into consideration, has the greatest number of appearance stories; and, with the possible exception of the first

---

[1] Thompson includes v. 12 in the sixth scene: Pilate has then remained in the palace and hears the Jews calling outside. There is, it is true, no indication of a change in scene by the evangelist, but the above interpretation, the possibility of which Thompson indeed accepts, seems to me to be the more correct one.

[2] The source critics have often, quite unreasonably, found fault with the composition of this act.

appearance to the disciples (20.19-23), which possesses just as few literarily effective elements as its counterpart in Luke (29.36-49), they are all highly graphic and dramatically effective, and could be performed on the stage, just as they have exercised a particular attraction for artists, too. That the pericopes of ch. 20 do not cohere organically, has been well demonstrated, especially by Wellhausen:[1] vv. 2-10, the first pericope, is an insertion; the appearance to Mary is narrated as if she is the only one intended; the appearance to Thomas is also an accretion, since the first appearance to the disciples is actually an appearance before all the disciples. Chapter 21 of course stands entirely on its own: it is originally the appearance of the Lord to his disciples. The Johannine Easter stories are thus a mosaic of pericopes, of a type not found elsewhere in John. The inconsistencies, however, are not disturbing. In ch. 20 rich variation and a certain intensification come into their own. If the message to Mary Magdalene once formed the conclusion of the Gospel, the confession of Thomas is now a much more effective ending, referring back as it does to the elevated introductory sentences in the prologue. By contrast, the present ending with the appearance tacked on finally in ch. 21, with its clumsy exegetical gloss, is a great anti-climax.

Noteworthy in the first Easter story, the two disciples' race to the grave, is the fact that though it is rich in action which suggests dramatic performance, it contains no conversation, not a single word, in fact, which makes it unique in the whole Gospel;[2] it is therefore a mime narrative, which, furthermore, serves apologetic purposes.

"Mary Magdalene at the grave" is the Johannine counterpart to the synoptic "Women at the empty grave". The charm of the narrative consists in Jesus' entrance—Matthew has this connection too—and in the way in which the recognition is described. The scene is one of the tenderest that John has transmitted. The occurrence is practically painted before one's eyes—one can almost reach out and grasp it, it is so vivid. The depiction of the scenes, the woman's originally depressed mood, and her change of mood, this is all drawn with mastery. What we call the "Easter morning atmosphere" is in the main drawn from this pericope. In no other Easter story does personal bonding with the master come to such sensitive and tender expression.

The first appearance to the disciples has little in the way of atmosphere, but all the more significance for apologetics and for the confirmation of the apostolate. The apologetic tendency of the appearance

---

[1] *Das Johannes-Evangelium*, pp. 91ff.

[2] In the account of the burial of Jesus there is an allusion to a conversation in the request to Pilate (19.38) and his giving of permission; the same is true of the removal from the cross (cf. 19.31).

to Thomas is even more strongly marked; similarly it has greater dramatic power. The "My Lord and my God", the penultimate utterance in the original form of the Gospel, sounds like a mighty chord in which the testimony of the apostle concerning the worthiness of Jesus echoes through the centuries. Its complete effectiveness is, it is true, mitigated to some extent by the Lord's critical words; as in the other Gospels, of course, he has to have the last word. But these last words are directed more to those who are not witnesses, to subsequent generations, and to them it is more of a comforting blessing.

The two disciple pericopes, moreover, together form an act divided into three scenes (Scene 2 is the report to Thomas of the first appearance); the addition has therefore been linked with particular skill to the first appearance report (vv. 19-23), which was not originally intended to have any sequel.

The appended chapter, the appearance at Lake Galilee, is, as has already been remarked, to be ranked with the greatest dramatic novellas. The play falls into two acts, the first of which is structured in three scenes, the second in two. Scene 1 of Act 1 evidently takes place in a house in Capernaum (vv. 2f.). Scene 2 takes in part of the lake and the beach as its setting. The action is rich and varied: first the disciples in the fishing boat, then the appearance of Jesus on the shore, then the catch of fish, then Peter's swim and the others' following by boat. Scene 3 follows on immediately; the disciples gather round the Lord, and a meal takes place, but without words. The narrative again suggests translation into dramatic form, despite the fact that it contains few words. In origin it is closely related to the Lukan story of Peter's catching of fish, but surpasses it by richer action and greater vividness.

Act 2 is the masterly Johannine version of the colourless "call" with which the Lukan counterpart (5.1ff.) ends. The two scenes into which it divides are of unequal worth. Scene 1, the Lord's courting of the love of Peter, his institution in the apostolic office and the prophecy of his tragic end is one of the most moving disciple narratives which John, and indeed the Gospel literature as a whole, offers. It is strange that this rehabilitation of the deeply fallen disciple is not found until the addendum to the latest Gospel. It fills a sensitive gap. Even stranger is the avoidance of any allusion to the preceding (threefold) denial. The Johannine Christ acts and speaks here, stirs and heals the conscience with a tenderness that is scarcely any longer human. However one thinks of the originator of this dramatic concluding chapter, he possesses the same mastery in the drawing of effective scenes and the stylisation of profound conversations as the creator of the other great dramatic narratives. The conclusion (v.

19) is something of an anti-climax; one would have expected some further comforting promise along the lines of 1 Pet. 1.6ff. or 5.1f.

The judgment is even more true, as we have already mentioned, of the second scene. The one who had just experienced the graciousness of the Lord in such a shaming and moving manner, shows jealousy towards the other great disciple—there is a faint reminiscence of the attitude of the unfaithful servant. He then experiences a cool reproach too; the repeated "Follow me" links the two scenes together into a unity and provides a 'last word of the Lord', which does not sound particularly formidable, but which remains in the reader's conscience as a last admonishment. The concluding remark was necessary in view of the later temporal circumstances, but it disturbs the mood awakened by the dramatic scene. It should be printed as an explanatory marginal note by the editor, in small type at the foot of the page. That it has the greatest significance for the theological critic is of no consequence at this point.

7

While the attempt to create in the Passion story a dramatically progressive narrative out of the original pericopes has been entirely successful, the Easter stories follow more the synoptic type of a linear sequence of pericopes; the material here was too sparse for an organic fusion, and the collection seems to have come into being in stages. It remains then to examine the 'pericopes' to be found scattered about in the earlier parts.

The Fourth Gospel appears to begin in entirely synoptic fashion with a necklace of pericopes: the Baptist scenes, the encounters between Jesus and the first disciples, then the wedding in Cana and the cleansing of the temple. We have seen above, however, that the two first-mentioned groups represent two acts structured in scenes, in which the individual images are connected much more organically together than for example the controversy narratives in Mark 2 and 3 or the miracle stories in Matthew 8 and 9.

By contrast, the wedding anecdote now seems to be a pericope that stands entirely isolated. Certainly the evangelist has taken it like this out of the tradition; but he has made an attempt to integrate it, on the one hand by connecting the event chronologically to the preceding scenes (2.1), and then by, on his own initiative, at the end proclaiming the miracle as Jesus' first sign (2.11), which marks it as the first link in a chain which stretches through the whole Gospel.[1] The narrative shows

---

[1] For an analysis cf. also K.L. Schmidt, "Der johanneische Charakter der Erzählung vom Hochzeitswunder in Kana" (Festschrift Harnack, pp. 32-43); for a relevant exegesis also my own article, "Der johanneische Weinregel", ZNW (1913), pp. 248-57.

dramatic impulses, as do most other Johannine miracle stories. Since there is no synoptic parallel it is difficult to say to what extent the evangelist has cast it in his own style. In every respect, including that of style, the narrative reminds one of the account of the miracle of the loaves. We miss an interpretation, of the kind John gave for the miracle of the loaves in the discourse. Not even an appended conversation with the disciples is added in explanation. The discourse concerning the vine (ch. 15) can be seen as a replacement and as an appended explanation; but no connection is made with the Cana episode at that point.

The account of the cleansing of the temple serves to introduce the first Jerusalem visit. By placing this at the beginning the evangelist manages to open the appearance of Jesus in the holy city with a dramatic action in the grand style. The literary form of the narrative is enhanced by comparison with the synoptic version by means of appending to the deed a conversation with the Jews as a second scene, in which the action is given an explanation, which is admittedly not understood until later. John has to some extent organically combined the story with a second pericope, the question of authority, and the scene that we missed in the Cana miracle is provided here. The conversation has two characteristics: Christ's words— already at this point—refer to the end of his life, thus tying a ribbon around the first and the last events in Jerusalem which the Gospel narrates. And the opponents have the last word, as is elsewhere the case from time to time in John. The evangelist does, it is true, add an explanation of the Lord's words (from the point of view of the disciples' community), so that this sticks as the last thing in the soul of the hearer.

Much more loosely connected to the composition as a whole than these two stories is the account of the healing of an official's son. The miracle precisely demonstrates features of ancient aretalogy, especially in the claim that word and healing occur simultaneously. In this connection the reproach against the seeking of signs seems rather strange. The father was seeking neither 'miracle' nor 'healing' for his terminally ill son. The idea is also touched upon in the Thomas story; Jesus' attitude (he feels indignation, not pity, when needy people come to him) has its counterpart in some synoptic stories.[1] It provides a certain amount of suspense in that it now has to be reported how Jesus overcomes his initial disinclination to intervene (cf. Mk 6.47; Mt. 15.22ff.; Mk 1.35ff.; Mt. 8.26a; perhaps also Mt. 8.7, if the saying is meant as a question). It is difficult to say why the evangelist has taken up this story in his Gospel, and why in this particular form. The fact that there was a desire for a Galilaean scene between chs.

---

[1] See my article, '"En hij wilde hen voorbijgaan" (Mk. 6,47)', *Nieuw theologisch Tijdschrift* (1920).

4 and 5, and that, as is brought out in v. 54, a second Galilaean sign was to be offered, does not explain everything. Perhaps the evangelist had a collection of Galilaean signs before him, which he intended to make use of again; perhaps he wanted to bring the number of Galilaean signs up to three (the third being the miracle of the loaves). Or was the pericope to have been inserted later?[1]

There remain the two Jerusalem pericopes which open the final act; it has already been shown how firmly they are inserted in the specifically Johannine presentation of the dramatic catastrophe.

So we come to the finding that John has consciously and successfully overcome the synoptics' system of pericopes. The few brief individual accounts which he presents are—with a single exception—removed entirely from their original isolation: either their significance for the subsequent course of history is indicated by means of pragmatic concluding remarks, or they are combined with related items into a dramatic unity. The Fourth Gospel is then a magnificent, varied and yet on the whole unified composition from (a) a number of individual stories thoroughly embodied in the whole, from (b) closed ranks of individual scenes, from (c) detailed, more or less dramatic conversa-tions, controversy accounts and sermons, from (d) dramatically structured, richly elaborated miracle stories, from (e) the Passion story which has been transformed into a self-contained drama, and from (f) a number of Easter stories that have been linked in more or less pericope-like fashion.

This is a literary masterpiece in a class of its own, which seems to stand somewhere in between a Gospel of the synoptic type and a drama, a tragedy. It would be wrong to seek a division into acts in the same way one would for the composition of Greek drama. John is too much 'biography' for this, i.e. too much concerned with the description of Jesus' journeys, deeds and sermons. One can juxtapose the main sections, but should not number them. And even if one tries to set up main sections, difficulties and great unevennesses occur: the John and disciple plays result in a 'pre-play'. But can one count the Cana miracle as part of this? The 'first visit to Jerusalem' is a good section. But how is one to group the John episode with the conversation with the Samaritan woman on the return journey and then the short and briefly described stay in Galilee? The scenes that follow, the second visit to Jerusalem, and the last appearance in Galilee, go together well. Then again various divisions are possible. Either: the events at the Feast of Tabernacles (7.1–10.21) (but are we still in the realm of this festival from 8.12 onwards?), the feast of

---

[1] On this, see now the hypothesis of Faure (*op. cit.*), that in chs. 1–12 a collection of 'signs' as the basic document (Grundschrift) or Vorlage is to be posited. Similarly, before him, Thompson in the *Expositor* (Jan. 1916).

the consecration of the temple (10.22-39), the Lazarus miracle and its
consequences, the passover festival—in public, in the circle of the
disciples, Passion and Easter. Or: the dispute with the world (chs. 7–12),
the farewell from the disciples (chs. 13–17), passion and Easter. It does
depend on making the right divisions, however. The evangelist was tied to
certain preconditions, to his materials and sources, to his preference for
particular materials, to his apologetic and edificatory tendencies and to his
inspirations. The main thing is that we see how in the stories and in most
of the conversation and controversy scenes he shows a sensitivity for
dramatic impulses and for the precise drawing of human characters, how
in the grouping of the various stylistic forms he is concerned for
variation, how he lets the basic, leading ideas of his Gospel have their
effect throughout the whole book in a fairly unified form[1] (the Son of
God reveals his glory to the world, he has to dispute with the world
which does not understand him and is intent on his destruction, he reveals
his nature to his disciples, he allows himself to be killed by the world, of
his own free will, and stands in the glory of his father, in order from then
on to be spiritually close to his disciples). John treats the epiphanies of the
divine Christ during his human life; he describes the 'work' that he had to
perform on earth, consisting of great signs, testimony discourses, the
Passion and the appearances after his death.

   To a much greater extent than the synoptics John is 'literature' because
he has quite a different mastery of his material than they do: in a
sovereign manner he chooses and he rejects. He collects and works only
with effective and significant material. He is able to shape the scenes
vividly and dramatically. He gives his Gospel the character of a
continuously unfolding drama, in which the conflict arises almost from
the beginning and all its danger rapidly becomes apparent but does not
explode until the moment when the hour is come. In the composition as a
whole, as in the shaping of its individual parts, John proves himself a
master of the literary art, who leaves the synoptics, these collectors and
redactors of popular tradition, far behind him. He is a greater artist than
they are, because he brings more of his own material than transmitted
material, more new things than old things out of his treasure-rooms, and
because even the transmitted and the old bears the stamp of his spirit. *It is
the great paradox of this Gospel that the same man who created the new
Christ-type, detached from the earth and from history, the man who has a
divine Christ from heaven appear on earth and has this Christ teach an
enlightened gospel, the testimony of the Son of God and his work and*

---

[1] Hitchcock (*op. cit.*, pp. 102ff.), whom I read after preparing this study, has some good
observations to make on this.

nothing else, that this same man almost constantly narrates more concretely, dramatically, novellistically, humanly, in a more down-to-earth manner and more literarily than the collectors of folkloristic tradition. Critics have paid too much attention to the unconcrete, unvivid and ethereal aspects of Johannine diction.[1] The traditionalist view has collected the many vivid details just as one-sidedly in order to prove that the work as a whole is historical tradition that rests on eye-witness reports. The two sides are to be viewed and evaluated equally. It is then clear, however, that the dramatic, true-to-life presentation is not to be explained from the fact that the narrator stands closer to the events than the synoptics, but that he was *a greater literary artist*, that he possessed *greater dramatic creativity*, that the urge to form something effective was stronger for him than the desire to reproduce events and traditions accurately. The special literary qualities of the Fourth Gospel are thus rooted just as much as its mystic-theological high-flying in the spiritual individuality of the evangelist. He was one of the most favoured people who have great inner vision and at the same time the urge and the gift for expressing what they see not only in testimony discourses and meditations but also moulding them in concrete forms and dressing them in vivid, dramatic narrative. No wonder that his composition has not been carried out completely evenly and has not turned out even in all respects, or that he occasionally loses interest in the historical situation and throws himself completely into the presentation of the testimony. Some inconsistencies can be explained by his dramatic creativity having temporarily gone lame or by his not having been willing and able to undertake his final revision at some points,[2] or by the supposition that students of his, working in his spirit but not with his artistry, undertook deletions or made insertions.

I hope that with these style-critical observations I have shown anew the high value of the style-critical method, which will always be associated with the name of Gunkel, for biblical studies. Gunkel pointed out to Old Testament scholars that scientific research into and appraisal of the historical books of the Old Testament is far from done by making source divisions, discerning seams and joins and showing the unhistorical character of the stories. In the same way, here the intention has been to show in the most elevated book of the New Testament how analysis and source criticism—the demonstration of the essentially ideal character of the Johannine tradition and the attempt to peel away basic writings and interpolations—though essential for a historical-critical assessment of the scripture, do not do full justice to its abiding significance. Such critical

---

[1] Cf. e.g. J. Overbeck, *Johannes-Evangelium*, pp. 299f.

[2] This impulse has now been rightly emphasised by Faure (*op. cit.*, p. 117).

work always runs the danger of leaving the truly significant aspects of the Gospel unexplained and making it a puzzle how it can have enjoyed such high esteem throughout the centuries. Often it has been seriously wrong in its evaluation of individual items. The investigation of style, which is not at all interested in suppressing critical occupation with the Gospel but rather presupposes it and wants only to supplement it (the same is true of its application to the Old Testament), simply wants to take the book, above all, just as it has come down to us, and to appreciate its stylistic-formal side; it aims by means of analysis of the stylistic forms to describe the direct effect that it has on the reader; putting aside all historical questions and all the numerous minor and major inconsistencies, it aims to bring out the measure of feeling on which, above all, the effect of his narratives rests. If historical criticism in application to John often has a cooling effect, so that the reader has to give up either interest in the criticism or interest in the Gospel, then the investigation of style is suited to dampening undeserved judgments about criticism and giving back to the Gospel reader something of its mood, which it demands if it is to be appreciated as a book of humanity, a book of world literature, and a book which brings the message of God to human beings. It can help us to bring once again to this unique and gentle principal Gospel, reverence and love.

LITERARY FORM IN THE FOURTH GOSPEL[*]

JAMES MUILENBURG

It is over fifty years now since Matthew Arnold wrote about the Fourth Gospel in these words:

> It may be said with certainty that a literary artist capable of inventing the most striking sayings of Jesus to Nicodemus or to the woman of Samaria would have made his composition as a whole more flawless, more artistically perfect than the Fourth Gospel actually is. Judged from an artist's point of view, it has blots and awkwardnesses which a master of imaginative invention would never have suffered his work to exhibit.[1]

And elsewhere he observes that the narrative of the gospel "might well be thought but a matter of infinitely little care and attention ..., a mere slight framework, in which to set the doctrines and discourses of Jesus."[2] Much water has flowed under the bridge since Arnold's day; yet it cannot be said that the difficulties of the literary composition of the Fourth Gospel have been resolved. J. Estlin Carpenter[3] confesses that he has no solution to the mystery of its composition, and Percy Gardner[4] ends his chapter on the gospel as biography by declaring the gospel a tangled skein. On the other hand, F.R. Montgomery Hitchcock devotes one chapter in his book, *A Fresh Study of the Fourth Gospel* (1911) to the dramatic development of the gospel and another to its artistic structure.[5] The climax of the drama is approached by scenes of rising interest; there is a development of plot, character, and purpose.[6] E.F. Scott is also impressed by the numerous marks of a deliberate artistic plan; the gospel unfolds itself, he

---

[*] This article first appeared in the *Journal of Biblical Literature* 51, (1932), pp. 40-53.
[1] Quoted by James Moffatt, *Introduction to the Literature of the New Testament,* 1923, p. 563, note.
[2] *God and the Bible,* Macmillan, 1883, p. 231.
[3] *The Johannine Writings,* 1927, p. 192. See pp. 255f., where he proposes his theory of communal authorship.
[4] *The Ephesian Gospel,* 1916, p. 122.
[5] Chapters V and VI, pp. 102-142.
[6] Hitchcock, *A Fresh Study of the Fourth Gospel,* p. 102.

says, "with something of the ordered majesty of a Greek tragedy."[1] And
Lord Charnwood can even go so far as to declare the gospel "in a very
high degree a compact and well-ordered whole, of which every part falls
in with a design thought out beforehand"[2] while Kenneth Saunders
compares the structure of the gospel to that of the early Christian
basilica.[3]

But the formal literary manner of the writer of the Fourth Gospel is
even more apparent in its lesser units. Rendell Harris,[4] Loisy,[5] Burney,[6]
Bacon,[7] and a score of others have commented on the structure of the
Prologue. Both as a unit in itself and as a preface to the gospel as a whole,
it illustrates the literary quality and form of the gospel. Many passages
easily resolve themselves into the acts and scenes of a drama with
astonishingly little change of text.[8] The stereotyped form of Fourth
Gospel controversy has been frequently observed. Lothar Schmid has
demonstrated the feeling for form in the conversation with the Samaritan
woman.[9] Hans Windisch, in his contribution to the Gunkel *Festschrift*,[10]
discerns a literary plan in the gospel, but the plan embodies a great
variety of literary materials. Yet the same definite structure is to be
observed within each pericope or witness discourse or detailed dramatic
narrative as the case may be. He presents the dramatic interest of the
writer by dialogue, stage directions, and division into acts and scenes.

There are few characteristics that are so apparent as the literary, yet it
is important to know which characteristics are significant. The value of
any literary undertaking will depend largely upon whether the right
questions are raised or not. How does the writer begin and end his
literary units? How does he develop his theme? How does he articulate his
materials? Is there unusual word order? What is the relation of words,
phrases, and clauses to each other, and to the whole? We shall naturally be
sensitive to these essentials of composition which we were taught to

---

[1] *The Fourth Gospel*, 2nd ed., 1908, p. 16. Compare this with the remarks of F.R.
Montgomery Hitchcock, "The Dramatic Development of the Fourth Gospel", *Expositor*,
Series 7, vol. IV, 1907, pp. 266-279.
[2] *According to Saint John*, 1926, p. 62.
[3] *The Gospel for Asia*, 1928, pp. 101f.
[4] *The Origin of the Prologue of St. John's Gospel*, 1917.
[5] *Le quatrième évangile,* 1921. The original form of the Prologue was "une sorte d'ode
au Verbe incarné, logiquement construite, exactement rythmée", p. 46.
[6] *The Aramaic Origin of the Fourth Gospel*, 1922.
[7] "Punctuation, Translation, Interpretation", *Journal of Religion*, 1924, pp. 243-260.
[8] See, e.g., F. R. Montgomery Hitchcock, *A Fresh Study of the Fourth Gospel*, Chap. VI;
J. M. Thompson, "An Experiment in Translation", *Expositor*, Series 8, vol. XVI, 1918, pp.
117-122.
[9] "Die Komposition der Samaria-Szene", *ZNTW*, 1929, vol. 28, pp. 148 to 158.
[10] "Der johanneische Erzählungsstil", *Eucharisterion*, Part II, pp. 174-213. [English
translation in the present volume.]

observe in our preparatory school days: unity, coherence, emphasis, and proportion. It is a primary canon of ours that form and content are interrelated. And in the case of the Fourth Gospel, where the dramatic element obtrudes itself so obviously, one will analyse his materials according to setting, inciting impulse, antagonistic forces, presence of obstacles, and the resolution of obstacles and conflicts. Analysis there must be, minute and painstaking, but the chief end should be the perception of the literary unity in which one gains a sense of form, a central purpose, and, if possible, the occasion which inspired the narrative. The more obvious are the signs of literary composition and art, the more important do such criteria become.

The passage selected for our study is the group of Baptist narratives immediately following the Prologue: first, because they begin the gospel proper, and secondly, because attention is usually directed to the longer narratives where the mode of composition is more apparent. The following analysis helps to visualise the structure:

JOHN 1.19-28

A. (19) And *this is the witness of John* (καὶ αὕτη ἐστὶν ἡ μαρτυρία τοῦ Ἰωάννου) when the Jews *sent* (ἀπέστειλαν) unto him from Jerusalem priests and Levites *to ask him, Who art thou?* (σὺ τίς εἶ)

    a. (20) And he confessed and denied not, and he confessed: *"I am not the Christ."*
    (21) And they asked him, "What then? Art thou Elijah?"
    And he said, *"I am not."*
        "Art thou the prophet?"
    And he answered: *"No."*
    b. (22) They said therefore unto him *"Who art thou* (τίς εἶ) that we may give answer to them that sent us. What sayest thou of thyself?"
Conclusion: (23) "I am the voice of one crying in the wilderness,
        Make straight the way of the Lord,
        as said Isaiah the prophet."

(24) And they had been sent (ἀπεσταλμένοι) of the Pharisees (cf. v. 19).

B. (25) And *they asked him* (cf. v. 19), and said unto him, "Why then baptisest thou, if thou art not the Christ, neither Elijah, neither the prophet?"
Conclusion: (26) "I baptise in water. In the midst of you standeth *one whom ye know not* (ὃν ὑμεῖς οὐκ οἴδατε), (27) even he that cometh after me, the latchet of whose shoe I am not worthy to unloosen."

(28) These things were done in Bethany beyond the Jordan where John was baptising.

The gospel proper begins with a demonstrative formula: "And this is the witness of John."[1] It serves as a title for the four following narratives, for it is John's witness that dominates the whole. Such formulae abound throughout the gospel.[2] John's is pre-eminently a demonstrative gospel. It seeks to prove and convince (cf. 20.30-31). It is centred about the conception of μαρτυρία. The controversies embody contemporary polemic and deal much with testimony. There are seven great asseverations of Jesus, all of them with the emphasis upon ἐγώ. The almost invariable result of Jesus' work is to inspire belief. There are frequent side-comments by the writer in order to indicate the true sense and correct interpretation of a word or statement.

The key to the narrative lies in the words addressed to John, "Who art thou?" This must be answered before the more central question "Who is Jesus?" can be faced.[3] The figure of the Baptist forms an obstacle which it is the purpose of this section to remove. After the threefold denial, the question is raised again, this time more urgently and emphatically. The question is repeated, it is paraphrased, and the reason for the request is given. Such repetitions are numerous, but they are usually motivated.[4] The effect is dramatic: "Who is he *then*, this leader with a tremendous following, if he is not the Messiah so many think him to be?" The answer is an accommodation to Synoptic tradition, but the notable difference illustrates the literary quality of John. In the Synoptic gospels, the quotation is given as such from Isaiah. In John it is put into the mouth of the Baptist himself and in the first person. The Synoptists give the quotation as part of a straightforward account. The emphasis in Mark and Luke is upon the coming of John; in Matthew, to be sure, the Baptist is directly equated with the voice. In the Fourth Gospel not only the setting and form are dramatic; the emphasis seems to have shifted from "making the paths straight" to "the voice crying in the wilderness."[5] **B** (vv. 22-23) also states its question directly, "Why do you baptise then?" That this was

---

[1] Observe the relation of these words to vv. 6-8, 15 of the Prologue.
[2] Note, for example, 1.15, 30, 33, 34; 2.11; 3.8d, 16, 19; 4.19, 29, 42, 54; 6.39, 40, 50, 58; 7.40, 41, 46; 14.25; 15.11, 12, 17; 16. 1, 4a, 4b, 25, 33; 17.1, 3, 13; 18.1; etc.
[3] This is the question which the Fourth Gospel seeks to answer. Cf. e.g. 4.10a; 8.25; etc.
[4] The explanation of Johannine repetitions is both literary and psychological. For an opposite view, see Stange, *Die Eigenart der johanneischen Produktion*, Dresden, 1915.
[5] Thus shrouding John in mystery and indefiniteness, which are gradually dispelled in the succeeding sentences not by emergence of a clear figure but by his complete disappearance.

another question in contemporary polemic we need have no doubt. And the answer to the question, evasive as it may seem, is "I baptise in water" without any reference to the greater baptism that is to follow.

The analysis has made clear the form of the pericope. It is set in a very clearly-marked framework with an introductory demonstrative formula as a possible title for all four sections, an introduction to each division, and a conclusion. There are two primary divisions, A (19-24) and B (25-28). Each has its own important question stated at the beginning, trebly important when read in the light of its historical context, and each its significant answer. Within each division we observe the same sense of form. In A (19-24) there is the threefold denial, each time with telling and increasing brevity[1] and the repetition of the question "Who art thou" just before the dramatic answer. The concluding sentence in the section serves more to separate the two sections than to unite them. That the author conceives them as part of the same section, however, is clear from the contents of B (25-28), from the chronological phrases at the beginning of the following section, and from the similar character of many Johannine literary units.[2] The question in B (25-28) recapitulates the substance of A (19-24) but presses the question further. The answer is most dramatic, and gains in significance when one compares it with the Synoptic parallels. There the statement "I baptise in water" is everywhere paralleled by "he shall baptise you in the Holy Spirit." Here the expected contrast is left incomplete, and in disagreement with the Synoptists John refers to the *one whom ye know not* who is soon to come and is even now standing in their midst (μέσος ὑμῶν στήκει). This device of dramatic anticipation is not uncommon in the Fourth Gospel. The reply creates an atmosphere of suspense and thus prepares the way for what is to follow. Its vagueness lends a feeling of mystery. We are now face to face with the Gospel's one question: WHO IS HE? Like the theme of a symphony, it recurs again and again with infinite variations: now quiet and pastoral, now mystic and passionate, now grand and sublime, now warm and intimate. After the reply the second episode is closed, but the writer completes his framework by adding a characteristic stereotyped comment.

Two or three further stylistic comments may be noted. First of all, the solemnity of v. 20. This solemn pronouncement "he confessed and denied not, but confessed"[3] at the beginning of the gospel attempts to express the

---

[1] Cf. the similar style of 9.8-9.

[2] Windisch makes B (vv. 25-28) a separate *Gesprächsfolge*.

[3] This type of repetition is included in Stange's list of "negierte Antithesen" or "doppelte Umkehrungen" ("eine Aussage wird unmittelbar hernach dadurch wiederholt, daβ der zum Hauptbegriff kontradiktorische Begriff negiert wird"). N.B. 1.3; 2.24-25a; 3.16b, 17, 16-17; 4.14; 5.19, 24; 7.18; 8.12b and c; 10.18; 12.47b, 49; 14.10; 15.4 and 5b, 15, 16, 19b; 16.13, 25-29; 17.9b; 18.20. Cf. also 1.33a-31; 6.51a-48; 7.8b-6a; 10.9-7;

writer's conviction of the significance of what he is about to testify. Again the section is for the most part in direct discourse. Indeed, so dramatic is the whole that one should have no difficulty in dramatising it.[1] The plot begins *in medias res*. We ask in vain concerning the history preceding the coming of the embassy, and the response of the Jews to the outspoken "confession". Finally it may be observed that every characteristic of the pericope finds frequent parallels throughout the entire gospel.

The analysis of the second pericope of the Baptist's witness may be presented as follows:[2]

JOHN 1.29-34

A. (29) *On the morrow he seeth* (βλέπει) Jesus coming (cf. v. 27) unto him, and saith: "Behold (ἴδε) the Lamb of God, that taketh away the sin of the world."

(30) "This is he of whom (οὗτός ἐστιν ὑπὲρ οὗ) I said, "After me *cometh* a man who is become before me: for he was before me." (31) *And I knew him not*; but that he should be made manifest to Israel;

Conclusion: "for this cause (διὰ τοῦτο) *came* I baptising in water."

B. (32) And John *bare witness* (ἐμαρτύσεν) saying, "*I have beheld* (τεθέαμαι) the Spirit descending as a dove out of heaven; and it abode upon him. (33) *And I knew him not;* but he that sent me to baptise in water, he said unto me, 'Upon whomsoever thou shalt see the Spirit descending, and abiding upon him, the same is he that baptiseth in the Holy Spirit'."

Conclusion: (34) "And I have seen (ἑώρακα) and have borne witness (μεμαρτύρηκα) that this is the Son of God" (ὅτι οὗτός ἐστιν ὁ υἱὸς τοῦ θεοῦ).

Again the evidences of form are most striking. The section is divided into two parts. Each has its introduction, and each its conclusion. Each contains a striking pronouncement from the Witness, and in each the pronouncement is followed by "and I knew him not, but" (cf. the ὃν ὑμεῖς οὐκ οἴδατε of the preceding pericope). This, in turn, is followed by the "witness" exactly as in the preceding pericope after "who art thou." The "on the morrow" binds the pericope with what precedes and what follows. It is a purely literary device, nothing more. The solemn words

13.3b-1a; 15.5-1; 16.18-17. Numerous other similar examples might be cited. Cf. e.g. Stange's list (II) of "repetitions for clearness".

[1] Cf. J.M. Thompson in the *Expositor*, 1918, "An Experiment in Translation", pp. 117-125.

[2] Windisch makes this Scene 3 of Act I but refuses to call it a separate pericope. It must be admitted that it does stand in intimate connection with the foregoing section. But its kinship with the following section, which Windisch makes a separate Act, is almost as intimate. The uniform structure of each pericope, according to my own division and quite evidently the author's, seems rather to argue for the above classification.

"he seeth Jesus *coming* unto him" are designed to furnish the setting, give emphasis to the momentous claim that is to follow, but above all to relate him with the Unknown Coming One of v. 27. The sentence "Behold the Lamb of God ..." is the culmination of the Baptist's witness. It stands out boldly at the moment when Jesus first appears. It is as inadequately motivated as the embassy of the Jews. It has nothing to do with the section as a unit. It stands in the way of the otherwise noticeable unfolding of testimony. It is not elaborated in what follows. On the contrary, the following words, *"this is he"* etc. are the real centre of the witness. It equates Jesus specifically with the *Unknown One*, the ἐρχόμενος of the preceding section. The new figure is coming to the foreground of the Johannine stage, but the Baptist is still there. The question "Why do you baptise, then?" of the preceding pericope must still receive an answer. Here it is plainly given: "in order that he might be manifested to Israel", even though this was an inadequate witness (κἀγὼ οὐκ ᾔδειν αὐτόν).

The unfolding of revelation progresses more strikingly in **B** (vv. 32-34). This is the Johannine counterpart to the baptism. But in John we have the account given as the direct testimony of the Baptist himself. The emphasis is on "beheld". But even yet the full significance of his experience does not dawn upon him. It is only when the heavenly token is interpreted directly from God (who acts as corroborative evidence) that he realises WHO it is that has come to him (v. 29). Here, finally, the incomplete contrast of the preceding section is completed: I baptise in water, he shall baptise in the Holy Spirit. The witness ends most solemnly and climactically: and I have seen and borne witness that this is the Son of God. This is the true literary climax of the section and in a sense the dramatic climax of the whole chapter. A milestone has been reached in the development of the central purpose (20.30f.).

"He must increase, but I must decrease." We have seen this process going on. The third section carries us further along until the Baptist disappears completely from the scene.

JOHN 1.35-42

A.a. (35) Again *on the morrow* (cf. 29.43) John was standing, and two of his disciples; (36) and he looked (ἐμβλέψας) *upon Jesus as he walked*, and saith,
"Behold the Lamb of God!"
(37) And the two disciples heard him speak and followed Jesus.

b. (38) And Jesus turned and beheld them following, and saith unto them, *"What seek ye?"* (τί ζητεῖτε)
And they said unto him, "Rabbi" (which is to say, being interpreted, Teacher), "where abidest thou?" (39) He saith unto them, *"Come and ye shall see."*

Conclusion: *They came therefore and saw* where he abode; and they abode with him that day.

It was about the tenth hour.

B. (40) One of the two that heard John speak, and followed him, was Andrew, Simon Peter's brother. (41) He first findeth his own brother Simon, and saith unto him, *We have found the Messiah* (which is, being interpreted, Christ).

(42) He brought him unto Jesus.

Conclusion: Jesus looked upon (ἐμβλέψας) him, and said, "Thou art Simon, the son of John: thou shalt be called Cephas (which is by interpretation, Peter)."

The literary features of this passage are at once observable. Its structure is the same as that of the two preceding sections. Again we have the two divisions, each with introduction and conclusion. There is a striking dramatic setting, the two figures stand alone in their grandeur, and John's representation of the scene is not without its element of augustness: John is *standing*, and he looks upon Jesus. His repetition of "Behold the Lamb of God" may seem at first to be at variance with our explanation above. But closer examination of the entire passage as well as of the gospel as a whole substantiates our view. In the first place, this repetition at the beginning of a section of something in a preceding section frequently acts as a transition. So we find the Baptist sections linked to the Prologue and with each other. In the second place, the repetition here gives an effect of solemnity and emphasis. Again, it acts as a summary statement of the Witness. And finally, there is a more specifically literary argument. From one point of view, literary technique would seem to demand "Behold the *Son* of God"; from another, however, there is good reason for placing a colossal assertion such as John's at the beginning of his witness for its dramatic effect. It is one of many foreshadowings of the Cross which occur throughout the gospel. Such evidences of what might appear to be a confusion in literary technique are encountered elsewhere in the Fourth Gospel, but usually the writer's reason for the confusion is not difficult to trace.

The narrative bears, throughout, the marks of literary structure. The central question of **A** (vv. 35-39) is "What seek ye?" (τί ζητεῖτε;). The answer is not an indirect but a direct question. "Rabbi" is motivated by theological interest, and the parenthesis accentuates this. Jesus utters the pregnant words: *"Come and See."* In Johannine style it is added "They came and saw where he abode", and the conclusion is "And they abode with him that day." The next sentence "It was about the tenth hour" has the same purpose as 1.24, 2.12, and numerous other similar sentences. These serve as much to separate units as to enclose them in a framework. The same vagueness and obscurity that we have observed in the first pericope is seen here. As there, we still ask "Why does John baptise then?" and "Who is the Unknown One?", so here we ask "What is it that they were really seeking?" or "What did they see?" But whereas in the first pericope we have to wait for a further narrative for a full explanation, here we get our answer in **B** (vv. 40-42).

The introductory clause of the second division (v. 40a) summarises the introductory sentences of **A** (35-36).[1] The prominence of Andrew is one of the many peculiar features of the gospel, and the position that Peter holds here in the centre of the stage may be variously explained as a reflection of the contemporary situation or as a Synoptic tradition in Johannine literary setting.[2] A comparison with the Synoptic account of Peter's call again reveals the strongly literary character of John. There is a degree of freshness, vividness, and colour in the former that is completely lacking here. On the contrary, we feel that behind the Fourth Gospel account there lies a long period of reflection. The writer seems to move in literary *grooves*. Whereas at the beginning of the narrative John looks upon (ἐμβλέψας) Jesus and is impelled to utter his lofty testimony, here Jesus looks upon (ἐμβλέψας) a disciple and confers upon him a distinction. Whoever is familiar with Johannine literary method will recognise that such phenomena are not accidental. *We have found the Messiah:* here is the complete answer to section **A** (35-39). The disciples were asking the gospel's pervasive question, WHO IS HE? They come to see, and they find the Messiah (cf. 20.31). It is a parallel to the vocative "Rabbi" in **A** as is also the parenthetical explanation. The answer to **A** is the inciting impulse to **B** (40-42). Andrew finds Peter, and the Christian mission continues until Samaritans and Greeks also come seeking Jesus.[3]

Our final pericope is still a part of the Baptist narratives. To be sure, the Baptist is now completely off the stage, but it is his influence and witness that conditions the narrative here.

JOHN 1.43-51

A. (43) *On the morrow* he was minded to go forth into Galilee, and *he findeth* Philip, and Jesus saith unto him, "Follow me." (44) (Now Philip was from Bethsaida of the city of Andrew and Peter.)

---

[1] Is there any such relationship, perhaps, between **A** and **B** of the preceding sections?
[2] Peter is second in importance only to the "beloved disciple." Cf. Wrede, *Charakter und Tendenz des Johannesevangeliums*, pp. 35-37.
[3] 4.30,36?; 12.20-21.

(45) Philip *findeth* Nathaniel, and saith unto him, "We *have found* him of whom Moses in the Law, and the prophets, wrote, Jesus the son of Joseph, of *Nazareth*" (cf. v. 41).

(46) And Nathaniel said unto him, "Can any good come out of Nazareth?" (ἐκ Ναζαρὲτ δύναταί τι ἀγαθὸν εἶναί)

Conclusion: Philip saith unto him, "Come and see."

B. (47) Jesus *saw* Nathaniel *coming* to him, and saith of him, "*Behold* an Israelite indeed in whom is no guile!"

(48) Nathaniel saith unto him, "Whence knowest thou me?"

Jesus answered and said unto him, "Before Philip called thee, when thou wast under the fig tree, I *saw* thee."

Conclusion: (49) Nathaniel answered and said unto him: "Rabbi, thou art the Son of God; thou art the King of Israel."

(50) Jesus answered and said unto him: "Because I said unto thee, I *saw* thee underneath a fig tree, believest thou? *Thou shalt see* greater things than these." (51) And he saith unto him: "Verily, verily I say unto you, *ye shall see* the heavens opened, and the angels of God descending upon the Son of Man."

The introductory τῇ ἐπαύριον indicates not only a transition but also identity of literary grouping. "He was minded to go forth into Galilee" is literary framework. This is the explanation of the constant shifting between Judea and Galilee in the Fourth Gospel. The idea of *finding* has been a thread running through the narrative ever since the dramatic pronouncement in v. 41. This is but one example of what is a most striking Johannine literary characteristic; namely, whenever a significant statement has been made, the author goes back again and again and plays upon and repeats the central words of significance. There are numerous such words in the gospel as a whole, and also in the individual sections. For our purpose here, it is well to see that the repeated inferences to "finding" enshrine the initial sentence with greater solemnity. The command of Jesus is characteristically brief. The parenthetical command is also typical. Philip bears the lighted torch further by *finding* Nathaniel and telling him that he has *found* him whom Moses and the prophets foretold. So Andrew had *found* Peter and had said, "We have *found* the Messiah." Thus another step is made in the advance of the witness. The cue is *Nazareth*, which in the Greek appears last in Philip's words. This serves both polemical and literary interests, for Nathaniel can ask in amazement, "From *Nazareth* can any good be" (literally), and Philip can answer quite effectively, "Come and see" (cf. v. 39), thus reaching back to the previous pericope and anticipating his discovery of Jesus in the next. And the question implies in the answer *what* (or *who*) is it that can come from Nazareth?

The second division begins in a fashion we have hitherto become familiar with (cf. 29, 35-36, 38). The greeting of Jesus is in the manner of all Johannine utterances which attempt to point out some great fact or introduce a new theme. So John greets Jesus, and so Jesus greets Peter. The short declaration, revealing unexpected insight and hence an unusual personality, is the inciting moment for the dialogue. On this basis most of the following narratives and controversial scenes are also constructed. To Jesus' manifestation of a secret and higher knowledge and of divine insight, Nathaniel can burst forth in adoring wonder, "Rabbi, thou art the Son of God; thou art the King of Israel!", which serves the purpose of all Johannine narratives and especially of this group of pericopes. This declaration of Nathaniel is, of course, the climax to the section. The last two verses form the completion of the framework into which the four little pericopes have been set. They were introduced by "Now this is the witness of John," and the "apocalyptical conclusion" is its fitting and, in the quality of its contents, majestic close. The words fit easily and admirably, it must be confessed, into the content and character of the fourth pericope, but their relationship must also be seen as a conclusion suitable to the whole chapter (after the prologue). The twofold introduction to Jesus' words reflects the fervency of the writer and the solemnity and majesty of his words. This is accentuated by the "Verily, verily, (only in John) I say unto you." The "things greater than these" is another Johannine theme, and the lofty prophecy at the close, together with this phrase is the final and the most dramatic of the anticipations we have met with in the chapter.

We may, then, conclude our examination of the Baptist narratives as follows:

1) The four little sections all exhibit a formal literary manner with a very definite method of literary composition.

2) The writer has a powerful dramatic sense. He loves to draw his narrative to a dramatic close. Climactic arrangement is evident everywhere: frequently he *begins* with some striking pronouncement, but more frequently he ends with the real "witness" of the narrative, and always the conclusion is of the revealing sort. His use of dialogue and his device of focussing the real point in some pithy phrased question accentuate the dramatic character of the whole. Similarly striking is the presence of dramatic anticipations. The element of suspense is well centred about the major interest of the gospel. It serves the purpose of drawing the pericopes into a unity and of giving progress to the whole.

3) A large question, and a difficult one, for the interpretation of the gospel concerns the degree to which one is to allegorise the contents. There are those who discover profound meaning in every sentence. Words and expressions are always being used cryptically. The truth is that this element is undoubtedly present. But to what extent? Commentators are sometimes Alexandrian Philos, only they use the Fourth Gospel instead of the Pentateuch as the object of their elucidations. How inward and spiritual a meaning are we to attribute to such words as *come, find, abide,* and *see*?

4) Repetitions and paraphrases abound everywhere. Erich Stange[1] has made a study of many of these in an effort to understand the workings of the Johannine mind. The above analysis of the Baptist narratives agrees with Stange's conclusion that the older partition theories do not furnish an adequate explanation of the literary phenomena of the gospel.

5) In general the order of the testimony is cumulative. At first it is only John who wins our attention, but John's mission is a self-effacing one. There is the Unknown One who stands over against him. Then the Unknown One appears, a momentous claim is uttered, but this falls out of the cumulative order. It is the Coming One, the One whom John knew not, that appears. The heavenly token reveals One who baptises not in water, but in the Holy Spirit. And John bears witness that this is the Son of God. Then the mission begins. The disciples seek, and find the Messiah, the one foretold by Moses and the prophets. Nathaniel's experience culminates in the witness of "Son of God" and "King of Israel."

6) John is the "one who baptises in water." It is a title designed to remind one of his inferior position. John is disposed of without a single word. After he has served his purpose, the author is no longer concerned with him. No exit is announced. So, too, the delegation in the first pericope is disposed of; so, too, Nicodemus; and so, too, are the Greeks.

7) Finally, one raises the question of the historicity of the narratives. The literary argument seems to tell against them. One may contend, perhaps, that historical material might very well be set in such a framework and dramatic form as have been revealed above. But if likelihood is to be a criterion, then the narratives must be viewed not primarily as historical accounts but as literary moulds embodying a theological theory.

---

[1] *Op. cit.*

THE STRUCTURE OF THE FOURTH GOSPEL*

DAVID DEEKS

It has long been recognised that the Fourth Gospel, the Johannine Epistles and the Revelation of St. John are closely related. C.K. Barrett, for example, writes in relation to these books: "the conjecture may be hazarded that the evangelist, the author of the epistles, and the final editor of Revelation were all pupils of the original apocalyptist".[1] It would not therefore be surprising to discover that similar principles of composition have been employed throughout the Johannine literature. In recent years new analyses of Revelation and 1 John have been made, and the purpose of this essay is to suggest a similar analysis of St John's Gospel. But the development of the structure of the Fourth Gospel is, of course, an independent inquiry; it does not presuppose any necessary connection between St. John's Gospel on the one hand, and Revelation and 1 John on the other.

The analysis of Revelation just referred to is that proposed by A.M. Farrer.[2] He has argued with great ingenuity that the clue to the understanding of Revelation lies in the "half-week scheme". Danielic apocalyptic imagery has been fused with the Christian traditions about Jesus' passion, death, and resurrection in the structure of Revelation. Farrer sums up his conclusions and their significance as follows:

> the whole Revelation has the form of a half-week of (halved) weeks: a greater half-week, embracing four lesser weeks, themselves also halved. But why should St. John use such a form? ... The meaning of the greater half-week is determined by the meaning of the lesser half-week it contains within it; for the sense of the lesser half-week was fixed in the tradition already. It was a literal three-and-a-half years, a period of acute distress limited and cut short by the advent of him who promised that he would come quickly. The greater half-week cannot be a literal forty-two months; but it may be taken as stamping the same essential character on the whole period of waiting from now until the end. It is a time of suffering patience, measured and predestined.[3]

---

* This article first appeared in *New Testament Studies* 15 (1968), pp. 107-29.
[1] C.K. Barrett, *The Gospel According to St John* (1955), p. 52.
[2] A.M. Farrer, *The Revelation of St. John the Divine* (1964).
[3] Farrer, *op. cit.* pp. 11f.

More recently J.C. O'Neill[1] has suggested that 1 John is not a letter, but a tract comprising twelve distinct sections. Each section is based upon a Jewish poem written by or used among members of a Jewish sect of the Diaspora, and showing linguistic and theological connections with the writings of the Qumran community and the "Testaments of the Twelve Patriarchs". In 1 John these poems have been "touched up" by a Christian editor who has perceived their fulfilment in Jesus Christ.

It may be noteworthy that the two books referred to have provided analyses of two Johannine writings in terms of what are known to have been significant numbers in the Jewish mind—three, four, seven, and twelve. Furthermore, the structure of Revelation has proved to be exceedingly complicated. From these data can we reasonably speculate that the structure of the Fourth Gospel also may be analysed into sections, the number of which would appeal to a Jewish mind? The purpose of this essay is to suggest just such an arrangement—told in terms of three, four, and seven.

No general agreement has emerged concerning the details of the arrangement of St John's Gospel. Each commentator has to provide his own analysis of the structure, and few commentators—with the notable exception of C.H. Dodd[2]—consider the results of their work are integral to their theological exposition. This illustrates the truth of Barrett's comment that "the structure of the gospel is simple in outline, complicated in detail".[3]

Certain conclusions are universally accepted. Jn 21 is clearly an appendix to the gospel proper, for which 20.31 is a fitting conclusion. Further, 1.1-18 is a self-contained section, the Prologue. Estimates vary as to the closeness of the relation between the Prologue and the bulk of the gospel. J.H. Bernard, for example, tends to divorce the two, regarding the Prologue primarily as an originally separate Hymn on the Logos which provides a philosophical explanation of the thesis worked out at length in the gospel—namely, that Jesus is the Revealer of God.[4] Barrett, however, believes that the Prologue was a prose introduction "specially written (it must be supposed) to introduce the gospel"—an idea confirmed by the fact that "many of the central ideas in the Prologue are central also in the body of the gospel".[5] R.H. Lightfoot brings the Prologue and the remainder of the gospel even more closely together; of the Prologue he writes: "These verses give the key to the understanding of this gospel, and

---

[1] J.C. O'Neill, *The Puzzle of 1 John* (1966).
[2] C.H. Dodd, *The Interpretation of the Fourth Gospel* (1953).
[3] Barrett, *op. cit.* p. 11.
[4] J.H. Bernard, *The Gospel according to St. John* (1928), p. cxxxviii.
[5] Barrett, *op. cit.* p. 126.

make clear how the evangelist wishes his readers to approach his presentation of the Lord's work and Person; and equally the rest of the book will throw light on the contents of these verses."[1]

The details of the analyses of the bulk of the gospel (1.19-20.31) vary enormously. This may be illustrated by summarising the structures of the Fourth Gospel proposed by the last three authors quoted. Bernard[2] concludes that, besides the Prologue and Appendix, the gospel comprises three parts: (a) 1.19-4.54 together with 6.1—71; (b) 5.1-47; 7.15-24, 1-14, 25-52; 8.12-9.41; 10.19-25, 1-18; 10.30-12.50; (c) 13.1-20.31. Barrett's solution[3] is that "the book falls into four clear parts, with an appendix, as follows: (a) 1.1-18; (b) 1.19-12.50; (c) 13.1-17.26; (d) 18.1-20.31." The second of these sections (1.19-12.50) is further analysed into eight episodes. Finally, we make mention of Lightfoot's proposed structure,[4] which is that, after the Prologue (1.1-18) and a preparation for the ministry (1.19-2.11), the book falls into two principal parts. The first of these (2.12-7.50) is seen to comprise six sections, and the second principal part (8.1-20.31) may also be considered as a seventh or final section.

One point immediately arises and needs to be settled. The Fourth Gospel has provoked much speculation about possible displacements in the original plan of the author. We have already seen, for example, how Bernard adopted certain displacements in his suggested outline of St. John's structure. The evidence on which displacement theories are based has been summarised as follows: "The narrative does not always proceed straight-forwardly; some of the connections are bad, and sometimes there are no connections at all. Occasionally a piece seems to be out of its proper setting."[5] Our task must be to give full weight to these observations but also, if at all possible, to explain the position of the sections in the gospel as we now have it—having recourse to displacement theories only as a last resort. (There is, of course, no textual evidence to support the various proposed displacements, except at 18.13-24.) We shall therefore take seriously the text as it stands, and shall propose a structure which involves no displacement theories, but which may throw some light on the reasons why, in the past, displacement theories have been so popular.

---

[1] R.H. Lightfoot, *St. John's Gospel* (1956), p. 78.
[2] Bernard, *op. cit.* pp. xxx-xxxiii.
[3] Barrett, *op. cit.* pp. 11-14.
[4] *Op. cit.* pp. 11-21.
[5] *Op. cit.* pp. 125f.

Fig. 1. Structure of the Fourth Gospel

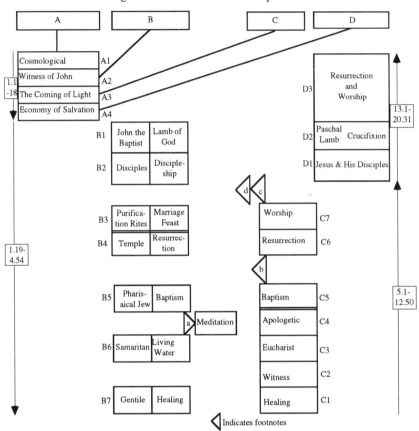

St. John's Gospel consists of four sections, as follows: (A) 1.1-18; (B) 1.19-4.54; (C) 5.1-12.50; and (D) 13.1-20.31. (John 21, as usual, is regarded as a later appendix.) We shall now consider each of these sections in turn, and the relationships between them.

SECTION A

The Prologue is to be seen in the closest possible connection with the remainder of the gospel. Indeed, the four subsections into which the Prologue naturally falls provide summaries of the contents of the four main sections of the gospel, A, B, C and D. Barrett[1] gives to the subsections of the Prologue the following titles, which we shall adopt for

---

[1] Barrett, *op. cit.* p. 18.

the present: A1 (1.1-5) is "Cosmological", A2 (1.6-8) is "The Witness of John", A3 (1.9-13) is "The Coming of the Light", and A4 (1.14-18) is "The Economy of Salvation".

It is apparent that "Cosmological" will serve as an adequate heading for section A as a whole. For, as we have already noted, it is much more philosophical in character than the rest of the gospel, and it attempts to relate the Incarnate One and His significance to the pre-existent being of God and His Will.

There is much debate as to whether the Prologue is a separate and self-conscious composition on the part of the author of the gospel, probably in prose form (so Barrett), or whether the Prologue comprises an original, fully metric hymn—'Urprolog'—into which the author has inserted prose interpolations. In arguing the latter case, J. Jeremias[1] appeals to the climactic parallelism found, for example, in 1.4f., and suggests that the interpolations are verses 6-8, 12b-13, 15, and perhaps 17-18. Whatever may be the outcome of this debate, advocates of both sides would agree that the Prologue has a marked liturgical structure. In other words St. John begins his gospel by reflecting the worship of the Church, and indeed the faith of the Church expressed in that worship. For while the first three subsections (1.1-13) are told in third-person clauses, the fourth subsection begins with a third-person clause (ὁ Λόγος σὰρξ ἐγένετο) and then immediately breaks into the first person plural (ἐθεασάμεθα)—a confession of faith.

SECTION B

The title which summarises the second subsection of the Prologue and which therefore stands as an appropriate heading for section B as a whole is "The Witness of John". This is particularly relevant because, as we shall see. Section B opens with an expanded form of John the Baptist's testimony to Jesus.[2] However, we must remember that Barrett's titles for the subsections of the Prologue were formulated with only the Prologue in mind. We would therefore not be surprised to find that when the subsections of section A are seen in their more intimate relationship to sections B, C and D of the gospel proper, Barrett's titles need a little adaptation. Perhaps a more comprehensive heading for section B would be: "Witness to Christ; Christ supersedes all earlier expectations."

Section B falls into seven subsections. The significance of the number seven in Jewish numerology immediately springs to mind: the witness borne to Christ in this section has a ring of completeness about it. The

---

[1] J. Jeremias, *The Central Message of the N. T.* (1963), chapter 4.

[2] See C.H. Dodd, *Historical Tradition in the Fourth Gospel* (1963), pp. 248f.

justification for the general title of section B we have just proposed lies in each of the subsections considered *in toto*. However, in the final column of the following table we shall give illustrative verses from each of the subsections in turn, which pinpoint the two aspects of the general title—first, the witness made to Christ, and second, the affirmation that the person and work of Christ go beyond any pre-Christian expectations. The first column of the table gives the number of the subsection; the second column delineates the subsection; the third column provides the name of the person or group bearing witness to Christ.

B1	1.19-34	John the Baptist	1.34;	1.30
B2	1.35-51	The Disciples	1.49;	1.50
B3	2.1-11 (12)	Jewish Purification Rites	2.11;	2.10
B4	2.13-25	Temple Worship	2.17;	2.20
B5	3.1-21 (22-36)	Orthodox, Pharisaical Judaism	3.2;	3.11ff.
B6	4.1-42 (45)	The Samaritans	4.29;	4.42
B7	4.46-54	The Gentiles	4.53;	4.51 (cf. 4.47)

NOTE: 3.22-36 is clearly a footnote to the story about Nicodemus. Its significance and the reason for its having been placed at this point in the gospel will be discussed later.

Most of the names of the bearers of testimony in column three, and their function as witnesses, are self-evident. It is clear, for example, that Nicodemus is used by St. John as a representative figure in this context: he is referred to as "a man of the Pharisees, a ruler of the Jews" (3.1) and "a teacher of Israel" (3.10). Similarly, the woman at the well represents a typical Samaritan, and it is therefore natural that the conversation between Jesus and the woman should involve the wider relationship of Samaritan religion and Judaism. Of the "official whose son was ill" (4.46), Barrett says he "is probably to be thought of as a Gentile".[1] In the light of these symbolic representations, it is reasonable to conjecture that St. John saw in the reference to "Jewish rites of purification" (2.6) the symbolical back-ground for the whole of subsection B3.

As we look at the list of testimony-bearers, it becomes obvious that St. John has deliberately arranged his subsections to form a linear development of thought. Witness to Christ begins with the one who was closest to him, namely John the Baptist. Did Jesus and John both belong originally to the same Qumran-type sect,[2] or was there, as St. Luke suggests,[3] a blood-relation between the two? Then comes the witness of the disciples, those who kept closest to Christ during his ministry.[4] This is

---

[1] *Op. cit.* p. 12.

[2] Dodd, *op. cit.* pp. 288-301.

[3] Luke 1.36.

[4] It may also be noted that there is a linear progression of witness among the disciples themselves: Rabbi (1.38) refers to a contemporary order of Jewish teachers; Messiah (1.41)

followed by the testimony proffered by Jewish ritual and religion—the typically Jewish ritual washing, and the Temple, a symbol which brings to a focus the religious insights of the Jews but which also tentatively offers some relationship with non-Jews. These two subsections (B3, B4) which point to the religious life of the race to which the Christ belonged, and which were the seed-bed for Messianic expectations, are now followed in their testimony by that of one who sums up the whole life of the Jewish nation, Nicodemus. From Judaism the witness expands outwards; testimony to Christ comes next from that ethnic group most closely connected to the Jews, the Samaritans. And finally, the whole world presents its witness through the symbolic Gentile. Thus we see how St. John has constructed successive spheres of witness, spheres of increasing influence. It is rather like the pebble dropped in the pond: the ripples gradually expand from the point where the pebble entered the water until the whole surface of water in the pond has been disturbed. This linear development of thought which St. John has devised is, as we shall discover, a common device by which he expresses the universality of Christ's influence through the Church. Men of all races are included in the one universal Church which bears testimony to the Person and work of Christ.

Of the seven subsections in section B, St. John brings our attention particularly to B3 and B7. This he does by a formula which occurs only in these two places in the gospel: "This, the first of his signs" (2.11) and "This was now the second sign" (4.54), i.e. enumeration of the signs. Furthermore, of the seven subsections under consideration only B3 and B7 occur in Cana, and therefore in Galilee. What is the significance of this? Probably that St. John wants to group the seven subsections into a group of three followed by a group of four; 7=3+4 (rather than, say, 7=4+3).[1] This observation is further confirmed by noticing that St. John has bound together the first three subsections by means of temporal references: "The next day" (1.29, 35, 43), "On the third day" (2.1). Thus B1-3 span a period of six days;[2] the remaining four subsections are not interconnected by a consecutive time sequence of this character. The role of this grouping together of the subsections in the total structure of the gospel will become apparent later.

---

picks one particular form of Jewish eschatological expectation, while Fulfiller of the Law and Prophets (1.45) broadens this Jewish hope to include the whole pre-Christian era; finally Rabbi, Son of God, King of Israel (1.49), grounds Jesus' status in his eternal relation to the Father—a category which supersedes Messianism.

[1] See Farrer, *Op. cit.* p. 9.
[2] Cf. Barrett's interpretation, *op. cit.* p. 158.

SECTION C

"The Coming of the Light" was the summary title of subsection A3 which we adopted earlier, and because we suggested A3 itself summarises section C, this should also serve as an appropriate heading for this whole section. Certainly section C is about the public ministry of Jesus. In addition, the important saying of Jesus, "I am the light of the world", occurs in this section (8.12). But we shall not be surprised to discover that section C is not only about the ministry of Christ; it deals also with the public work of the Church. Our previous two sections, A and B, have revealed a strong ecclesiastical interest already: section A took us into the liturgical life of the Church, and section B pointed to the witness made to Christ by the members of his Church throughout the world. Now section C delineates the public functions and ministries of the Church by pointing to the pioneer of the Church's mission, Christ himself. We may therefore propose a comprehensive title for section C in the following form: "The public work of Christ (the Church) in the world, and the world's reaction to Christ (the Church)."

Section C comprises once again the significant number of seven subsections. The work of Christ, like the mission entrusted to the Church, is complete and without defect. In the following table the first column gives the number of the subsection, the second column lists the extent of the subsection, and the third column gives the ministry of Christ (the Church) expounded at length in the subsection.

C1	5.1-30	Healing
C2	5.31-47	Witness
C3	6.1-71	Eucharist
C4	7.1-8.59	Apologetic
C5	9.1-10.21 (22-42)	Baptism
C6	11.1-57	Resurrection
C7	12.1-26 (27-50)	Universal devotion, praise and service

NOTE: At this stage it will be tentatively suggested that 10.22-42 and 12.27-50 are appendices to the basic sevenfold sub-structure of section C. The reasons for their inclusion and the positions in which they have been placed will be discussed below. In 6.1-71, the story of Jesus walking on the water (6.16-21) probably provides no material for eucharistic theology (unlike the sign and discourse on either side of it). The reason for its inclusion here is almost certainly its relation to the story of the feeding of the five thousand in the tradition from which St John was drawing;[1] the actual way it has been written up may suggest other speculations as to its role in the total structure of the gospel, for which see later.

---

[1] Barrett, *op. cit.* p. 233.

The headings given in the table above to subsections C1, 3 and 6 are, I believe, self-evident. More needs to be said about the other subsections. The subsection C2 does not follow smoothly upon the discourse which comes after the healing by the pool called Bethzatha, and this break probably suggests the beginning of a new subsection with the theme of Witness. In comparison with the other six subsections in section C, C2 is short and lacking in full development. This is natural enough, for St. John has already dealt at length with the theme of Witness throughout section B. Admittedly there is a shift of emphasis in comparing section B with C2. The former builds up the idea of the universal witness to Christ; the latter provides the authoritative grounds upon which the former stakes its claims. For subsection C2 offers a fourfold testimony: by John the Baptist, the works of the incarnate Christ, the Father, and the scriptures.

We have already said that C2 is rather brief and undeveloped. But the situation is not as bad as it appears at first sight. For we would now suggest that at significant points in the rest of the gospel, St. John has deliberately included units of tradition (written up in his own inimitable style) which develop in turn the four witnesses mentioned in C2. First of all, John's testimony is developed in 3.22-30,[1] a unit of tradition appropriately placed in a footnote to the Nicodemus story because of the baptismal imagery which colours both. The second witness mentioned in C2—"the works which the Father has granted me to accomplish" (5.36)— is reiterated and developed in 10.22-42 (see especially v. 25). The reason why these verses are placed after 10.21 is not difficult to see: Jesus' words about sheep (10.26ff.) make a fitting footnote to his claims to be the good shepherd (10.14).[2]

The Father and the scriptures are the third and fourth witnesses made explicit in C2. We may tentatively propose that they are developed further at the end of section C3—i.e. in 12.27-36, and in 12.37-50 respectively.[4] The former of these two passages centres around a voice which came from heaven, "I have glorified [my name], and I will glorify it again" (12.28) . The other passage provides a summary of the response of the Jews to Jesus' public ministry, which is seen as a fulfilment of Isaiah's prophecy.[5] One further comment must be made before we leave

---

[1] See above, p. 82.
[2] Cf. Lightfoot, *op. cit.* p. 209.
[3] See above, p. 85.
[4] It may be that the witness of scripture is found only in 12.37-43; 12.44-50 would then be a free summary of Christ's offer, written by the author. 10.24 f. and 12.27f. are based on traditional stories of Jesus' trial before the Sanedrin and his visit to Gethsemane respectively. Perhaps St. John has deliberately removed these from his Passion story (cf. the Synoptists) to serve his theological scheme. See C.H. Dodd, *op. cit.* pp. 69-71, 91 f.
[5] See below, pp. 88-89.

subsection C2: the tenses of the verb μαρτυρέω in 5.31-47 are present
indicative active in relation to Christ's works and the scriptures, but
perfect indicative active in relation to John the Baptist and the Father.
These tenses make quite good sense in the context of the earthly ministry,
although it is a little difficult to understand the perfect tense for the
Father's witness—"It is not clear to what witness John refers at this
point";[1] the tenses make even better sense in the context of the Church in
which St. John was working, for the works of Christ are continued in the
life of the Church and the scriptures are still read there, while the
testimonies of John the Baptist (3.22-30) and the Father (12.27-36) are
things of the past although their effect and authority are contemporary.
This confirms that section C is not only about Jesus; it is also about his
Church.

"Apologetic" is the heading which has been given to subsection C4. It
is a heading which is designed to convey the dominant impression of what
is probably the most difficult and least attractive section of the Fourth
Gospel. That impression is one which sees Jesus standing aloof from the
petty and ignorant taunts and questions of the crowds; they cannot
possibly understand in any depth the real issues—the divine origin of
Jesus' Person, his divine–human status during the Incarnation, and his
future heavenly 'place'. And Jesus makes little attempt to draw the crowds
into any deeper insights; indeed throughout these chapters (7.1-8.59)
there is hardly any real dialogue at all. Rather, it seems, Jesus views his
task as simply stating the deep truths with which he has been entrusted,
and maintaining them publicly and without compromise in the face of
abuse and foolish speculation. This is what apologetic is all about.
Religious knowledge about God and his Word comes not by intellectual
debate but by faith; and the religious man has the task of affirming the
content of his intuitions of faith although it appears as foolishness in the
eyes of the world.

That 10.1-21 belongs to chapter 9 in a single subsection (C5) may be
seen from Barrett's comment:

> No break is indicated by John between chapters 9 and 10; but the
> present passage [10.1-21] is rather a comment upon chapter 9 than a
> continuation of it. A signal instance of the failure of hireling shepherds
> has been given; instead of properly caring for the blind man the
> Pharisees have cast him out (9.34). Jesus, on the other hand, as the
> good shepherd, found him (9.35) and so brought him into the true
> fold.[2]

---

[1] Barrett, *op. cit.* p. 222.
[2] Barrett, *op. cit.* p. 304. For a fuller discussion see Lightfoot, *op. cit.* pp. 205f. and
209f.

Furthermore, the final paragraph of this subsection, 10.19-21, ties 10.1-2 very closely into chapter 9; the σχίσμα of 10.19 parallels that of 9.16, and 10.21 reflects the puzzlement aroused by the sign of 9.1-7.

The title which is suggested for C5 is "Baptism". Perhaps we could express it more fully with the phrase: "Baptism, and the pastoral oversight which ensuing membership of the Church brings." Certainly the main ideas of the subsection—water and illumination (opening of blind eyes)—are not inconsistent with the thesis that St. John has written up his traditional material to bring out his baptismal theology. That theology would then hinge upon the twin ideas that baptism has to do with insight into the Person of Jesus (especially 9.35ff.), and also with the removal of sin and guilt (9.2, 40f.).[1] Other clues which point to the suggestion that C5 has become a meditation on Baptism are as follows: (i) The use of ἐπιχρίω (9.11, and possibly in 9.6, if the reading of 𝔓⁶⁶ ℵ A D W Θ, etc. be accepted), which reminds one of the occurrence of χρῖσμα in John.[2] (ii) The twice-mentioned sequence of 'baptismal events', namely 'Going, washing, and seeing' (9.7, 11). (iii) The public confession of Jesus as the Christ (9.22)—a common demand upon early baptisands. Finally, (iv), the outline of a primitive credal confession (9.35-8) of an interrogatory character. There is, then, probably sufficient evidence to justify the claim that in this subsection St. John affirms that the rite of Baptism properly belongs to the public ministry of the Church.

Subsection C7 brings us once again into close contact with the public worship and liturgy of the Church. These verses bring together the significant number of three pericopae—Mary anointing the feet of Jesus with costly ointment and wiping them with her hair, the crowds greeting the entrance of Jesus into Jerusalem with palm branches and cries of "Hosanna!" and the Greeks making their appeal through Philip to see Jesus. Immediately there springs to mind the idea that St. John once more deliberately arranged these three stories to form a linear development of thought: the devoted and pious woman closely attached to the circle of Jesus' friends, the crowds of Jews, and the representatives of the non-Jewish world at large, the Greeks. The devotion and praise and service (12.26) which are given to Jesus in these stories represent the universal devotion and praise and service which belong to him and which the universal Church endeavours to offer him.

When we look at section C as a whole, a very striking fact may be observed. In each of the seven subsections there is either a reference to a threat on Jesus' life, or a direct or allusive pointer towards his

---

[1] See further p. 95 below.
[2] 1 John 2.20, 27.

crucifixion. In other words, the public ministry of Jesus was enacted in the shadow of the cross; his ministry brought forth opposition and hostility and provided the impetus which led to his death. And from the theology of the Church which St. John has written in the very arrangement of his gospel, we may further deduce that the public ministry of the Church—in its sevenfold aspect—is conducted in the face of fierce hostility and persecution. In the following table are listed the references which set the whole of section C in the context of suffering (and it should be noted that this impregnation of the subsections with references to hostility is peculiar to section C, which is, perhaps, further evidence for the analysis of the gospel into four sections as suggested).

	Threats on Jesus' life	Pointers towards Jesus' death
C1	5.16, 18	
C2		5.36-47*
C3	6.64, 71	6.51-8
C4	7.1, 19f., etc.†	
C5	(10.31, 39)	10.11, 15, 17
C6	11.8, 50, 57	
C7		12.7, 24-6 (27ff.)

* There is no direct evidence in C2 which mentions Christ's sufferings or death. However, if we follow the suggestion made above[1] that the four witnesses of C2 are expanded at other points in the gospel, we can see that in three of these expanded witnesses the theme of suffering is made clear. In the section on works (10.22-42) we have threats to stone (10.31) and arrest (10.39) Jesus. The expanded sections on the witnesses of the Father (12.27-36) and the scriptures (12.37-50) contain many references to Christ's death and the crowd's hostility (e.g. 12.32-4, 36, 40), and it must be remembered that they have been placed immediately prior to the account of Christ's passion and death.

† The threat to kill Jesus and the attempt to arrest him are made particularly clear in C4. This is fitting, for this fourth subsection is the central subsection in section C—both by having three subsections on either side of it, and also by being the longest subsection. At the beginning of C4 there is a series of references which speak of the Jews' desire to kill Jesus (7.1, 19f., 25), and at the end of the subsection there is a complementary series (8.37, 40, 59); Jesus' apologetic begins and ends in the same threatening atmosphere. In the middle of the passage is a group of verses which describe the elaborate plans of the religious officials to arrest him: 7.30, 32, 44f.; 8.20.

It was suggested above[2] that section B is arranged into a group of three subsections followed by a group of four. In section C the converse is true, thus preserving an attractive symmetry between the two main sections of

---

[1] P. 85 above.
[2] P. 84 above.

the gospel. In section C, 7=4+3 (rather than 7= 3+4). This arrangement may be demonstrated in at least three ways.

(*a*) St. John brings our attention to C4 and C7 by having only these two subsections without a description of a sign or a reference to Jesus' works (5.36). (Notice once again the reversed technique for bringing our attention to the significant subsections in section C compared with section B. In the latter the presence of signs was the identifying agency of B3 and B7.)

(*b*) St. John has written up C1 and C5 (the first subsections of the groups of four and three respectively) so as to bring out parallels of situation and activity on the part of Jesus. The whole tenor and approach of the two passages show a close similarity, the details of which are given by Lightfoot.[1]

(*c*) We have referred immediately above to the centrality of C4 in section C considered as a whole. This is important because this subsection marks the end of the first group of four subsections. The centrality of this passage is further emphasised when we note that within it there may be references backward and forward to all the other subsections in section C. Thus while the Church's apologetic is primarily concerned with the major themes on the lips of Jesus in C4, there is also an apologetic role in relation to the whole public ministry of the Church; these 'notae ecclesiae' are to be firmly defended against opponents and unbelievers. This extension of the apologetic work may be demonstrated as follows: the backward references are to healing (7. 23), witness (8.18), and the eucharist (7.37); the forward references are to baptism (8.12), resurrection and life (8.51f.), and glorifying the Son (8.54).

SECTION D

"The Economy of Salvation" is Barrett's title for the fourth stanza of the Prologue, and if our initial presupposition is correct, that final stanza should serve as a summary of the theme of section D as a whole. This is evidently true, for section D records the final words and deeds of Jesus as he prepares for his death, the death itself (which is simultaneously glorification), and the vindication of the glorious death—the resurrection. St. John never leaves us in any doubt that the death of Christ, voluntary and in obedience to God's will, is the sole ground of his saving power. But, as we have discovered in the previous three sections, so here St. John cannot rest content with being simply a reporter of events. For he tells the story of Jesus' death and resurrection, as he tells the story of his ministry,

---

[1] Lightfoot, *op. cit.* p. 16.

in such a way as to throw light upon the life and purpose of the Church which he inaugurated. Section C elucidated the public, or external, work of the Church; section D, in contrast, concerns the inner life of the 'gathered' Church. Now cease the squabbles and taunts of the Jews, and Jesus, in complete and quiet control of the situation, draws together his disciples to be with himself. Certainly all things point to the cross, but the atmosphere is different: Jesus deliberately moves towards his destiny in God's good time. And as he goes, he displays to the pristine congregation the true character of the love which makes possible a united fellowship, the humble service which breaks down the barriers of pride and self-sufficiency, and he pioneers the teaching and praying activities whereby the Church is built up. But chiefly he indicates the purpose of the inner life of the Church—the world mission (13.35; 17.20, 23, etc.)—and the true basis of the Church's fellowship and mission. This basis is Jesus himself—the Prophet (13.1-11), the Priest (17.1-26), and the King (18.33-7; 19.3-22)—who is at one and the same time the Crucified One and the Glorified One. We may, therefore, suggest as a full title for section D: "The Economy of Salvation and the inner life of the Church which is grounded upon the saving work of Christ." Perhaps it is not without significance that the fourth stanza of the Prologue (which summarises section D) contains the clauses in the first person plural;[1] the fruit of the cross is the Church and it is within the Church that faith is confessed and deepened, and the work of Christ is remembered and taught, by the guidance of the Holy Spirit.

Section D comprises three subsections, and each subsection consists of four parts. Subsection D1 is 13.1-17.26, and may be divided into a prophetic symbol with explanation (13.1-30), two parallel discourses (13.31-14.31; 15.1-16.33), and Jesus' final prayer (17.1-26). Subsection D2 recounts the climax of Christ's earthly life (18.1-19.42), describing in detail his arrest (18.1-14) his trial (18.15-19.16), his death (19.17-37) and burial (19.38-42). Finally, we have subsection D3, 20.1-31, which consists of the visit of Peter and the Beloved Disciple to the tomb (20.1-10), the appearance to Mary Magdalene (20.11-18), the appearance to the disciples on Easter Day (20.19-23), and the rebuttal of Thomas' unbelief (20.24-9). (St John concludes with a brief statement of his purpose and ambition, (20.30-1.)

Little more may be said about the structure of section D; what remains is only the need for exposition. However, a few notes on this section may be added at this point. With regard to D1 (Jesus alone with his disciples), one of the most striking features is the absence of detailed structure in

---

[1] See above, p. 81.

such a comparatively long subsection. St. John has possibly included two parallel farewell discourses so as to have four parts to this subsection, and thus provide the significant number of twelve parts in section D as a whole. The themes touched upon in the two discourses are clearly closely related; Lightfoot, for example, says that in the second discourse

> the instruction given deals more fully with certain subjects briefly treated in the first [discourse], especially the relation of the disciples to the Lord after his return to them, and, through him, to the Father, and the work of the Holy Spirit.[1]

But it must be admitted that St. John has not drawn out the parallels in the two discourses in any mechanical or rigid way; rather, the themes have been freely expounded with quite different metaphors and images. Probably the purpose of this subsection in the overall ecclesiology of the gospel is to point to those activities which nourish the united fellowship of the Church as it gathers around its Lord to prepare for its universal mission: and those activities are mutual service, meditation on the Lord's teaching, and prayer in the power of the Holy Spirit.

D2 pictures Jesus alone—in his suffering and death. Significantly this subsection stands at the centre of section D. The crucifixion, which is glorification, is the centre and ground of the Christian Church. From the side of the Crucified One flow the blood and water which give life and cleansing to the Christian community (19.34).

Subsection D3 depicts the return of the risen Lord to his Church. The structure and content of this subsection repeat what we have suggested before: the inner life of the Church (as developed in section D) is to be viewed only in the context of universal mission. For the first three parts of the subsection are arranged to provide once again a linear development of thought. The first part (20.1-10) tells only of hesitant and partial faith on the part of the two disciples, and the pericope ends without any missionary motif: "the disciples went back to their homes" (20.10). The second part (20.11-18) tells of a gradually dawning 'vision' of the risen Lord, a primitive and inadequate faith, and a limited missionary charge: "Go to my brethren" (20.17). The third part (20.19-23), however, speaks of immediate and joyful recognition of the risen Lord on the part of the disciples, a full faith (implied by the contrast with doubting Thomas), and a universal missionary commission: "As the Father has sent me, even so I send you" (20.21). We see here another example of St. John's technique of linear development of complete numbers of parts (three or seven) for proclaiming the world-wide significance of Jesus Christ and the world-

---

[1] Lightfoot, *op. cit.* p.280.

wide task of his Church. The subsection ends with a pericope which explores the relation between faith and sight and worship; so the gospel comes to a conclusion as it began, with faithful believers making an adoring confession of faith in Christ.

We are now in a position to look back over the gospel to see the pattern which St. John has deliberately constructed in order to convey his theological insights. The suggestion of a deliberate and complex structure makes no judgement upon the historicity of the pericopae the author used; but it does contend that the imaginative creator of the Fourth Gospel saw in the form of literature pioneered by at least the three Synoptic Evangelists new possibilities as a vehicle for conveying his own religious understanding. The structure of the gospel is complicated, yet beautiful. It comprises four sections, the first of which brings together the themes elaborated in the subsequent sections. Each section is meaningfully divided into subsections to provide the following pattern: 4; 3+4; 4+3; 3. One naturally brings together the first and last sections to present a third group of seven subsections. Thus the whole gospel comprises 3x7=21 subsections; in Jewish numerology, a more significant combination of numbers can hardly be imagined. If one were to use the terminology proposed by Farrer,[1] one could argue that the Fourth Gospel is constructed so as to have a week divided into two half-weeks (sections A and D): in between the two half-weeks are inserted two further weeks (sections B and C), each of which is divided into two half-weeks.

May we not go further? May we not see the same approach to the construction of their books by the author of the Fourth Gospel and the author of the Apocalypse? For Farrer has analysed the Apocalypse also into four sections (each having seven subsections), the first of which points the way for the other three. He writes:

> The apocalyptic drama occupies the last three sevens; the first seven, the messages (1-3), introduce the figure of the Revealer, exhort the recipients, and promise a disclosure of the things that shall be hereafter. They also state the themes of the three sevens to follow.[2]

One may see in this similarity of literary technique between these two Johannine writings evidence that the Fourth Gospel and the Apocalypse spring from the same theological school, and therefore probably from the same geographical area and from roughly the same period of time.

---

[1] Farrer, *op. cit.* pp. 7 ff.
[2] Farrer, *op. cit.* p. 10. See also pp. 83-6.

The plan of composition suggested above accounts for all the material in the gospel except 3.31-6. But one cannot help being left with the suspicion, particularly in section B, that the allusive details of St. John's subsections have not been given due weight. Certainly it would seem that the theme of witness binds together the subsections of section B, but is there not more to be said, for example, about the baptismal language in the Nicodemus story, 3.1-21? It could be argued that these allusive details were present in the pericopae St. John used, and that, while he selected and arranged his material to fit the scheme already outlined, he could not remove these subsidiary themes from the actual contents of the pericopae themselves. If this were so, we could safely ignore these allusions in our reconstruction of the Evangelist's plan of the gospel. But St. John was a more skilful artist than this would suggest. The general impression of his book is that everything is carefully and deliberately worded in a self-conscious manner. Of course he inherited traditional material; but equally certainly he has rewritten or edited this material so that it is now composed in his own distinctive yet limited vocabulary. In the light of this observation we must conclude that the allusive details in the gospel are to be taken with great seriousness.

The proposal that will be put forward for consideration to explain the details hitherto ignored will be much more speculative than what has gone before. This is inevitable because of the complexity of the situation. The proposal is that, in addition to the structure of the gospel already stated St. John has arranged his material so that the latter two sections (C, D) repeat in reverse order the themes of the first two sections (A, B), and *vice versa*. That is, the gospel is arranged as a huge chiasmus: A, B; B′ (=C), A′ (=D).

To justify such a bold superimposed structure is a difficult task; occasionally the arguments will be allusive rather than direct. But surely it is not unreasonable to suppose that an author who has already devised a complicated ground-plan will find a little difficulty in fitting in the details of a complex chiasmus on top of the ground-plan. For St. John is an author who never becomes tied to his structure in such a way that he loses his creative flair. The best writing is always disciplined by a tidy and tight structure; but a too mechanical approach kills the spirit of creative literature.

In the following table we set out, in the first two columns, the references and titles of the subsidiary themes in sections A and B. The third column contains the references to the subsections of sections C and D. It will be seen that the first two columns should be read from top to bottom, and the third column from bottom to top, to obtain a continuous record through the gospel. Reading across the table will reveal the suggested parallels which justify an overall chiastic structure for the gospel. See further Figure 1.

Subsidiary themes in A, B		Chiastic reversal in C, D
1.1-18	Prologue	20.1-31
1.19-34	Lamb of God	18.1-19.42
1.35-51	Discipleship	13.1-17.26
2.1-12	Marriage Feast	12.1-26*
2.13-25	Death and Resurrection	11.1-57
3.1-21*	Baptism	9.1-10.21*
3.31-6	Meditation	7.1-8.59
4.1-45	Living Water and Worship	6.1-7.1
4.46-54	Healing	5.1-30†

* We have already offered explanations of why the footnotes, 3.22-30, 10.22-42, 12.27-36, and 12.37-50, have been inserted into the main structure, and why they have been added at the points where they have been included.[1] We may perhaps note here, in addition, the wisdom of inserting these footnotes at simple points in the gospel: the first two have been added at those points where Baptism is alluded to (on the same horizontal line in the table above); the latter two have been added consecutively at the end of the third section, section C, of the gospel.

† It may be wondered why 5.31-47 has been omitted in the table. We have to admit freely that no compelling reason springs to mind. But it is fair to say that the theme of witness, with which these verses deal, has had a very full treatment elsewhere in the gospel. The plan and contents of section B were devoted to it; more particularly the four witnesses enumerated in 5.31-47 have been elaborated in the four footnotes we have just mentioned. Could not the very fact that these sections which elaborate the four witnesses have been placed as footnotes to the structure proper be St. John's allusive way of suggesting that 5.31-47 may itself be a footnote when the overall chiasmus is being considered?

We shall now draw out the parallels implied in the table above. Some need little, if any, explanation. It is obvious, for example, that the healing of the official's son in 4.46-54 links up with the story of the healing of the man who had been ill for thirty-eight years (5.1-30); in each case the extremity of the sickness is overcome by the word of Jesus. Similarly, there are clearly baptismal echoes in the conversation between Jesus and Nicodemus—being born again (or, from above), of water and the Spirit—and these echoes chime in with the baptismal framework which, it has been argued,[2] pervades 9.1-10.21. Nor is there any difficulty in understanding the parallels between 2.13-25 and 11.1-57. The former incident concludes with Jesus' reference to the destruction of the temple

---

[1] See above, p. 85.
[2] See above, p. 87.

of his body and the raising up of this temple in three days—a truth which dawned on the disciples only after his resurrection; the latter section describes how Jesus—"I am the resurrection and the life" (11.25)—brought back Lazarus from death to life.[1] Finally, among these self-evident parallels in the chiastic structure, we refer to 1.35-51 and 13.1-17.26. The first passage recounts the call of the first disciples; the second passage, as we have illustrated at length, has to do with the spiritual development of the disciples, and all Christian people, within the Church.

The five remaining parallels require more comment. We shall begin at the top of the table and work down. First, then, 1.1-18 and 20.1-31. There is something to be said for the fact that these obviously self-contained sections begin and end the gospel respectively. More important is the worship-theme which unites both: the "Heilsgeschichte in Hymnenform"[2] and the wonder of Thomas' exclamation, "My Lord and my God!" (20.28). Further, the two sections show structural affinity. Both comprise four clearly distinguished parts, the fourth part in each case exploring the relation between faith, worship, and sight. In the former case (1.14-18) we have phrases such as "The Word became flesh"..."We have beheld his glory"...and "No one has ever seen God; the only Son, who is in the bosom of the Father, he has made him known"; in the latter case (20.24-9) the climactic speech of Jesus is "Have you believed because you have seen me? Blessed are those who have not seen and yet believe". In other words, the Prologue offers the Incarnation of the pre-existent Word as the proper ground for Christian faith; the final chapter of the gospel shows how fullness of faith and richness of worship do not depend upon the continued physical presence of the Incarnate One.

In 1.19-34 the most striking phrase is that of John the Baptist, "Behold, the Lamb of God, who takes away the sin of the world!" (1.29). Immediately we are directed to the climax of Christ's saving work on the cross, and so it is only natural that we should look for a parallel to this saying in the record of the crucifixion, 18.1-19.42. There is much disagreement among scholars about the identity of the "Lamb" in John the Baptist's exclamation. But if our suggested chiastic structure is correct, we are led to suppose that there can be little doubt about identifying the "Lamb" as the Paschal Lamb. For in his crucifixion account St. John brings out very forcibly paschal imagery: Jesus dies on the day (and at the time of day) when the passover lambs were being slaughtered in the Temple (19.14); the sponge full of vinegar was put on "hyssop" (19.29),

---

[1] Cf. Lightfoot, *op. cit.* p. 17, who suggests a link between 10.40-11.53 and 1.19-28.

[2] Jeremias, *op. cit.* p. 76.

which played an important part in the Passover ritual;[1] and like the Paschal Lamb,[2] Jesus dies without a bone being broken (19.36).

We must now illustrate the parallels between 2.1-12 and 12.1-26; this we shall do by listing the ideas and phrases which link together in the two sections. (i) The former passage describes events at a marriage feast—a prolonged period of rejoicing and festivity. (The marriage feast, it may be noted, was a popular analogy for the joyous life of the New Age.) The latter passage, as we have suggested above,[3] speaks of lavish devotion and joyful worship and service offered to the Lord. (ii) The "third day" which introduces the narrative in 2.1 brings us to the sixth consecutive day recounted since 1.19; the succeeding subsection begins with the phrase "The Passover of the Jews was at hand" (2.13). These temporal relationships are paralleled exactly by the opening words of 12.1: "Six days before the Passover."[4] (iii) The marriage feast took place at Cana in Galilee (2.1, 11) and afterwards Jesus moved to Capernaum (2.12), another Galilean town. Could it be that we are told so emphatically in 12.21 that Philip was "from Bethsaida in Galilee" to link up with the geography of 2.1-12?[5] (iv) At the marriage feast we find Jesus, Jesus' mother, and his disciples (2.1f.)—that is, Jesus and those closest to him. At the supper at Bethany were Jesus, Mary, Martha, Lazarus, and at least Judas Iscariot from among the disciples—a similar clientèle. (v) At the marriage were standing six stone jars "for the Jewish rites of purification" (2.6). At Bethany Mary squandered on Jesus' feet "a pound of costly ointment of pure nard" (12.3), a proleptic cleansing and embalming of the crucified Jesus. Moreover, only in the two passages under consideration (and in the burial story, 19.38-42) does St. John relate quantities of materials: six jars, each holding μετρητὰς δύο ἢ τρεῖς; a pound of ointment worth three hundred denarii. (vi) Jesus' sign at Cana "manifested his glory" (2.11). In chapter 12 Jesus looks forward to the glorification of the Son of man on the cross (12.23).[6] Although these points are not of equal weight, together they provide perhaps sufficient data to justify the parallelism of the two sections.

3.31-6 is a passage which previously we have not discussed at length and whose position we have not explained. Our suggestion is that these verses are the free composition of St. John; they have been written as a summary of the long section of apologetic, 7.1-8.59. These verses have

---

[1] Exod. 12.22.
[2] Exod. 10.46; Num. 9.12.
[3] P. 87.
[4] Barrett, *op. cit.* p. 158. See also p. 86 above.
[5] Cf. Lightfoot, *op. cit.* p. 251; but note Barrett's comment, *op. cit.* p. 351.
[6] This theme is further developed in 12.27-36.

then been included at this point in the gospel to form a parallel with chapters 7 and 8 in the overall chiastic structure. The strength of this hypothesis may be tested by investigating the contents of 3.31ff. They concern the divine origins of Christ (and his subsequent responsibility in the divine economy), the truth of his words, the Spirit, and the duality between faith and life on the one hand and disobedience and wrath on the other. It is also true that these ideas are highlighted in 7.1-8.59: Christ's divine origin is a constantly recurring theme (7.16f., 27-9; 8.14, 18f., 23, etc.), as is the truthfulness of his teaching (7.16-18; 8.13ff., 31f., 40, etc.); the gift of the Spirit is briefly dealt with (7.37-9), and throughout the demand of faith is made clear, together with the consequences of ignorance and unbelief—the Jews are children of the devil (8.44).

Only one more parallel in the table above remains for investigation: 4.1-45 and 6.1-71. Chapter 6 obviously deals with the Eucharist, the bread of life. "It will be remarked at once that the 'bread of life' chapter forms a complement to the 'water of life' discourse (4.10-26)."[1] It might also be said that in its own right the incident concerning the woman at the well has been written up by St. John to reveal eucharistic ideas:[2] the drink which gives unceasing nourishment (4.13), the woman's repentance (4.17), the discussion of true worship in the light of Jewish and Samaritan antecedents (4.20-4), and the confession of Christ (4.29, 42). Besides this broad thematic agreement between the two sections, we may suggest more tentatively further evidence for their being linked together. First, we mention the references to patriarchal donors of the Jewish forerunners of the Christian eucharistic symbols: the well of water in the field which Jacob gave to Joseph (4.6), and the manna which, according to the Jews, Moses gave the Israelites in the wilderness (6.32). Second, we speculate why the incident of Jesus walking on the water (6.6-21) has been written up as it has been.[3] For when we investigate the sequence of confessions of Christ's person in 4.1-45, we can list a developing insight through the section as follows: "a prophet" (4.19), "Messiah (he who is called Christ)" (4.25), ἐγώ εἰμι (4.26), and "the Saviour of the world" (4.42). Now chapter 6 as we have it provides a very similar development of Christological confession, as follows: "the prophet who is to come into the world" (6.14), "king" (6.15) ἐγώ εἰμι (6.20), "I am the bread of life" (6.35, 48), "the Son of man" (6.62), and "the Holy One of God" (6.69).

---

[1] Barrett, *op. cit.* p. 11. In particular, the verses on food and the food which is the doing of God's will (4.31-4) form a direct link with 6.35-40; the latter section, interestingly, has a reference back to chapter 4 in the words of 6.35: "He who believes in me shall never thirst."

[2] Cf. O. Cullmann, *Early Christian Worship* (1953), pp. 80-4.

[3] See above, p. 87.

(It must be remembered in particular that in the Fourth Gospel the titles Μεσσίας, Χριστός and Βασιλεύς are used interchangeably.) Dare we suppose that St. John has deliberately evolved these sequences of titles for Jesus in the two sections under discussion to point out their parallel themes in the overall chiasmus of the gospel?

Having now considered the similarities of theme and vocabulary in the relevant sections as we have tabulated them above, it is possible to give credence to the thesis that the Fourth Gospel has imposed upon its complicated ground-plan a chiastic structure. Thus, while the gospel reads progressively through its four sections A, B, C, and D, there is also a continual interplay between the theological themes of the early sections (up to 4.54), and those of the later sections from 20.31 to 5.1. The Fourth Evangelist was not only a brilliant theologian; he was also a master of a very specialised literary technique.

By way of conclusion we shall draw out briefly certain consequences which spring from this investigation of the structure of the Fourth Gospel. We have already dwelt upon the critical conclusion that the Fourth Evangelist and the author of the Apocalypse seem to have used similar sophisticated techniques for organising their material. This would seem to indicate a proximity of 'milieu' for the two writers.

There is still no compelling argument to which to appeal to settle the problem of whether the gospel was written for the Church, or from the Church for the world. But if the discussion about the gospel's structure is broadly correct, the most likely thesis is that the gospel was written for the Church. Then we could understand why St. John has gone to such pains to elucidate, in the plan of the gospel, the public ministries of the Church, the activities which edify the inner life of the Church, and the call to the Church to fulfil its universal mission and witness. The gospel was written from the ecclesiological viewpoint of St. John, and addressed to the Church, in order that, through the Church, the world might believe.

As to whether the recipients of the Fourth Gospel were Jews or Gentiles, again the analysis of the gospel's structure provides no clear adjudication. On the one hand we have encountered a love for significant numbers—particularly three and seven—which would indicate that the author, at least, was well versed in Jewish thought-forms. On the other hand, the universalist strand which runs through the gospel would demand even of a Jewish readership involvement in a mission in which ethnic barriers were of no account. Perhaps the best solution is still that which postulates that St. John was writing for people immersed in Greek culture; he was bringing to them deeper religious insights through the fusion of their inherited Hellenist environment and his own Jewish background—a fusion made possible by the Church's incentive to take the story of the Jewish Messiah into the gentile world.

From the earliest times St. John's liturgical interest has been recognised.[1] What has emerged from our study of the gospel's detailed structure is that this liturgical interest must be set in the context of a comprehensive ecclesiology. At every point, as it were, the author has the Church in view—its public life, its secret discipline. The Church, he believes, follows directly upon the course the Lord himself pioneered; so much so, in fact, that the stories about Jesus and his ministry provide simultaneously material elucidating the work and witness of the Church. Whatever Jesus did in the narrow geographical limits of Palestine and in a relatively brief period of time the Church must now do on a world-wide scale and constantly. In its sevenfold public life the Church, like its Lord must bear with persecution; indeed, the Church's suffering, like all its words and deeds, must point to the cross as the source of eternal life and object of faith.

We may speculate about the particular problems to which St. John addressed himself. The full section of the gospel (section B) on universal witness, the demand for a universal worship (12.1ff.), and the final call to a universal mission (20.1-23) might suggest that the Church to which St. John was writing was one which had lost its proper evangelical concern. Perhaps it had become self-satisfied, perhaps introverted; it may have fallen from its early faith. But in the gospel St. John insists again and again on the transcendental significance of Jesus and the role of his Church in manifesting this truth to the world. The Church is mission.

St. John is certain that the significance of the Person of Jesus is not matter-of-fact, descriptive knowledge. He insists, rather, that only religious experience can illuminate men's minds and prevent trivial misunder-standings. For this reason the Evangelist grounds the life of the Church—both its public and its private life—in the atmosphere of worship. As we have gone through the gospel we have noted numerous liturgical references. By way of further illustration we may mention here the details of sabbaths and Jewish religious feasts which crop up at so many points in the narratives: "St. John invites the reader to see the Lord's whole work in close connection with the Jewish festivals, especially the passover."[2]

The most original contribution to liturgical and ecclesiological thinking may be found by considering St. John's attitude to the

---

[1] Cullmann, *op.cit.* p. 59.
[2] Lightfoot, *op. cit.* p. 20.

sacraments. To begin with we must insist that the Evangelist is deeply concerned with the two sacraments of Baptism and Eucharist. This contrasts with R. Bultmann's opinion that "it is permissible to say that though in John there is no direct polemic against the sacraments, his attitude toward them is nevertheless critical or at least reserved".[1] On the other hand, it would seem that Cullmann[2] has overstated his case in so far as he tends to find in every reference to water an allusion to Baptism, and in every reference to blood, or body, or bread, a reference to the Eucharist. It is better to adopt a 'via media': if our analysis of the gospel is correct, the passages giving the author's theology of Baptism or Eucharist are fairly rigidly defined. Eucharistic theology, for example, is found in 4.1-45, 6.1-71 and 7.37. But can we suggest why an author so concerned with, say, the eucharist does not even record its inauguration?[3] Once again we can appeal to St. John's ecclesiology. He refused to include the institution of the sacrament at, say, the Last Supper because that would have rooted the rite in the private life of the Christian community, and its purpose would have been only the Christians' edification. Instead St. John chose to refer to the eucharist in the sections of his gospel dealing with the public, or external, life of the Church: the eucharist (and baptism) are public portrayals, 'converting ordinances'. The cost he had to pay for this method of conveying his sacramental theology was that he could refer to the rites only by allusion; his historical sense was so keen and the Christian tradition so fixed that he could not transfer some of the events of the Last Supper to another part of his gospel without explanation.

We return, finally, to a critical problem associated with the Fourth Gospel. Can we now offer any explanation of the phenomena in the style of the gospel which have given rise to a variety of displacement theories? If our analysis of St. John's structure is anywhere near correct, it is obvious that the business of writing the gospel must have been exceedingly complicated. Certainly St. John's literary flair was let loose on the individual pericopae he was using; but when it came to putting the pieces together to form the total pattern, St. John naturally had to adopt fairly mechanical procedures. We have had to draw up several tables to try and rediscover his plan of action, and the author himself must have done something at least as naïve to clarify his mind. We have even suggested that at one point (3.31-6) St. John had to summarise a long

---

[1] R. Bultmann, *Theology of the New Testament*, §47. 4.

[2] *Early Christian Worship*, part II.

[3] Cf. "The problem set by St. John's method here is usually explained by his unwillingness to disclose to non-Christian readers of his book the origin and ground of the eucharist—and similarly of the sacrament of baptism" (R.H. Lightfoot, *op. cit.* p. 262, n. 1.).

discourse section to complete his overall scheme. In the light of this it is hardly surprising that the author has not always smoothed out the harsh breaks between succeeding subsections; the disjointed character of the text is due not to displacements in an early copy of the gospel, but to the mathematical structure to which the author was conforming for theological purposes.

To illustrate this we can look at 3.22-36.

> It has often been supposed that this section, or part of it, is out of place. Two conjectural improvements are worthy of consideration. (*a*) vv. 22-30, which interrupt the connection between vv. 21 and 31, should be removed from their present position and read after 2.12. (*b*) vv. 22-30 and vv. 31-6 should be transposed. V. 31 is thus brought into immediate connection with v. 21 and v. 30 with the next chapter, the connections being improved in each case.[1]

Barrett himself, from whom that quotation is taken, rejects these conjectures, believing the passage flows as an essential unity. Our own explanation is different: 3.1-21 was one of the subsections in St. John's plan for section B; 3.22-30 was added as a footnote—added at this point because of its common baptismal imagery, and inserted in the gospel at all to illustrate the Baptist's witness mentioned in v. 33; 3.31-6 is the free composition of St. John summarising subsection C4 and placed here to fit in with the overall chiasmus in the gospel. This explanation has the advantage of giving full weight to the disjointed character of the text but does not hide behind speculative and subjective displacement theories.

---

[1] Barrett, *op. cit.* p. 183.

THEOLOGY AND IRONY IN THE FOURTH GOSPEL*

GEORGE W. MACRAE, S.J.

The vitality of recent scholarship on the Fourth Gospel is virtually unparalleled in the history of exegesis—at least since Origen and the Gnostics. In the last half-century, the period since Rudolf Bultmann's first major article on John,[1] the volume of publication on the Fourth Gospel is wholly unprecedented. There has been some pattern to it, of course. The best of this scholarship has tended to concentrate on such issues as the history of Johannine sources and redaction, the problem of the historical *Sitz im Leben* of the Gospel, the meaning and origin of the Johannine symbolism, and themes of Johannine theology, especially the implications of eschatology. It is a tribute to the genius of Bultmann, the acknowledged master of modern Johannine scholarship, that a large majority of significant modern studies are devoted to exploiting, continuing, sometimes challenging the insights of his articles and his great commentary. But the exploration of Johannine literary techniques, especially in relation to their significance for Johannine theology, has been somewhat neglected.[2] In particular, neither Bultmann nor many of the other recent interpreters have had more than passing things to say about the obvious and long-noted Johannine predilection for the literary device of irony.[3]

* This essay first appeared in Clifford. R.J. & MacRae G.W. (eds) *The Word in the World: Essays in honour of F.L. Moriarty.* (Cambridge, Mass: Weston College, 1973), pp. 83-96.

[1] "Der religionsgeschichtliche Hintergrund des Prologs zum Johannes-Evangelium", ΕΥΧΑΡΙΣΤΗΡΙΟΝ, *Festschrift Hermann Gunkel* (FRLANT, 19: Göttingen, 1923), 2, 3-26. Bultmann's commentary on John finally appeared in English near the end of the half-century period, *The Gospel of John, A Commentary,* tr. G.R. Beasley-Murray *et al.* (Philadelphia, 1971).

[2] A few significant works were devoted, in the wake of Bultmann's source analysis, to the study of the Johannine discourses: e.g. H. Becker, *Die Reden des Johannesevangeliums und der Stil der gnostischen Offenbarungsrede,* ed. R. Bultmann (FRLANT, 68; Göttingen, 1956); S. Schulz, *Komposition und Herkunft der johanneischen Reden* (BWANT, 5.1; Stuttgart, 1960). One of the more important recent works, which does relate literary analysis to theology, is H. Leroy, *Rätsel und Missverständnis* (BBB, 30: Bonn, 1968).

[3] H. Clavier is an exception; he has dealt with the theme of irony in a series of articles from 1929 to 1959; see "L'ironie dans le quatrième Evangile", *Studia Evangelica* I (TU: Berlin, 1959), 261-276 (with references to earlier articles). D. W. Wead, *The Literary Devices in John's Gospel* (Theologische Dissertationen, 4: Basel, 1970), points out some of the

In the following pages, I propose, not to furnish a detailed study of the Johannine irony as a literary technique, but rather to raise a more general question: What does the Fourth Evangelist's use of the literary device of irony imply for our understanding of his theology? It is a great privilege to be able to offer these reflections to F.L. Moriarty, whose unflinching openness to the multiple methodologies of the biblical interpreter has emboldened the author to enter the domain of the modern literary criticism of an ancient literary work.

At the outset it would be appropriate to state what is understood here by "irony," since the term itself is at once obvious and unclear. But that is in part the problem. Perhaps we can most profitably begin by employing the description of irony used by E.M. Good in his very perceptive study on irony in the OT.[1] Thus we shall understand irony in its most generic sense to be a "perception of incongruity" that is characterised by two specific qualities. First, it is normally expressed in understatement or suggestion, for example in double or multiple meanings perceptible on different levels by different hearers, or in saying the opposite of what is meant. Secondly, the ironic perception of incongruity rests upon the ironist's claim to an insight into the truth of things that is not shared by everyone.

It is not useful for our present purposes to dwell on the origin of irony as a literary device or on the well-known conflict of the $\epsilon\check{\iota}\rho\omega\nu$ and the $\grave{\alpha}\lambda\alpha\zeta\acute{\omega}\nu$ in classical comedy. The author of the Fourth Gospel would probably not have recognised the term $\epsilon\grave{\iota}\rho\omega\nu\epsilon\acute{\iota}\alpha$ as a designation of what he was doing, since the particular form of dramatic irony he used most has only in modern times inherited that name. The word had in John's time lost its pejorative sense, however, and the Socratic practice of dissimulation was not looked upon askance. But "irony" is a modern concept—though an ancient practice—and precisely because the modern concept has such a broad extension, there are some distinctions yet to be made.

1. TYPES OF IRONY

These may be briefly dealt with by way of elimination. First, the irony of the Fourth Gospel is not that which we usually associate with humour or with satire, whether humorous or biting. It is not the "militant irony" of Northrop Frye's "mythos of winter."[2] I would not want to exclude

---

irony in John but does not relate it to Johannine theology; J. Jónsson, *Humour and Irony in the New Testament* (Reykjavík, 1965), deals only superficially with John.
[1] *Irony in the Old Testament* (Philadelphia, 1965), pp. 30-31.
[2] *Anatomy of Criticism, Four Essays* (Princeton, 1957), p. 223.

humour entirely from the Gospels, of course. It may well be that such stories as those of the Syrophoenician woman (Mk 7.24-30) or the tribute money (Mt 17.24-27) are intended to be at least wryly humorous. But the Fourth Gospel, though often heavily ironical, seems singularly humourless. To use the literary critic's terms again, John's Gospel does not, like satire, assume the guise of the world of romantic idealism in order to demolish the romantic delusion.

Secondly, the irony of the Fourth Gospel is not Socratic irony, properly speaking. The Socratic irony was a didactic method employed by the philosopher in the well-known manner and with the well-known results. Socrates as εἴρων feigned ingenuousness to provoke the discovery of truth. G. G. Sedgewick, in his perennially readable lectures on the topic of irony,[1] has pointed out how our concept of Socratic irony has been purged of its offensiveness in part through the admiration of Socrates in later ages, to become an "urbane pretence." "It is a war upon Appearance waged by a man who knows Reality: now it is a process deadly to empty pretence, now a sort of kindly pruning vital to growth in truth." Socratic irony no doubt lies at the base of any concept of the ironical, but as a didactic method elaborated in dialogue it is not the main component of Johannine irony. This is not to say that it is wholly foreign to the Johannine presentation of Jesus. For example, the question of Jesus to those who "took up stones again to stone him": "I have shown you many good works from the Father; for which of these do you stone me?" (10.32). But if this stance is Socratic, the response of "the Jews" is another kind of irony, one that as we shall see gets more to the heart of the Johannine method: "We stone you for no good work but for blasphemy; because you, being a man, make yourself God."[2]

Thirdly, Johannine irony should not be identified with what is commonly called "tragic irony" (or "Sophoclean irony") either, though here again there are points of contact. The irony of the classical Greek tragedy (and of course of Shakespeare and others) functions as a dramatic technique in the service of undoing the tragic hero because of his fatal ὕβρις. One of the clearest examples is the powerful dialogues of the *Bacchae* of Euripides,[3] in which the god Dionysus in disguise confronts the king Pentheus of Thebes, maddened by a spell of Bacchic frenzy. Pentheus' opposition to the god is requited by his death at the hands of the frenzied Maenads, his own mother among them, and his downfall begins with his mad desire to witness the mysteries. Of course the spectator

---

[1] *Of Irony, Especially in Drama* (Toronto, 1935), p. 13.
[2] Clavier's emphasis on the Socratic origin of Johannine irony ("L'ironie dans le quatrième Evangile") has led him to miss some of its theological significance.
[3] Also cited by Sedgewick, *Of Irony*, pp. 24-25.

knows the story and waits with fascination the sight of Pentheus' head in
his raving mother's hands.

Pentheus:	True—true: we must not overcome by force
	The women. I will hide me midst the pines.
Dionysus:	Hide?—thou shalt hide as Fate ordains thine hiding.
	Who com'st with guile, a spy on Bacchanals.
Pentheus:	Methinks I see them mid the copses caught,
	Like birds, in toils of their sweet dalliance.
Dionysus:	To this end then act thou appointed watchman:
	Perchance thou shalt catch them—if they catch not thee.
Pentheus:	On through the midst of Thebes' town usher me!
	I am their one *man*, I alone dare this!
Dionysus:	Alone for Thebes thou travailest, thou alone;
	Wherefore for thee wait struggle and strain foredoomed.
	Follow: all safely will I usher thee,
	Another thence shall bring thee,—
Pentheus:	Ay, my mother!
Dionysus:	To all men manifest—
Pentheus:	For this I come.
Dionysus:	High-borne shalt thou return—
Pentheus:	Soft ease for me?
Dionysus:	On a mother's hands.
Pentheus:	Thou wouldst thrust pomp on me![1]

For comparison, several scenes in the Fourth Gospel suggest themselves,
most notably the scene of the Pilate trial, which we shall deal with below.
There the ironic interplay between "the Jews," symbols of the opponents
of the Johannine community, and Pilate, and between both and Jesus rests
on the same principle that the spectators know the story and what it
means. But in John the issue is not the ὕβρις of a tragic hero; not even
Caiaphas, who unwittingly "prophesies" the true meaning of Jesus' death
(11.49-52),[2] functions like Pentheus or Oedipus or Prometheus or
Agamemnon, even though the conflict with the divine is central. For the
Fourth Gospel we must distinguish dramatic from tragic irony.

Fourthly, and finally, we must distinguish the Johannine irony from
the "metaphysical irony" identified by modern literary critics, though
again the distinction is not a complete one. I borrow the term
"metaphysical irony" from the fascinating study of modern literature by

---

[1] *Euripides,* vol. 3, tr. A.S. Way (Loeb: Cambridge, Mass., 1930), lines 953-969.
[2] Bultmann, *The Gospel of John,* 411, refers to this remark as an example of tragic irony.

Charles I. Glicksberg.[1] What he understands by the "modern ironic vision" is the resultant of a set of contributory causes: "romantic individualism, the conflict between illusion and reality, the limitless aspirations of the self and its constraining finitude, the contradiction, always present, between freedom and necessity, spirit and matter, life and death."[2] What is specific about this form of irony is that it is "an expressive form of the metaphysical vision, the fruit of the growing suspicion that life is essentially meaningless."[3] Modern "metaphysical irony" is typified by the tragic absurdity of life, the image of Albert Camus' *Myth of Sisyphus*. The "world" of the Fourth Gospel is of course anything but absurd, yet the work borders on a dualism of God and world in which irony functions as a form of expression. This aspect of Johannine irony is reflected in the dialogue that concludes one section of the Farewell Discourse of Jesus. Here the disciples say, "Ah, now you are speaking plainly (ἐν παρρησίᾳ), not in any figure (παροιμίαν)! ...by this we believe that you came from God." And Jesus answers, "Do you now believe?... I have said this to you, that in me you may have peace. In the world you have tribulation; but be of good cheer, I have overcome the world" (16.29-33).

2. JOHANNINE IRONY

The four types of ironic expression that we have identified are not completely distinct from one another, nor is any of them completely distinct from the irony of the Fourth Gospel. But it is time to turn to a more positive statement about the latter. And here we must begin with the observation that the Johannine irony is first of all dramatic irony in that it presumes upon the superior knowledge of the reader to recognise the true perspective within which the Gospel's assertions are ironical.

Sedgewick singles out the following characteristics of dramatic irony:[4] the conflict of forces or elements, the ignorance of reality on the part of one of the forces, and the spectator's recognition of both the appearance and the reality. "Dramatic irony, in brief, is the sense of contradiction felt by spectators of a drama who see a character acting in ignorance of his condition." I do not wish to dispute this definition, but I should like to call attention to a few characteristics of Johannine dramatic irony which seem to me the most significant.

---

[1] *The Ironic Vision in Modern Literature* (The Hague, 1969).
[2] Glicksberg, *The Ironic Vision*, p. 10.
[3] Glicksberg, *The Ironic Vision*, p. 13.
[4] *Of Irony*, pp. 48-49.

First, like any dramatic irony, Johannine irony is born out of a *conflict* in situation. The conflict is one that takes place on a variety of levels simultaneously: it is the conflict between Jesus and "the world" or "the Jews," between the Christians contemporary with John and the Jewish communities which have ostracised them, between the power of truth and error, between glory and suffering, between the divine and the human. Conflict arises out of a disparity of vision. It can be historical (the debates between Christians and Jews) or theological (the conflict of immanence and transcendence) or metaphysical (the dualism of world and God). In some cases it is clearly the conflict of appearance and reality, as with the mystery of the incarnation. The Johannine statement "and the Word became flesh," as it is elaborated thematically in the Gospel, denotes not merely the fact of the incarnation, but the conflict created by the act of judgement in the human sphere on the part of the revealing word of God.[1]

Second, like the irony in tragedy, Johannine irony presumes the factor of *distance* from the events narrated. But precisely where the distance of tragedy is meant to bring about catharsis without actual terror, in the Fourth Gospel this distance has the effect of involving the spectator in the challenge of faith.[2] For the factor of distance in John is precisely the post-Easter perspective, the perspective of faith in Christ as the Logos vindicated by death and resurrection. It is this knowledge, which the Evangelist shares with the reader, which creates the ironical atmosphere that surrounds Jesus in his earthly career. "These [signs] are written that you may believe [i.e. go on believing, if the present subjunctive may bear this weight] that Jesus is the Christ, the Son of God, and that believing you may have life in his name" (20.31). It is important to note that the Evangelist does not say "these *happened* that you may believe," but "these *are written* that you may believe," that is to say that the *literary* perspective of the Gospel is designed to appeal to and nourish faith. In this sense, the irony in question lies in the Evangelist's perception and literary presentation of the reality of God's dealings with men.

---

[1] Cf. Bultmann, *The Gospel of John,* pp. 61-62.

[2] S. R. Hopper, "Irony—the Pathos of the Middle", *CrossCurr* (Winter, 1962) p. 35, refers to the "ironic dénoument of irony" in which the ironist's own ironic perception turns back upon him, involves him. The phenomenon may be somewhat analogous to the relationship between the process of faith in the situations of the Fourth Gospel—perceived ironically by both Evangelist and reader—and the process of faith in the reader himself. In a very important essay (which does not, however, deal with the theme of ironic perception in John), W. A. Meeks remarks: "The book functions for its readers in precisely the same way that the epiphany of its hero functions within its narratives and dialogues" ("The Man from Heaven in Johannine Sectarianism", *JournBibLit* 91 [1972] 44-72, quotation from p. 69).

Third, like the so-called modern metaphysical irony, Johannine irony shares the view that the world itself and the symbols it uses are *ambiguous*. These can be used as an avenue of access to the divine, but they can also lead only to themselves. Not only is the person of Jesus ambiguous, but the symbolisation of his identity as the bread of life or the living water is also an essentially ambiguous process. I should like to return below to illustrate this ambiguity as a form of the Fourth Evangelist's ironic vision.

I use the term "ironic vision," for in John irony is not confined to the dramatic device but represents a whole literary (and quasiphilosophical) outlook, such as Frye identifies with the "ironic mode."[1] It is through this ironic vision that the contact with Johannine theology is made, for it is in irony that John expresses his own insight into the meaning of Christ for the world. Indeed, as we shall try to show, in the Fourth Gospel theology *is* irony. But it is time to turn to some illustrations of both the dramatic and what we shall call the "thematic" irony of John.

3. DRAMATIC IRONY: THE PILATE TRIAL

The techniques of drama which the author skilfully employs in such episodes as that of the woman at the well (4.4-42) and the story of the man born blind (9.1-41) are brought to bear with great sophistication upon the Pilate trial (18.28-19:15). In addition to the obvious device of alternating scenes outside and inside Pilate's Prætorium and the meticulous balancing of characters in these scenes, the entire passage is the clearest example of Johannine dramatic irony. My intention at the moment is not to offer an exegesis of the passage nor to claim any new insights into it, but merely to call attention to some elements of the irony as a Johannine reflection on the Passion narrative. The Pilate trial is a narrative, of course, and not a drama, and consequently the irony is not confined to the dialogue but also appears in the descriptive remarks. For convenience let us group our observations on the irony of the passage around the *dramatis personae*.

Bultmann points out that in this passage, as often elsewhere in John, οἱ Ἰουδαῖοι are symbols of "the world" which is opposed to Jesus and to his revelation.[2] Other interpreters prefer to draw attention to the Jews as representative chiefly of the synagogue contemporary with the Evangelist, which has come to a clear position on the expulsion of the Christians.[3] It

---

[1] *Anatomy of Criticism*, pp. 40ff.

[2] *The Gospel of John*, pp. 652ff.

[3] Cf. e.g. the penetrating study of J.L. Martyn, *History and Theology in the Fourth Gospel* (New York, 1968).

is not of course necessary to choose between these interpretations as long as we realise that the significance of this group is not exclusively, perhaps not even primarily, on the level of a historical narrative. Whether accurately or not it may be impossible to ascertain—and it is certainly not my purpose—but the Fourth Evangelist clearly places upon "the Jews" the major element of blame for the condemnation of Jesus, which he regards as the real criminal act that (ironically) underlies the trial. In the light of his stance, his mention of the prosecutors remaining outside the Praetorium to avoid ritual defilement (18.28) serves not only to justify the alternating scenes but to set the tone of irony. The irony develops with some curious and no doubt quite deliberate cross-references between the individual scenes. For example, in the first scene "the Jews" protest that they are not allowed to execute anyone (18.31); in the fifth scene they are made to insist, "We have a law and according to the law he must die" (19.7). A similar cross-reference is made between Pilate's taunting attempt to escape the confrontation of decision, "Take him yourselves and crucify him" (19.6) and the Evangelist's conclusion to the drama, "Then he handed him over *to them* to be crucified" (19.16). The apex of the dramatic irony with regard to "the Jews" appears, as is well known, in their climactic rejection of Jesus, "We have no king but Caesar" (19.15), which also functions as a desperate rejection of the very values they are portrayed as claiming to defend.

In the figure of Pilate we are confronted again with a choice of symbolism: he may represent, as Bultmann suggests,[1] the state faced with the option of yielding to the world or confronting the issue of the source of its own authority, or he may represent the Gentile faced with the option of a decision when confronted with Jesus. In any case, Pilate plays the role of an ironical figure. Here I do not refer primarily to his famous question, "What is truth?" (18.38), which may or may not be sarcastic. Indeed if one sees in Pilate a symbol of the power of the state it might be better understood as not sarcastic at all but as reflecting the incapacity of the state to deal with issues involving the truth as Jesus reveals it from the Father. But there is irony in the brief dialogue about Pilate's authority (19.10-11): his power or to crucify is a power of life or death, but it is an empty boast in the presence of one who has the power from his Father to give the gift of eternal life. In some ways Pilate appears at his most ironical in his repeated protestation that he can find no guilt in Jesus (18.38; 19.4, 6): Jesus' innocence is ironically proclaimed by a person who is himself portrayed as incapable of understanding what the issue of guile or innocence really means.

---

[1] *The Gospel of John,* pp. 652ff.

Finally, the figure of Jesus is the centre of the strongest irony in the passage. Here the irony arises from the reader's faith-understanding of who Jesus really is, and the issue throughout is less that of Jesus' guilt or innocence than that of his true identity. It is the distance of the reader's— and the Evangelist's—stance, the post-Easter perspective, which makes the irony possible. The most obvious example is the issue of Jesus' kingship which pervades the whole passage and is expressed both in the description and in the words of Pilate (18.33, 37, 39; 19:3, 14, 15). Jesus is the messianic King "of the Jews," but everyone in the scene—Pilate, the soldiers, and Jesus himself—is made to proclaim this kingship, except "the Jews" (who do so only indirectly in 19.12). This irony is a central theme of the Passion narrative, and it is carried over from the trial scene into the crucifixion scene when, by affixing the inscription to the cross, Pilate revenges himself on those who tried to provoke him to judgement. For the believer, for whom the Fourth Gospel is written, Jesus is God's Son, and in the trial this supreme acknowledgement of his identity comes from "the Jews" as an implicit accusation of blasphemy (19.7).

Throughout the Gospel, Jesus' mission appears as that of provoking judgement. In the trial scene it is he who is ostensibly being judged, but in fact his presence forces the Jews to bring judgement upon themselves— perhaps it so affects Pilate also, though the text does not clearly indicate this. In light of the irony accompanying the judgement theme, I am inclined to opt for the controversial rendering of 19.13: "Pilate, then, hearing these words, brought Jesus outside and sat *him* on the judgement-seat." The arguments for this understanding, apart from the predominance of irony in the context, are conventional and need not be rehearsed here.[1]

In light of the Johannine irony, it appears that the most ironical and theologically most profound assertion made in the Pilate trial is the *ecce homo* scene (19.5). Whether or not one wishes to relate the use of ἄνθρωπος here to an anthropos myth, the assertion of Pilate, in view of its parallelism with "Behold your king" a few verses later (19.14), must call our attention, ironically, to the spectacle of the Son of God appearing as man in the lowest degradation of human suffering and humiliation. This affirmation is not intended to contradict Käsemann's insistence that Johannine Christology is not based on the humiliation-exaltation theme,[2] but it does mean that the Fourth Evangelist takes seriously the Passion narrative as a revelation of the "scandal of the cross"—the scandal of the transcendent divinity revealing itself in the paradox of humanity suffering

---

[1]See the commentaries, esp. R.E. Brown, *The Gospel according to St. John*, vol. 2 (Anchor Bible: Garden City, 1970).

[2] *The Testament of Jesus*, tr. G. Krodel (Philadelphia, 1968).

out of the motive of love. But the Fourth Gospel is precisely not docetic,
for the Evangelist does not assert that the divinity of the Son merely
appears to be present in man suffering. Rather, by consistently orienting
his Gospel to the supreme revelation of the Passion narrative, the
Evangelist asserts that man's quest for the divine must terminate in the
irony of man's supreme act of self-giving in love. A thoroughly docetic
Christology might indeed be expressed ironically, but it would be the
irony of pretence in which man's capacity for love does not figure at all.

4. THEMATIC IRONY: JOHANNINE SYMBOLS

Besides his use of dramatic irony, the Fourth Evangelist, as we have tried
to suggest in general terms above, also expresses his ironic theological
vision in some of the dominant themes throughout the whole Gospel.
Given the limitations of a short essay, it is scarcely possible to do more
than list some examples here, but it should easily become clear how these
contribute to the ironic vision.

In the first category I would include the miracles of Jesus which the
Evangelist carefully designates as signs.[1] I take it with Bultmann, Robert
T. Fortna,[2] and many others that the Evangelist draws upon a signs-
source and that he is critical of the Christological implications of
presenting Jesus as miracle worker. But I do not place the irony merely in
the fact that he makes use of a traditional theme with which he is not
wholly in sympathy. Instead, it is the function of the signs as revelations
of Jesus' glory (2.11) to those who understand them, from the post-Easter
perspective, and at the same time as obstacles to true faith in Jesus as
revealer ("Unless you see signs and wonders..." 4.48). The ambiguity of
the signs becomes ironical, too, in the reactions that they provoke in
people without the discovery of the revealing word: wonderment,
eagerness, fear, opposition.

A second manifestation of irony is to be found in the predicative "I
am" sayings and other Christological symbols which have the inherent
capability of being understood on several levels. For example, the woman
at the well responds to Jesus' partial revelation of himself in the symbol
of living water, "Sir, give me this water so that I will not thirst nor come
here to draw water" (4.15). Here the irony is heightened by a dramatic
touch, the exchange of roles between Jesus, who first asks the woman for
water (v. 7) and the woman, who now asks it of Jesus. Or again, the

---

[1] Clavier, "L'ironie dans le quatrième Evangile", and others also list these as examples
of irony.

[2] *The Gospel of Signs: A Reconstruction of the Narrative Source underlying the Fourth
Gospel* (SNTS Monograph Series, 11; Cambridge: Cambridge University Press, 1970).

Galileans who follow Jesus not because they have seen signs, but because they have eaten the loaves and been filled (6.26), respond to his mention of life-giving bread, "Sir, give us this bread always" (6.34). The more explicit revelation through the symbol of bread, "I am the bread of life" (6.35), only elicits murmuring (6.41) and eventually rejection even on the part of some disciples (6.66). The way of self-revelation through the diverse signs and symbols of the first part of the Gospel is less than effective (cf. 12.37-43), not only because the world of human symbolisation of the divine is inadequate and ambiguous,[1] but because the very presence of the divine in human experience is, in the Evangelist's view, ironical.

A more specific, yet even more fundamental, example of Johannine thematic irony occurs in the Fourth Gospel's transformation of the triple prediction of the Passion into the threefold allusion to the "lifting up" of the Son of Man (3.14-15; 8.28; 12.32-34). Here there is consummate irony in choosing the image of an apotropaic magic rite—the bronze serpent on the pole (Num 21.8-9)—to suggest the mystery of the cross. The incongruity of the serpent, instrument of death (in the OT context to which the Evangelist refers[2]), as source of life, parallels the incongruity of the ignominious death of Jesus as source of eternal life. But again, the irony reveals a deeper perception of reality that is contrary to the appearance. For the Fourth Evangelist accepts the fundamental Christian belief in both the incarnation and the reality of the Passion. His interpretation of the death of Jesus as exaltation and return to the Father, the "lifting up of the Son," is his unique and crowning irony.

In a word, the heart of the Johannine theology is itself the irony of the Logos becoming flesh and dwelling among men, the revealing Word graciously announcing to men their own potential for eternal life in the self-giving act of love that is the return to the Father.

---

[1] Cf. G.W. MacRae, "The Fourth Gospel and *Religionsgeschichte*", *CBQ* 32 (1970) pp. 13-24, esp. p. 23.

[2] Even though in the Roman Hellenistic world at large the serpent did not in itself imply death—quite the opposite, in fact, in the Asclepius cult.

JOHN 9: A LITERARY-CRITICAL ANALYSIS*

JAMES L. RESSEGUIE

C.H. Dodd refers to John 9 as "one of the most brilliant passages in the gospel." The imagery, the structure, the movement of the plot, and the characterisation all work together to form a tightly knit narrative. The narrative has been carefully shaped so that everything it shows serves to tell. The purpose of this paper is to show how the form and content of John 9 are closely woven together to form a unity.

The chapter may be divided into seven scenes with each scene containing a dialogue between two characters or sets of characters. In scene 1, the dialogue occurs between the disciples and Jesus; in scene 2, the blind man and his neighbours; in scenes 3 and 5, the blind man and the religious authorities; in scene 4, the religious authorities and the parents of the blind man; in scene 6, Jesus and the blind man; and in scene 7, the authorities and Jesus.

SCENE 1: VV. 1-7

The opening scene introduces a blind man and two other characters, Jesus and the disciples. If we compare the structure of chapter 9 with other healing stories in the Gospel, we see that this chapter does not conform to the basic form of other similar stories. John 9 departs from the structural pattern of the other stories in one significant way: the characterisation of the healed man is fully developed. In John 5, for example, a lame man at the pool of Bethzatha is healed by Jesus; yet within the miracle story itself there is no attempt by the narrator to develop the character of the lame man. Only once does the lame man speak, and that is in response to a question by Jesus. The blind man of chapter 9, however, not only speaks in 13 of 41 verses, but he uses irony and sarcasm, and he even takes the initiative to lecture the religious authorities on some basic theological insights. Unlike any other healing story of the Gospel of John, the blind

---

* This article first appeared in Gros Louis, K. (ed) *Literary Interpretations of Biblical Narratives*. Vol.II. (Nashville: Abingdon Press, 1982).

man in chapter 9 does not fade into the background. He remains not only in the foreground but as the centre of attention for the entire chapter.

As the scene opens, the disciples ask Jesus to make a judgement concerning the cause of the man's blindness. However, Jesus prefers not to answer that question; instead he points to the purpose of the man's blindness (v. 3: "that the works of God might be made manifest in him"). The literary import of this should not go unnoticed. By having the disciples raise a question that is not immediately answered, the entire narrative can then be structured so that the reader is shown the answer to that question instead of being told the answer. Also, postponing the answer to the disciples' question creates a dramatic tension for the readers. Ironically, it will be the religious authorities who will illustrate the cause of blindness, not the blind man.

The opening scene introduces some important images, which create a mood of urgency and set a tone of opposition. The images of night and day are set in opposition to each other in v. 4: "we must work the works of him who sent me while it is day; night comes, when no one can work." Verse 5 introduces the imagery of night with the saying by Jesus: "I am the light of the world," while the healing of the man's blindness sets before the readers another set of images: blindness and sight. The dualistic imagery of day and night, of blindness and sight, of light and darkness, creates a pronounced tone of opposition and helps to establish a mood of urgency. The works of the day and of light can not be delayed even for a short period of time, for the night and the darkness may come at any time. For this reason the healing of the blind man cannot be postponed even one day, even though the laws that govern the sabbath are violated in the process (cf. v. 14).

The imagery of the opening scene also has the effect of establishing a figurative context for the interpretation of the narrative. Similar imagery of light and darkness is used figuratively in the prologue of the Gospel. There light is not only opposed to darkness, but light also represents the "enlightenment" that Jesus brings. "The true light that enlightens every man was coming into the world" (1.9). Therefore, the reader is already alert to the figurative significance of John 9. Light and the reception of sight represents enlightenment, while night and darkness represent blindness and continued opposition to the light.

The method of healing the blind man is striking; yet similar techniques are recorded in the Synoptics (cf. Mark 7.31-36; 8.22-26). Jesus spits on the ground, makes clay, and anoints the man's eyes. He then sends him to the pool of Siloam to wash. At this point the narrator intrudes into the narrative to inform the reader that the word Siloam means "sent." Although it is not unusual for the narrator to translate Hebrew words or to explain Jewish customs, the translation of Siloam as "sent" draws the reader's attention to the symbolic meaning of washing in the pool of Siloam. The narrator expects the reader to make a connection between Siloam, which means "Sent," and Jesus as the "one who is sent." Several times throughout the gospel Jesus refers to himself as the "one who is sent" from the Father (e.g., John 3.17; 3.34; 5.35, etc.). As recently as verse 4 of chapter 9 we are told that Jesus does the work of "him who sent me." The blind man received his sight after washing in the pool of Siloam. By association "enlightenment" comes from the "one who is sent." Scene 1 closes with the creation of the blind man's sight, and Jesus moves offstage.

SCENE 2: VV. 8-12

The neighbours of the blind man enter and discuss among themselves whether this man who received sight was "the man who used to sit and beg." There is a division among them. Some say he is the man; others say he is someone else. The contrasting imagery of scene 1 is now replaced by contrasting opinions. Several times throughout the Gospel the narrator draws attention to divided opinion: "there was a division among the people over him" (v. 43). In chapter 10 there is a division among some of the Jews over who Jesus is. Some say that he has a demon; yet others believe that he could not open the eyes of the blind if he had a demon (vv. 19-21). Again the narrator specifically underscores the division with the narrative comment: "there was again a division" (v. 19). Later in this chapter the Pharisees will be divided over who Jesus is (9.16). Some conclude that Jesus is not from God; others remain uncertain. The narrator once again feels it is important to draw attention to the division: "There was a division among them." First the narrator shaped for us contrasting images (day/night; light/darkness; blindness/sight); now he moulds contrasting opinions, pro/con. the dualistic imagery of light and darkness is reflected in the divided opinions, and the tone of opposition created by the imagery becomes concrete in the contrasting opinion. The scene closes with the healed man's story of how Jesus healed him. When asked where Jesus is, he confesses his ignorance. "I do not know."

SCENE 3: VV. 13-17

We have seen the development of contrasting imagery and of divided opinion, and now the narrative focuses on the development of the characters. The antagonists, the religious authorities, appear on the scene. Because Jesus healed the blind man on the sabbath and kneaded clay—a double violation of the laws governing the sabbath—the religious authorities are consulted by the neighbours of the healed man. The breach of the sabbath laws suggest that Jesus is a sinner and not from God, and yet the miracle itself seems to suggest that he is from God. The authorities are divided in their opinion concerning Jesus' action. The division serves not only to focus attention upon who Jesus is, but it sets an atmosphere for a trial. A verdict concerning Jesus' action of healing on the sabbath needs to be reached.

Therefore, the narrative takes the form of a trial. At first the religious authorities interrogate the healed man; then the parents of the healed man will testify, followed by a second interrogation of the man born blind. Finally, in a dramatic peripeteia, the verdict will be pronounced not on Jesus by the religious authorities, but on the authorities by Jesus.

Scene 3 closes with the testimony of the healed man concerning Jesus. "He is a prophet."

SCENE 4: VV. 18-23

Unwilling to accept the testimony of the healed man, the religious authorities attempt another course of action. Perhaps the man was not born blind. Therefore, the authorities call the parents to testify. "Is this your son, who you say was born blind? How then does he now see?" The parents, however, seem reluctant to get involved in the trial. In fact their response is so evasive that the narrator intrudes to provide an explanation for their curt response to the authorities. "His parents said this because they feared the Jews, for the Jews had already agreed that if anyone should confess him to be the Christ, he was to be put out of the synagogue." It seems to make no difference to the narrator that the parents were not asked who Jesus is, only to provide an explanation for the fact that their son now sees. This puzzling comment by the narrator has been seen by many scholars as a later redaction added to the narrative. J. Louis Martyn, for example, suggests that the community of the Fourth Evangelist is experiencing a situation similar to this comment. If the members of the community confess that Jesus is the Messiah, then they are in danger of being expelled from the synagogue. Therefore the narrative intrusion serves to identify the *Sitz-im-Leben* of the Fourth Evangelist, but it does not fit into the present narrative.

However, if the intrusion is seen as a rhetorical device on the part of the narrator, it does fit smoothly into its context. The parents are a foil for the action of the healed man in the subsequent scene. While the parents are fearful of the authorities and are fearful to confess Jesus as Messiah, the man born blind is fearless and bold in his confrontation with the authorities. The characterisation of the healed man is markedly enhanced by contrasting his response to the authorities with that of his parents.

SCENE 5: VV. 24-34

The scene shifts now to the dialogue between the religious authorities and the healed man; for the second time, they interrogate him. The division among the religious authorities concerning who Jesus is, is now replaced by a single authoritative voice. "We know that this man is a sinner." The confident assertion of the first person plural, "we know," clearly states the judgement of the religious authorities concerning who Jesus is.

The characterisation of the healed man is most pronounced in this scene. With biting irony he asks the authorities if they too want to become disciples of Jesus. In the opening scene the blind man appeared more as an object to settle a theological discussion than as a person in his own right. In the third scene he still lacks colour: to the questions of the authorities he responds with short, declarative sentences. He takes no initiative of his own, and his comments lack the biting sarcasm of the fifth scene. This scene, however, marks the development of the healed man as a person in his own right. His irony leads to sarcasm, and his sarcasm opens the way for him to lecture the religious authorities on some basic theological principles. When the authorities admit that they do not know from where Jesus comes, the healed man sarcastically says, "Why, this is a marvel! You do not know where he comes from, and yet he opened my eyes." The lecture continues: "We know that God does not listen to sinners, but if anyone is a worshipper of God and does his will, God listens to him. Never since the world began has it been heard that any one opened the eyes of a man born blind. If this man were not from God, he could do nothing." The confident assertion of the first person plural, "we know", underscores the authoritative posture of the healed man. His singular action of lecturing the authorities has penetrated the barriers of a stratified society. The narrative's development of the healed man's character is actually the development of his personhood. It is not accidental that the blind man appears in scene 1 as a colourless object of theological speculation and that not until this scene does he appear as a character in his own right. The reception of sight in scene 1 and the "enlightenment" he receives concerning who Jesus is parallels the development of his own character. When he comes to the point of seeing who Jesus is, he also comes to the point of seeing who he himself is. No longer is he that nameless blind man of scene 1; now he is confident in his own identity, and he confronts the religious authorities.

The scene closes with the expulsion of the healed man by the religious authorities from their midst.

SCENE 6: VV. 35-38

Jesus comes back onstage. When he hears that the healed man has been cast out by the authorities, he goes and finds him. Then narrative places the final set of contrasts before us. First the narrative shaped for us the opposing contrasts of day and night, of light and darkness, of blindness and sight; they were followed by the divided opinions, pro and con, towards Jesus; then there were the contrasting responses of the parents and of their son to the religious authorities. Finally we have the contrast of the blind man's being cast out and then found by Jesus, the contrast of rejection and acceptance.

The scene closes with the healed man's confession of Jesus as the Son of man.

SCENE 7: VV. 39-41

The final scene of the narrative is an exchange between Jesus and some of the religious authorities. It opens with a solemn pronouncement by Jesus concerning his mission. "For judgement I came into this world, that those who do not see may see, and that those who see may become blind." Some of the religious authorities overhearing what Jesus said ask, "Are we also blind?" In the opening scene the disciples ask Jesus to make a judgement concerning the cause of blindness. That judgement, however, was deferred so that the narrative could show the reader the true cause of blindness. The closing scene now has Jesus make the judgement so that the reader is told as well as shown the cause of blindness, which is simply the reluctance of some of the religious authorities to see the light when given the opportunity. As a result, the verdict is pronounced upon them. "If you were blind, you would have no guilt; but now that you say, 'We see,' your guilt remains." With the verdict given, the trial is now completed.

The literary unity of form and of content makes John 9 a brilliant passage in the Gospel. The imagery, the structure, the movement of the plot, and the characterisation work together to form a unified whole. Each part contributes to the whole and advances the plot, no action or event is unrelated to the main theme of the narrative. The theme that shapes the form and content is the concept of judgement. It is the individual's response or judgement concerning the light that determines whether he or she remains in darkness or enters into the light. The man born blind receives his sight because he is healed by the One who is the Light, and his positive judgement concerning Jesus parallels the reception of sight. But when the religious authorities are confronted with the Light or knowledge of the Light, they remain obdurate and unwilling to see the Light.

The structure of John 9 also derives its meaning from the theme of judgement. The form of a trial is singularly appropriate to show the dramatic reversals brought about by the presence of light and the resulting judgement. Light and judgement are interrelated concepts in this Gospel, for light causes division or separation so that light and darkness cannot coexist. Actually the judgement that Jesus brings is nothing more than the specific manifestation of this process of division, which results because the light has come into the world. Although John 3.19 brings together the concepts of light and judgement ("And this is the judgement, that the light has come into the world, and men loved darkness better than light, because their deeds were evil"), it is John 9 that shows the reader the relationship between light and judgement.

The movement of the plot is also directly related to the theme of judgement. The comic movement, or the movement from ill-being to well-being on the part of the healed man, parallels the judgement he makes concerning who Jesus is. In the second scene, he refers to Jesus merely as "the man called Jesus" (v. 11). In scene 3 he confesses that Jesus is a prophet (v. 17), and by scene 5 he has become an ardent defender of Jesus as the one from God (v. 33). Finally, in scene 6 he sees that Jesus is the Son of man.

The comic movement of the plot contrasts with the tragic movement, or downward movement from well-being to ill-being on the part of the religious authorities. Initially the authorities' opinion is divided; some say that he is not from God, but others are uncertain (v. 16). However, by scene 5 this divided opinion is replaced by the judgement that Jesus is not from God (v. 24). The last scene completes the tragedy when the authorities, not Jesus, are pronounced guilty.

Finally, the characterisation contributes to the theme of judgement and to the unity of John 9. The contrasting characterisations of the religious authorities and of the blind man parallel the opposing judgements made by the characters concerning Jesus. The characterisation of the religious authorities keenly illustrates their tragic fate because they believe that they do see, when in fact they are the ones who are blind to who Jesus is. It is with tragic irony that they ask at the end of the trial, "Are we also blind?" The development of the blind man's character on the other hand, parallels his positive judgement concerning Jesus' identity. He moves from a colourless character in scene 1 to an engaging, attractive personality in scene 5 who badgers the authorities with irony and sarcasm. In the process of confrontation he discovers who he is. In other words, the development of the blind man's character is also the development of a person, of a new-found selfhood that penetrates a stratified society and that breaks down the walls that divide. John 9 shows us a new selfhood developing, one that is no longer captive to one's own sin or to the sin of one's parents. The creative act of giving the man sight enabled him for the first time to see both who Jesus is and who he himself really is.

Because the form and content are so carefully woven together, John 9 is a superb piece of literature. Dualistic images, contrasting opinions, opposing movements of plot, and diverse characterisation all work together to show the reader the interrelationship between light and judgement. At the same time everything John 9 shows also serves to tell.

WOMEN IN THE FOURTH GOSPEL AND THE
ROLE OF WOMEN IN THE CONTEMPORARY CHURCH*

SANDRA M. SCHNEIDERS

The question, what does the Fourth Gospel say about women, obviously arises within the context of the contemporary discussion concerning the role of women in the Church. Indeed, this question could only be asked in such a context because the subject of women as such is simply not a conscious concern of any of the New Testament writers.

Except for the theological declaration in Gal 3.27-28 that all natural distinctions, including that of sex, are transcended by the unity of the baptised in Christ, the New Testament says nothing at all of a theological nature about men *qua* male or about women *qua* female. With the exception of a few disciplinary injunctions in the pauline and pastoral letters (e.g., 1 Cor 11.3-16; 14.34-35; 1 Tim 2.8-15) whose evident cultural specificity limits their relevance to the people, time and place where they were formulated, everything in the NT which is addressed to human beings is addressed to them as actual or potential believers, regardless of age, sex, family connections, ethnic background, nationality, race, political affiliations, economic conditions, or social status. Consequently, the legitimacy of addressing a clearly twentieth century question to a first century document which was not concerned with the subject matter of the question must be examined at the outset. Why address such a question to the NT? Can a valid response be expected? If not, why not? If so, under what conditions?

Let us start with the first question. Christians want to know what the NT says about women because many members of the contemporary community, from simple believers to the bishop of Rome, are embroiled in the practical questions of whether centuries-old restrictions on the role of women in the Christian community can and should be maintained today (PCB: 92-96; CDF: 517-524) when, in every other sphere of modern life, discrimination on the basis of sex is being recognised as baseless, unjust, and dysfunctional. If Scripture, and particularly the NT, within the living context of tradition, is the primary source of divine revelation, then change

---

* This article first appeared in *Biblical Theological Bulletin* 12.2 (1982), pp. 35-45.

in patterns of behaviour based on an understanding of revelation must be warranted by, or least not contrary to, the NT message. Operative in this line of reasoning is the firm, but erroneous, conviction that if the church restricted the roles of women in the Christian community this restriction was probably based on an explicit understanding of revelation (CDF: 521-522; Paul VI: 718-719).

The discussion would be immensely simplified by the recognition of what research shows to be the case, namely, that the treatment of women in the church was never based on any careful study of the sources of revelation. The application in the Church of the patriarchal patterns of the surrounding culture was 'proof-texted' from Scripture, 'tradition', and whatever sources lay ready to hand whenever the question was raised. But the repressive treatment of women was never based on Scripture any more than was the practice of slavery which was also defended for centuries by reference to biblical texts. Consequently, to abandon such repressive treatment needs no Scriptural warrant. On the contrary, to restrict the freedom of the children of God (male or female) to exercise the gifts they receive from the Spirit demands the very strongest basis in revelation because the quenching of the Spirit is plainly contrary to the NT message (cf. 1 Thes. 5.19-22; 1 Cor. 12.7; the example of Jesus in Mk. 9.38-40 and par.; the instruction to Peter and the Church in Acts 10.1-11, 18). In other words, the only people who really need to search the NT for what it says about women are those who are convinced, for non-biblical reasons, that women should be restricted in some way within the Church, and who must justify their sexual discrimination (which they admit is unjust in any other context except the ecclesial one [cf. Gaudium et Spes # 29]) by an appeal to Scripture.

The immense effort which is currently being expended to show from Scripture that discrimination against women in the church is not justified is, in my opinion, open to serious misunderstanding unless those doing the work (e.g., the Chicago Theological Union faculty and the contributors to the Swidler volume who are primarily criticising the faulty methodology of discriminatory arguments) make it clear from the outset that such effort is not demanded by the issue itself. The sex of believers is not an issue in the NT and we should not allow ourselves, either as believers or as scholars, to be manipulated into acting as if it is. The burden of proof lies with those who wish to set limits to the exercise of Christian freedom by female members of the community.

Nevertheless, the contemporary question about the NT data on women need not be restricted to a spurious apologetic effort to ground the equality of women in the Church. It might also be motivated by the legitimate desire and real need to balance some 1700 years of male-dominated exegesis which has systematically (even if not deliberately) masculinised our appropriation of revelation. The NT message is not essentially patriarchal, despite the fact that an unreflective patriarchal ideology pervades it as does an unreflective mythological cosmology. What is patriarchal is the history of exegesis and appropriation and this can only be corrected by a deliberate and sustained effort to revalourise that which has been ignored, to surface that which has been suppressed, and to interpret correctly that which has been falsified (cf. the work of Platt: 29-39; Trible). For this reason, we do need to address ourselves seriously to those passages in the NT which concern women and to attempt to read these texts with eyes purified, to some degree at least, of male bias.

This leads to the second question: can we expect a valid response on the subject of women from a document which was not concerned with this question? That depends on how we understand our question, "What does the Bible say about women?" If, by this question, we mean: "What did Jesus explicitly intend to teach about the nature and roles of women?" then the only valid answer we can expect is, "Nothing" (cf. Schneiders: 227-233).

We might, however, mean: "What did Jesus, by his own attitudes, words and behaviour, manifest about his own understanding of women and to what extent is his understanding normative for us?" Here we must distinguish between what Jesus did in accord with his culture and what he did in contrast to his culture. When he follows the patterns of his society we have no way of knowing whether he reflected on those customs, approved of them, or in any way intended to reinforce them. First century cultural patterns do not become normative for us simply because Jesus followed them. Just as we cannot maintain that Jesus, by the fact of speaking Aramaic, canonised that language as uniquely suitable for the expression of the Word of God, so we cannot assume that if Jesus followed the cultural pattern of appointing only men to public positions he thereby canonised the exclusion in perpetuity of women from such roles.

Jesus taught in Aramaic and appointed men to public roles because he was a first century Palestinian Jew. Beyond this we cannot go except in respect to what Jesus did in contrast to his environment. In these cases we can confidently expect that we are in touch with Jesus' deliberate choices. In such cases it makes better sense to at least raise the question of the normativity of his behaviour for us. However, our task as believers is to put on the mind of Christ, not to slavishly reproduce the behaviour of the historical Jesus. Consequently, the NT data about Jesus' behaviour towards women as a solution to how we should behave in the present situation is highly problematic. To know that something is normative is not the same as knowing how the norm functions. In other words, there is a crucial difference between a norm and a prescription.

A third way of understanding our question would be to regard the Gospels as reflections of the faith and practice of the earliest Christian communities and to ask what they reveal about the role of women in these communities and to what extent this earliest practice is normative for us. This enquiry can be very fruitful in surfacing much within our tradition that has been obscured, repressed or trivialised by a masculising exegesis and a patriarchal ecclesiastical practice. It can also help us to distinguish between arguments from ontology, from morality, and from discipline.

If women in the NT communities actually exercised certain roles then there can be no valid argument to the effect that they are incapable by nature of exercising such functions today. However, the fact that something was done, and therefore that it can be done, does not necessarily mean that it should be done. Christians held slaves in NT times (cf. Philem. 16) but, in retrospect, we see that they should not have done so and that their practice does not justify our owning slaves today. Something may be ontologically possible but morally reprehensible. Likewise, some practices which are morally indifferent were legitimately imposed as discipline in the earliest communities but are totally irrelevant today, e.g., the obligation of women to wear head coverings in the liturgical assembly (1 Cor 11.5-6, 13). In other words, we have the same problem in respect to the behaviour of the historical Jesus. It is difficult enough to establish what, historically, was done; more difficult still to establish what, in the practice of Jesus or the community in respect to women, is normative; but practically impossible to decide, on the basis of Scripture alone, how to apply the normative to the concrete contemporary situation.

All of the foregoing amounts to saying that a strictly historical approach to the NT texts, i.e., an exegesis which assigns itself to the sole task of unearthing and explaining the historical material relevant to women in the NT, is of very limited value as a resource in our discussion of the roles of women in the contemporary Church. However, this type of exegesis, which regards the text primarily as a source of historical information, uses exclusively historical-critical methods to discover that information, and considers the application of that information to the contemporary situation as a second and independent process is not the only legitimate approach to the biblical text.

In what follows, I will use a different hermeneutical process on the Johannine texts concerning women. This process assumes that the Gospel is not primarily a source of historical information but religious literature whose purpose is to bear witness to the faith of the first Christians and thereby to enlighten the faith understanding of the reader in such a way as to challenge him or her to ongoing conversion and increased fidelity to Christ. It will be further assumed that this text, like any other, is semantically independent of the conscious and explicit intentions of its human authors (Ricoeur: 29-30). This implies that, when reading from the vantage point of twentieth century faith, standing within the tradition of the believing community, the gospel text will undoubtedly yield more and richer meaning than the author was aware of expressing when he wrote it (cf. Tolbert: 62-66; Gadamer: 264). This surplus meaning is not arbitrary, nor is every interpretation valid. But the process of validation consists in seeking the continuity of the interpretation with the direction of the author's intention and its coherence with the totality of the NT message as embodied in the lived faith of the community, rather than in verifying that the interpretation coincides by identity with the explicit intention of the author.

It is thus assumed that the contemporary meaning of the text is the primary question addressed to the text and that it is integral to the interpretative process (Gadamer: 274-305), not (contrary to Stendahl), a secondary question to be dealt with after the exegesis is completed. The effect of these hermeneutical presuppositions will be evident in the treatment of the Fourth Gospel material on women which follows.

THE MOTHER OF JESUS MATERIAL

The material in the Fourth Gospel involving women consists of the following passages:

1. The First Sign at Cana	Jn 2.1-12	Mother of Jesus
2. Dialogue at Jacob's Well	Jn 4.4-42	Samaritan Woman
3. Raising of Lazarus	Jn 11.1-44	Martha & Mary
4. Anointing at Bethany	Jn 12.1-8	Martha & Mary
5. Word from the Cross	Jn 19.25-27	Mother of Jesus, Mary Magdalene, 2 other women
6. Discovery of the Open Tomb	Jn 20.1-2	Mary Magdalene
7. First Easter Christophany	Jn 20.11-18	Mary Magdalene

Obviously, there are a number of possible ways of dividing this material, e.g., chronologically: women in the public ministry (1-4) and women during the Hour of Jesus (5-7); by character: the Mother of Jesus (1,5), the sisters of Bethany (3,4), The Samaritan (2), and Mary Magdalene (5-7). I propose a theological division between the Mother of Jesus material and the other material. I am going to exclude the former from detailed consideration for both practical and theological reasons.

The practical reason is that the sheer quantity of scholarly work on the Mother of Jesus in the Fourth Gospel precludes any exhaustive original treatment of it in an essay of this length and I do not think such a treatment necessary at this point in the history of Johannine research. The studies made in the decade 1960-1970, which take account of those which precede them, have been competently surveyed in a lengthy article (Collins: 1970). Furthermore the subject of Mary in the Fourth Gospel has been thoroughly re-examined and judiciously presented (although almost exclusively from an historical-critical perspective and with a tendency towards minimalism that is quite legitimate in view of its purposes) in the recently published ecumenical study, *Mary in the New Testament.*

The theological reason for excluding the Mother of Jesus material from this study is that the femaleness of Mary, as she is presented in the Fourth Gospel, is irrelevant for the issue under discussion. First, it is obvious that the Mother of Jesus, unlike his interlocutors in Samaria, at Bethany, or in the garden of the tomb, could not have been other than female. Secondly, whatever role Mary is assigned in the Fourth Gospel, it is either unique to her or universal, in neither of which cases it is more significant for women than for men. John does not seem to imply that the Mother of Jesus had some special role in relation to the salvific role of Jesus. If she is understood as the New Eve in relation to the New Adam, or as Sion giving birth to Messiah, her role is unique and is not shared by other Christians, men or women. Just as men do not participate any more than women in Jesus' unique role as Saviour of the World, New Adam or Messiah, so women do not participate any more than men do in Mary's unique role as New Eve or Lady Sion. If Mary is seen as a symbol of the Church, as Mother of the Church, or as Mother of all believers, these roles also are unique to her and not shared by other Christians of either sex. Finally, if Mary is seen as a model of disciples, she is equally so for men and women. As a representative figure in the Fourth Gospel (Collins: 1976) Mary must be assigned the same universality as the figures of the Beloved Disciple and Judas. The historical Judas was a male, but this does not imply that men are more typically the locus of unbelief and betrayal than women. The historical Beloved Disciple was also a male, but men are not more called to the ideal of discipleship than women. The same must be said of Mary as a model of conversion and discipleship (cf. Reese: 41). In summary, the femaleness of the Mother of Jesus is both an historical fact and an integral part of the symbolism attached to her in the Fourth Gospel, but it is theologically irrelevant for the contemporary question of the role of women in the Church because Mary's role is either unique to her or universally significant for all Christians. The only observation about the Mother of Jesus in the Fourth Gospel that is truly significant for our study is the one on which the ecumenical task force was unanimous: John is in substantial agreement with the Synoptics in presenting Jesus as relativising the significance of physical relationship with himself (whether of motherhood, sorority, fraternity, or distant kinship) and recognising discipleship, expressed in hearing the word of God in Jesus and keeping it, as the truly meaningful relationship with him (Brown, et al: 1978, 283-294). If physically based human relationship with Jesus is rejected as salvifically irrelevant it should be obvious to all that biological similarity is even less relevant in the order of faith.

GENERAL REFLECTIONS ON THE MATERIAL ABOUT WOMEN IN JOHN

In this section I would like to make some general observations, which I think might be significant for our discussion about women in the church, about the way women actually appear in the text of the Fourth Gospel. In accord with the hermeneutical presuppositions set forth in the introduction, no claims are being made that the evangelist explicitly intended to present women in this way or even realised that he was doing so. Rather, just as art critics have seen that Michelangelo, whether or not he intended to do so, frequently presented women as amazons, so it is possible for scholars to discern some overall characteristics of the Johannine women, regardless of the possibilities of demonstrating the evangelist's intentions in this respect.

First, all the women in the Fourth Gospel are presented positively and in intimate relation to Jesus. No woman is shown as resisting Jesus' initiatives, failing to believe, deserting him, or betraying him. This is in sharp contrast to John's presentation of men who are frequently presented as vain (13.37), hypocritical (12.4-6), fickle (13.38; 16.31-32), obtuse (3.10; 16.18), deliberately unbelieving (9.24-41; 20.24-25), or thoroughly evil (13.2, 27-30).

However, and this is the second characteristic, John's positive presentation of women is neither one-dimensional nor stereotypical. Women do not appear as bloodless representatives of the 'eternal feminine'. On the contrary, John's women appear as strikingly individual and original characters, especially in contrast to the shadowy male figures who frequently appear in close proximity to them. Compare, for example, the stereotypical scribe, Nicodemus (3.1-12) with the Samaritan Woman (4.7-41) who realistically negotiates an incredible range of emotions from suspicion, to almost brassy defiance, to a complex mix of intelligent curiosity and blank misunderstanding, to half-hearted deviousness, to total and selfless enthusiasm and commitment. Or again, compare the shadowy Lazarus with his sisters, the warm and dominant Martha and the strong, contemplative Mary (11.1-12.8). The disciples in the Easter narratives, with the exception of Thomas, (20.2-8; 19-29) are not nearly so realistically drawn as is Mary Magdalene (21.12, 11-18) who displays the blind folly, tough-minded devotion, desperate despair, and rapturous joy of the ardent lover.

Whoever the author of the Fourth Gospel was, it was someone who had a remarkably rich and nuanced understanding of feminine religious experience. Historically, this knowledge could have been the product of an active literary imagination, but it was more likely that it was the result of actual experience of Christian women who played prominent roles in the community of the Fourth Evangelist (cf. Brown: 1979, 183). If women Christians in John's community had been restricted to the domestic and religious roles of women in the Jewish world of that period it is very difficult to imagine where the evangelist got his extraordinarily rich insights into the relationships of women with Jesus.

The third characteristic of John's women is the unconventionality of the roles they play. The Samaritan Woman with her chequered past (about which she is not unduly embarrassed!), her uncommon theological knowledge and interests, and her spontaneous assumption of the role of public witness to Jesus; Martha running the public aspects of funeral and mourning; Mary of Bethany extravagantly anointing the feet of Jesus over the protests of the devious Judas; Mary Magdalene roaming alone in a darkened cemetery, questioning a strange man, and responsibly bearing apostolic witness to the assembled disciples, cannot help but suggest that the Christian women of John's experience were not uneducated domestic recluses. Surprisingly, none of John's women figures except the Mother of Jesus and Mary of Clopas is represented as wife or mother in any way essentially defined in relationship to men. On the contrary, Lazarus is identified through his relationship to Mary and Martha and named after them in relation to Jesus in Jn 11.15 (Brown: 1979, 192, n. 341). Again, John's presentation leads to speculation about the roles of women in the community of the Fourth Gospel. It seems more than likely that real women, actually engaged in theological discussion, competently proclaiming the Gospel, publicly confessing their faith, and serving at the table of the Lord, stand behind these Johannine characters.

These three general observations, that women in the Fourth Gospel are all presented positively and in particularly intimate relationship to Jesus, that they have richly complicated and various religious personalities and experiences, and that they play quite unconventional roles, suffice to suggest that the women Christians in at least one of the earliest communities, John's, were fully participating and highly valuable community members (Brown: 1979, 198). It also suggests that the evangelist considered such feminine behaviour as fully according to the mind of Jesus who is never presented as disapproving of the women and in two scenes, as we shall see, defends the women from explicit or implicit male objections. But quite apart from the evidence which the material concerning women in John's Gospel supplies about the historical community of the Beloved Disciple, the text as it stands is significant for what it plainly says about the discipleship of Christian women regardless of time or place.

First, women, according to the Fourth Gospel, relate to Jesus directly and never through the mediation and/or by the permission of men.

Secondly, according to John's Gospel, there is no such thing as "women" whose "place" and "role" are to be decided and assigned once and for all by some third (male) party. There are only highly individual and original women whose place is wherever Jesus calls them and whose role is whatever their love for him suggests or his desires for them indicate, however unconventional. Their ministry to Jesus and to others in his name requires no approval or authorisation of anyone.

Thirdly, unlike most of the male disciples in the Fourth Gospel, the women are remarkable for their initiative and decisive action. The Samaritan Woman assumes on her own her mission of bearing witness to the people of her town; Martha and Mary immediately send for Jesus when Lazarus is ill; they prepare and host the supper on the eve of the Passion and Mary performs the unusual anointing on her own initiative; Mary Magdalene is first at the tomb on Easter morning determined to find and remove the body of her Lord; she alerts the male disciples to Jesus' disappearance and she alone remains to continue the search while they hide for fear of the Jews. If leadership is a function of creative initiative and decisive action the Johannine women qualify well for the role.

SPECIFIC REFLECTIONS ON THE PERICOPES ABOUT WOMEN

It is beyond the scope of this article to undertake a detailed exegesis of the four pericopes involving women in the Fourth Gospel. Excellent historical-critical and theological analyses of these texts are available in the standard commentaries (e.g., Brown: 1966, 1970). What I will try to do here is highlight aspects of these passages which have been overlooked or underestimated and which are potentially useful for the contemporary discussion of the role of women in the Church.

The Samaritan Woman (4.4-42)

Three aspects of this long and theologically rich pericope deserve special attention: the self-revelation of Jesus to the woman; the woman's role as witness; and the discomfort of Jesus' male disciples. Commentators generally agree that it is very difficult to place this scene within the public ministry of the historical Jesus, and especially within the Johannine account of that ministry (Brown: 1966: 175-176). We have no evidence from the Synoptic Gospels that Jesus carried on a ministry in Samaria. However, Samaria was one of the first missions undertaken after Pentecost (Acts 8.1-8) and John was involved in that mission. It is fairly certain that the Johannine community had a significant Samaritan component (cf. Meeks; Cullmann; Brown: 1979, 34-54) and, in all probability, the scene recounted in Jn 4 has its real context not in the ministry of the historical Jesus but in the history of the Johannine community. The conversion of Samaria is projected back into the ministry of Jesus to establish that this important element of the community was called directly by Jesus as were the Jews and, in the mind of the Fourth Evangelist, every disciple of all time.

The central concern of the Fourth Gospel is the saving revelation which takes place in Jesus. This revelation, however, must be understood as a dialogical process of Jesus' self-manifestation as the one being continuously sent by the Father (7.16-18) who is thereby encountered in Jesus (10.30; 14.9-11) and the response of belief on the part of the disciple (17.8). After the glorification of Jesus on the Cross, through the gift of the Spirit, this belief bears fruit in the disciples bearing revelatory witness to Jesus and thereby bringing others to him (16.26). This process is anticipated three times in the account of the public ministry; in the witness of John the Baptist (1.29-36); in the calling of the first disciples (1.35-51); in the conversion of Sychar (4.39-42).

The story of the Samaritan Woman is remarkable for the clarity and completeness of its presentation of the revelation process in the Fourth Gospel. Jesus' self-revelation to the woman as the Messiah whom the Samaritans expect (4.25) is given in the "I am" formula which has such christological importance in the Fourth Gospel. It is the first use of this absolute formula in the Gospel and its impact on the woman is that she immediately leaves her water jar where it is and hastens into the town to bear witness to Jesus as the expected Messiah, i.e., the one who would tell them all things (cf. 4.25 and 29). We should not fail to note the feminine version of the standard Gospel formula for responding to the call of apostleship, namely to "leave all things," especially one's present occupation, whether symbolised by boats (e.g., Mt. 4.19-22), or tax stall (cf. Mt. 9.9), or water pot.

The witness which the woman bears is quite clearly apostolic in the Johannine perspective (cf. Brown: 1979, 188-189). First, its effect is that those who hear her "come to him" (4.30) which is the Johannine expression for the first movement of saving faith in Jesus (6.37). In 4.39 we are told explicitly that many Samaritans "believed in him because of the woman witnessing" (διὰ τὸν λόγον). The force of this expression as apostolic identification of the woman appears when we compare it with Jesus' prayer in 17.20 describing, in essence, the apostolic mission: "I do not pray for these only [i.e., those present at the supper] but also for those believing in me through their word" (διὰ τοῦ λόγου). John ascribes at least the conversion of at least one Samaritan town (probably symbolising the whole Samaritan mission) to this woman apostle who acts out of her belief in Jesus' self-revelatory word and whose own witnessing word brings others to believe in him.

That her apostleship is fully effective is indicated by 4.41-42, according to which the Samaritans come to full faith in Jesus as "Saviour of the World" (another indication that this is a post-glorification account retrojected into the historical ministry). They claim that their faith is no longer dependent on the words of the witness but is now based on Jesus' own word. In John's perspective the witness of a believing disciple brings a person to Jesus but then the disciple fades away and the prospective believer encounters Jesus himself (cf. Jn 1.35-41). Anyone who believes is personally called by name by the Good Shepherd (10.3), becomes a branch directly enlivened by the True Vine (15.4-5). Essentially, no one mediates between Jesus and his own (cf. 10.3-5) in this Gospel's perspective for the immediacy of their relationship is patterned on that of the Father and the Son (10.14-15).

The third item of note in this account is the reaction of Jesus' disciples (presumably male) who return from their trip to town and discover Jesus conversing with the woman (4.27). We are told how they "marvelled" or "wondered." Raymond Brown is undoubtedly correct to translate it "they were shocked" (Brown: 1966, 167). They are not shocked, as we might expect, because Jesus was violating the religious prohibition against a Jew conversing with a Samaritan. By the time this Gospel was written converted Samaritans were an integral part of the Johannine community. But if the members of the community were well beyond anti-Samaritan prejudice, some were evidently not beyond the cultural patterns, characteristic of Semitic societies in general, of exclusion of women from public affairs. It seems more than a little likely that this detail about the disciples being shocked at Jesus' dealings with a woman, since it is in no

way necessary to the story itself, is aimed at those traditionalist male
Christians in the Johannine community who found the independence and
apostolic initiative of Christian women shocking. The point is quite clearly
made, however, that they knew better than to question the profound
purposes (indicated by the verb "to seek," [Schnackenburg: 444]) of Jesus
for his women disciples. Jesus alone decides to whom he will reveal
himself and whom he will call to apostleship. Jesus is evidently filled with
joy at the woman's work (4.35), which he recognises as a realisation of his
own mission to do the will of the one who sent him (4.34), and is an
anticipation of the later work of the other disciples (4.38).

In summary, the Samaritan Woman episode shows us a woman disciple
presented as such within the lifetime of the historical Jesus but surely
reflecting also the life of the Johannine community, in whom is realised the
typically Johannine revelation process: Jesus' self-revelation to her as
Messiah (or Christ) and "I am" (God) which is the content of Christian
faith according to the Fourth Gospel (cf. 20.31); her believing in him and
leaving all things to bear effective apostolic witness to him among the
Samaritans; and the acceptance of her work by Jesus who claims as his
own those who come to believe in him through her word. The detail about
the silent shock of the male disciples vindicates her discipleship,
apostleship, and ministry in the face of the cultural patterns which might
have challenged its appropriateness or even legitimacy.

In the history of exegesis and preaching a great deal has been made of
this woman's irregular marital situation, very little of the clear indications
of her apostleship, and virtually nothing of the vindication of her role
against the implicit disapproval of the male members of the community.
The importance of this scene for the contemporary discussion about the
role of women is obvious enough, but we can see that it is only when we
put a new question to the Gospel text that certain heretofore unseen aspects
of the NT message come to light.

Martha and Mary (Jn 11.1-53; 12.1-8)

The Johannine material on Martha and Mary of Bethany, who are sisters of
Lazarus according to John, no doubt stems from a cycle of traditional
women-disciple material that was common to all of the evangelists. The
Fourth Evangelist, however, has made a very original use of this traditional
material. In Jn 11, the account of the raising of Lazarus, we will focus on
Martha who plays the leading role in relation to Jesus. Mary's part in this
scene (11.28-32) serves merely to introduce her in preparation for her role
in the anointing scene in Jn 12.1-8, and to introduce the Jews who witness
the sign which will divide them into those who believe in Jesus (11.45) and

those who report him to the authorities (11.46). Mary herself simply
repeats what Martha has already said.

Within the Gospel narrative the raising of Lazarus functions as the crisis
which determined the Jewish authorities to kill Jesus (11.47-53). Within
the Johannine community it probably functioned in the context of the death
of believers which constituted the ultimate crisis of faith for those left
behind. If to believe in Jesus is to possess eternal life in him (6.40) what is
to be made of the fact that faithful disciples die? And what answer is to be
given to outsiders, especially Jews, who challenge the Christian faith in the
presence and power of the glorified Jesus by asking why, if the Jesus of
their faith is really the same Jesus who worked the signs of the public
ministry, he cannot save his disciples (symbolised by the representative
figure of Lazarus) from death (cf. 11.37). Lazarus, whom Jesus loved
(11.5, 36), is the faithful disciple who has died. Martha is the representative
of the community left behind which must face the challenge to its faith in
Jesus as the Life. This is the point at issue in the dialogue between Jesus
and Martha in 11.17-27.

Martha expresses (11.21-24) the real but inadequately enlightened faith
of the community which must be purified by a new and deeper encounter
with Jesus in the crisis event of physical death: if Jesus had been there, i.e.,
with the community as he had been during his public life, the brother
(Johannine terminology for a member of the community) would not have
died; whatever Jesus asks for from God will be granted, and here the
implication is that Jesus should do something to remove the scandal of
death, for death, even given the promise of resurrection on the last day,
cannot be integrated into the faith experience of the community of eternal
life.

Jesus challenges Martha with the word which must finally be accepted
by anyone who wishes to belong to Jesus (11.25-26): that he is the
resurrection and the life and that the eternal life which he gives to his
disciples transcends physical death without abolishing it. This must be
believed in and through the crisis experience of death, that of others and
finally one's own. Jesus asks Martha for a total acceptance of his self-
revelation and its implications for her: "Do you believe this?"

Martha rises to the challenge, giving the response which, according to
the conclusion of John's Gospel (cf. 20.31), is the saving confession of
faith, i.e., that Jesus is the Christ, the Son of God, the one coming into the
world. (In contrast, Simon Peter's confession in John's Gospel [6.68-69] of
Jesus as "the holy one of God" lacks the fullness of Johannine faith).

Several points are to be noted here. First, Martha in this scene represents
the Johannine community making the full Christian confession of faith in
Jesus as Simon Peter represented the community of the disciples in an

analogous scene in Mt. 16.15-19. In the Matthean scene Jesus also posed the ultimate faith question about himself: "Who do you say that I am?" and Simon Peter answered, "You are the Christ, the Son of the living God." In the Matthean pericope this confession is the foundation of the primacy conferred on Peter in the following verses (16.17-19). In John, the primacy seems to be a shared charism. The Beloved Disciple has primacy as the authoritative witness to revelation (cf. 19.35); a certain pastoral primacy is recognised in Peter (cf. 21.15-17); apostolic primacy as witness to the paschal mystery belongs to Mary Magdalene (20.17-18). In this scene Martha seems to be the locus of the primacy of faith. She speaks the faith of the community as it overcomes the ultimate scandal of death by belief in the one who is Life itself. Faith in the glorification of Jesus is not mature unless it enables one to face physical death with full confidence that one's possession of eternal life is not simply a guarantee of resurrection on the last day but is a present and ongoing participation in the life of the ever-living Jesus. Those who believe in him never die, despite appearances to the contrary.

Secondly, it is important to realise that Martha's confession of faith is in no way a response to the sign of the raising of Lazarus. It is a response to the word of Jesus revealing himself as the Resurrection and the Life. The sign comes later and does not function as a guarantee of Martha's faith but as a crisis for the Jews who have gathered. Martha does not expect it (cf. 11.38-39) any more than the disciples of any time or place can expect physical death to be overcome by miracle. Her faith, like ours, responds not to the signs of the public ministry but to the revealing word of the present Jesus. It is not those who believe who will see the glory of God (11.40), no vice versa. After the glorification it is not the seeing of signs which leads to faith (cf. the Thomas incident in 20.24-29) but faith which enables one to see the glory of Jesus.

In summary, Martha appears in this scene as the representative of the believing community responding to the word of Jesus with a full confession of Christian faith. It is a role analogous to Peter's as representative of apostolic faith in Matthew's Gospel. This representative role of Martha is difficult to understand unless women in John's community actually did function as community leaders. But whatever role women held in the Johannine community, the Gospel text as it stands presents Jesus as addressing the foundational question to a woman and the woman as making, on her own responsibility, the Christian confession. If this confession, given during the public life of Jesus, grounds the promise of the primacy to Peter, it is no less significant as foundation of community leadership when given by a woman.

Let us now turn to the scene in which Mary plays the major role, the anointing at Bethany (12.1-8). The scene has certain eucharistic overtones which ought not to be overlooked. It is situated six days before the Passover, which according to John's chronology of the Passion, falls on the following Saturday (cf. 19.31). The meal at Bethany, therefore, took place on Sunday evening, the customary time of the Eucharist in the early Church. Those whom Jesus loved (cf. 11.3, 5) gave a supper for him, and we are told that Martha "served". The Greek verb for "serve" is διάκονειν. By the time John's Gospel was written at the end of the first century the term διάκονος (servant) had become the title of a recognised ministerial office in some Christian communities (cf. Phil 1.1; 1 Tim 3.8, 12-13; Rom 16.1) and waiting on table a function conferred by the laying on of hands (Acts 16. 1-6). Alf Corell (1958:40-42) has made the interesting suggestion that if any established ministry existed in the Johannine community it was probably that of deacon. And it is certainly not unlikely that, if any Christian community had some form of foot-washing in its eucharistic liturgy, it would have been the Johannine community. I do not wish to defend the hypothesis that the supper at Bethany is presented explicitly as a sacrament in the strict sense of the term. But it does seem to be evocative of Eucharist and in that perspective it is worth noting that Jesus is the guest of honour and Martha and Mary are the ministers, a presentation of Eucharist that would fit well in the setting of the Johannine community. A loved male disciple, Lazarus, was present, but simply as one of those at table with Jesus.

A second characteristic of the scene's setting is that it evokes the entirety of the paschal mystery. It is a supper, Jesus' last with these disciples whom he loves. A beloved disciple is reclining with Jesus and Judas is also present as he will be at the Last Supper. Mary performs an act which recalls Jesus' washing of his disciples' feet signifying his death for them and for this act she incurs the money-motivated enmity of Judas. Her act is connected by Jesus himself to his burial. The scene ends with Jesus' prediction of his imminent departure.

Within this scene we are particularly concerned with Mary's action of anointing the feet of Jesus with costly perfumed ointment and then wiping his feet with her hair. The act, a combination of the Mark-Matthew account of the anonymous woman's anointing of Jesus' head (Mk 14.3-9; Mt 26.6-13) and Luke's account of the sinful woman washing Jesus' feet with her tears and drying them with her hair (Lk 7. 36-50), is so strange if taken literally that we are virtually forced to attach primary importance to its symbolism.

Perhaps the reference to Mary's wiping the feet with her hair is an effort to attach her act to the Footwashing, not that of the sinful woman in Luke

but that of Jesus, who at the Last Supper performed for his disciples an act
that would normally have been performed by a devoted disciple for his
teacher. The anointing with precious ointment, on the other hand, is a
proleptic anointing of Jesus for burial (12.7), which occasions Judas'
objection.

Three points are particularly worth noting. First, if Mary's wiping of
Jesus' feet with her hair is meant to evoke the Footwashing then we have a
presentation of Mary as a disciple of Jesus in the strict sense of the word.
To wash the feet of one's master was an act of veneration by a disciple
(Brown: 1970, 564). It is also the act which Jesus commanded his disciples
to perform in imitation of himself (13.14-15). This presentation of Mary as
a disciple would accord well with the picture of this same Mary that we get
from Lk 10.39 where she sits at the feet of Jesus listening to his teaching in
the attitude of a Torah scholar with a rabbi. John has separated the two
aspects of discipleship, that of listening to the master's teaching and that of
actively expressing devotion to the person of the teacher. In Jn 11, after her
confession of faith, Martha runs to Mary and says, "The Teacher is here
and is calling for you" (11.28) and Mary goes quickly to him and falls at
his feet (11.32). In Jn 12, Mary anoints her Teacher's feet in an act that
resembles (because of her wiping them with her hair) a footwashing. In
other words, it seems likely enough that John is deliberately presenting this
woman as a disciple of Jesus the Teacher, a role generally forbidden to
Jewish women (Stagg: 53). When we remember that discipleship is the
primary relationship with Jesus according to the Fourth Gospel and that, as
Robert Culpepper has shown (1975: 270-271), the community of the
Beloved Disciple had the characteristics of an ancient "school" in which
the members devoted themselves to the study of the Scriptures and the
teaching of Jesus, it becomes especially significant that John presents a
woman in this role. It is unlikely that he would have done so unless women
in his community were active members of the school who devoted
themselves to sacred study and discussion.

Secondly, we have in this scene another example of a male objection to
a woman's unusual expression of her relationship with Jesus. Judas objects
to Mary's extravagant act of devotion and suggests a more conventional
form of piety for her, almsgiving (12.4-5). The Evangelist tells us that
Judas' real motive was theft (12.6) but Jesus replies not to his hidden
motive but to his expressed objection. His defence of Mary's ministry to
him is blunt and harsh, "Let her alone" (12.7).

What is important to our purposes here is the fact that Jesus approves of
this woman's original religious initiative. Mary does not express her
relationship to Jesus in a conventional way nor does she seek permission of
anyone, not even Lazarus who was presumably head of the house, to act as

she does. She assumes the right, as a disciple, to decide what form her ministry to Jesus should take, and when another disciple objects he is silenced by Jesus himself. It is to be noted that each of the Synoptics has a version of this element of the episode, each with a different male or group of males objecting (cf. Mt 26.8-10; Mk 14.4-6; Lk 7.39) which makes one aware of how early the attempt of men to control the discipleship and ministry of women began in the Christian community. Jesus' opinion of male attempts to control the relationship between his women disciples and himself is so clear in the NT that one can only wonder at the institutional Church's failure to comprehend it.

Our third point concerns the Martha and Mary material as a whole. Chapters 11 and 12 of John constitute a proleptic presentation of the "Hour" of Jesus. The raising of Lazarus both foreshadows Jesus' resurrection and finalises the intention of the authorities to kill him. The anointing at Bethany foreshadows Jesus' burial and exposes Judas as the one who will precipitate the Hour by his betrayal. Throughout this anticipation of the paschal mystery women disciples play the leading positive roles not only as witnesses but as faithful participants. In the persons of Mary Magdalene and the Mother of Jesus women will participate in the reality of the Hour in a similarly intimate and public way.

Mary Magdalene (Jn 19.25; 20.1-2, 11-18)

Like the Beloved Disciple, Mary Magdalene does not appear in the Fourth Gospel until the Hour of Jesus' glorification has come. Her role is that of witness to the paschal events. She is at the foot of the cross at Jesus' death (19.25), discovers the opened tomb on Easter morning (20.1-2), and receives the first Easter christophany including the apostolic commission to announce the exaltation of Jesus and its salvific effects to the disciples (20.11-18). Mary Magdalene is, without any doubt, the disciple whose place in the paschal mystery is most certainly attested by all four Gospels. She holds a place in the tradition about Jesus' women disciples analogous to that of Peter among the male disciples, and for the same reason, namely, the tradition that she received the first appearance of the glorified Jesus and the foundational apostolic commission (Hengel: 256). Consequently, we will concentrate on these two aspects of the Mary Magdalene material.

The question of who first saw the risen Jesus is theologically significant because the early church regarded the protophany as the manifestation of the primacy of apostolic witness which is the foundation of the Church's faith (Gils: 1962). According to Paul (1 Cor 15.3-8) and Luke (24.34) Jesus appeared first to Simon Peter. According to John (20.14-17), Matthew (28.1, 9-10), and the Markan appendix (16.9-11) he appeared first to Mary Magdalene, who, in Matthew is accompanied by another woman. There are no scholarly grounds for questioning the authenticity of the tradition that the first christophany was to Mary Magdalene. In fact, since this tradition clearly challenged the Petrine tradition, there would have been strong motivation for suppressing it if the evidence for it were at all weak. The fact that it has survived in two independent witnesses, John and Matthew, (the Markan appendix is a collage that cannot be considered independent) is excellent evidence that it was a primitive and authentic tradition, carefully preserved by some Churches.

In the history of orthodox exegesis (in contrast to the liturgy which celebrates Mary Magdalene as "apostle to the apostles" [cf. Brown: 1979, 190, n. 336]) the christophany to Mary Magdalene has been constantly trivialised as a "private," i.e., unofficial event without ecclesiastical significance. The only grounds for such a position, which is clearly contrary to the evidence of the text, is the long-standing and unjustified assumption that all of the early Christian communities shared the Jewish proscription of testimony given by women. As we saw in regard to the Samaritan Woman passage, John regarded the apostolic testimony of women as valid, effective, and approved by Jesus.

The only conclusion that an unbiased interpretation of the Mary Magdalene episode in John 20 can yield is that, according to the Fourth Gospel, Jesus did appear to Mary Magdalene on Easter morning and that that appearance was the first christophany. He assigns no individual christophany at all to Peter. That the theological significance of the protophany to Mary Magdalene is the same as that intended by Paul and Luke in assigning the protophany to Peter, namely, that it identifies the "apostle to the apostles" in the respective traditions, will be clearer once we have examined Jesus' commission to Mary.

The commission that Jesus gives to Mary is "Go to my brothers and sisters and say to them: I ascend to my Father who is now your Father, to my God who is now your God" (20.17). It is not necessary to enter into all the detail that a complete exegesis of this text would require in order to make the point that this message is the Johannine version of the kerygma.

First, it is addressed to Jesus' "brothers and sisters" (ἀδελφοί, the plural of "brother", means siblings of both sexes) whom Mary understands to mean the "disciples" (20.18). This is the first time in the Fourth Gospel that Jesus refers to his disciples as brothers and sisters because it is only by his exaltation that he accomplishes the purpose of the Incarnation, namely, to give the power to become children of God to those who believe in his name (cf. 1.12). The message entrusted to Mary is precisely that Jesus' Father is now truly Father of the disciples and thus they are now truly the sisters and brothers of Jesus.

The second part of the message is equally vital: that Jesus' God is now the God of the disciples. This is an expression of the new Covenant mediated by Jesus, the new Moses, through whom comes the grace and truth (*hesed* and '*emet*) foreshadowed by the Sinai covenant (cf. Jn 1.16-18 [Léon-Dufour: 180-181]). Until his glorification Jesus alone possessed the Spirit of the New Covenant (cf. Jn 7. 37-39) but the very meaning of his return to the Father is that the Spirit is now handed over to his disciples (cf. 16.7; 19.30). In short, the message Jesus entrusts to Mary Magdalene is that all is indeed accomplished and that by his exaltation Jesus has become the source of the Spirit of filiation and of the New Covenant for those who are doubly his brothers and sisters, children of the same Father and members of the same Covenant. There can be no question of regarding this message   as anything but the Good News of salvation in its characteristically Johannine formulation.

Mary Magdalene, unlike the women in Mark (16.8), hastens to fulfil the commission by announcing the Gospel to her co-disciples. The formula with which she opens her proclamation is the Fourth Gospel's technical credential statement of revelation as the basis of one's witness: "I have seen the Lord" (cf. 20.18 with 20.25 in which the disciples announce the message to Thomas; also 3.11; 19.35). The disciples in John, unlike those in Matthew (28.17), the Markan appendix (16.11), and Luke (24.10-11), give no indication of not accepting Mary's testimony. Indeed, when Jesus appears to them later that day they are not astonished or unbelieving but rather filled with joy (20.20).

The Mary Magdalene material in the Fourth Gospel is perhaps the most important indication we have of the Gospel perspective on the role of women in the Christian community. It shows quite clearly that, in at least one of the first Christian communities, a woman was regarded as the primary witness to the paschal mystery, the guarantee of the apostolic tradition. Her claim to apostleship is equal in every respect to both Peter's and Paul's, and we know more about her exercise of her vocation than we do about most of the members of the Twelve. Unlike Peter she was not unfaithful to Jesus during the Passion and unlike Paul she never persecuted Christ in his members. But like both she saw the risen Lord, received directly from him the commission to preach the Gospel, and carried out that commission faithfully and effectively.

SUMMARY AND CONCLUSIONS

Let us now briefly summarise our findings about the evidence of the Fourth Gospel on the role of women in the Christian community. We have seen that both general impressions and analyses of particular passages about women supply us with a picture of a first century community in which original and loving women played a variety of unconventional roles which the Fourth Evangelist presents as approved by Jesus and the community despite the grumblings of some men. These women do not appear dependent on husbands or other male legitimators, nor as seeking permission for their activities from male officials. They evince remarkable originality in their relationships with Jesus and extraordinary initiative in their activities within the community. They are the privileged recipients of three of Jesus' most important self-revelations; his messiahship, that he is the resurrection and the life, and that his glorification is complete and its salvific effect given to his disciples. Women are the two most important witnesses to him during his public life and during his Hour. We have seen that women officially represent the community in the expression of its faith (Martha), its acceptance of salvation (Mary Magdalene), and its role as witness to the Gospel (Samaritan Woman, Mary Magdalene). Two women in John hold the place occupied by Peter in the Synoptics: Martha as confessor of faith and Mary Magdalene as recipient of the Easter protophany and the commission as apostle to the Church. Women were disciples in the strict sense of the word as students of the word of Jesus (Mary of Bethany) in the Johannine School. We have also seen that women were considered to have played the leading roles, along with the Beloved Disciple, in the paschal mystery. Finally, we saw two examples of male objections to the activity of women (the disciples in Samaria and Judas at Bethany), both of which were effectively suppressed by Jesus, and two examples of the acceptance and effectiveness of the witness of women (the Samaritans and the disciples after the glorification).

If the material on women in the Fourth Gospel were released from the shackles of a male-dominated exegesis and placed at the service of the contemporary Church there is little doubt that it would help to liberate both men and women from any remaining doubts that women are called by Jesus to full discipleship and ministry in the Christian community. Hopefully, our investigation of this concrete question has also helped to demonstrate that the Word of God given to us in the New Testament is a word of liberation not only for first century Christians but for each succeeding generation of believers who will faithfully and creatively address new questions to the text in the well-founded expectation that this Word is indeed living and active.

SOURCE MATERIAL

Brown, R.E. *The Gospel According to John,* 2 vols. (Garden City/New York: Doubleday, 1966,1970).

Brown, R.E. "Role of Women in the Fourth Gospel", *The Community of the Beloved Disciple* (New York/Ramsey/Toronto: Paulist, 1979) 183-198.

Collins, R.F. "Mary in the Fourth Gospel. A Decade of Johannine Studies", *Louvain Studies* 3: (1970) 99-142.

Collins, R.F. "The Representative Figures in the Fourth Gospel", *Downside Review* 94 (1976) 26-46, 118-132.

Corell, A. *Consummatum Est: Eschatology and Church in the Gospel of St. John* (London: SPCK, 1958).

Cullmann, O. *The Johannine Circle* (Philadelphia: Westminster, 1976).

Culpepper, R.A. *The Johannine School: An Evaluation of the Johannine School Hypothesis Based on an Investigation of the Nature of Ancient Schools* (Missoula: Scholars Press, 1975).

Gadamer, H.G. *Truth and Method* (New York: Seabury, 1975).

"Gaudium et Spes", *The Documents of Vatican II.* Eds. W. M. Abbott and J. Gallagher (New York: Guild/ America/Association, 1966) 199-308.

Gils, F. "Pierre et la foi au Christ ressuscité", *Ephemerides Theologicae Lovanienses* 38 (1962) 5-43.

Hengel, M. "Maria Magdalena und die Frauen als Zeugen", *Abraham unser Vater: Juden und Christen im Gespräch über die Bibel,* Eds. O Betz et al. (Leiden: E.J. Brill, 1963) 243-256.

Léon-Dufour, X.. *Resurrection and the Message of Easter* (London: Geoffrey Chapman 1974).

Mary in the New Testament:A Collaborative Assessment by Protestant and Roman Catholic Scholars, Eds. R. E. Brown, K. P. Donfried, J. A. Fitzmyer, J. Reumann (Philadelphia/ New York: Fortress/Paulist, 1978).

Meeks, W.A. *The Prophet-King: Moses Traditions and the Johannine Christology* (Leiden: E.J. Brill, 1967).

P. Paul VI. "Women/Disciples and Co-Workers", *Origins* 4 (1975) 718-719.

Platt, E.E. "Ministry and Mary of Bethany", *Theology Today* 34 (1977) 29-39.

Pontifical Biblical Commission. "Can Women be Priests?" *Origins* 6 (1976) 92-96.

Reese, J.M. "The Historical Image of Mary in the New Testament", *Marian Studies* 28 (1977) 27-44.

Ricoeur, P. *Interpretation Theory: Discourse and the Surplus Meaning* (Fort Worth: Texas Christian University Press, 1976).

Sacred Congregation for the Doctrine of the Faith. "Vatican Declaration: Women in the Ministerial Priesthood", *Origins* 6 (1977) 517-524.

Schnackenburg, R. *The Gospel According to John,* vol. 1. Tr. K. Smith (New York: Herder and Herder, 1968).

Schneiders, S.M. "Did Jesus Exclude Women from Priesthood?" *Women Priests,* Eds. A. and L. Swidler (New York: Paulist, 1977) 227-233.

Stagg, E. and F. *Women in the World of Jesus* (Philadelphia: Westminster, 1978).

Stendahl, K. "Contemporary Biblical Theology", *Interpreter's Dictionary of the Bible,* vol. 1. Eds. A. Buttrick et al. (New York/Nashville: Abingdon, 1962) 418-432.

Trible, P. *God and the Rhetoric of Sexuality* (Philadelphia: Fortress, 1978).

Tolbert, M.A. *Perspectives on the Parables: An Approach to Multiple Interpretations* (Philadelphia: Fortress, 1979).

Women and Priesthood, Ed. C. Stuhlmueller (Collegeville: Liturgical Press, 1978).

Women Priests: A Catholic Commentary on the Vatican Declaration. Eds. A. Swidler and L. Swidler (New York: Paulist, 1977).

IT IS WRITTEN: A STRUCTURALIST ANALYSIS OF JOHN 6*

JOHN DOMINIC CROSSAN

> If it recedes one day, leaving behind its works and signs on the shores
> of our civilisation, the structuralist invasion might become a question
> for the historian of ideas, or perhaps even an object. But the historian
> would be deceived if he came to this pass: by the very act of
> considering the structuralist invasion as an object he would forget its
> meaning and would forget that what is at stake, first of all, is an
> adventure of vision, a conversion of the way of putting questions to
> any object posed before us, to historical objects—his own—in
> particular. And, unexpectedly among these, the literary object.
>
> Jacques Derrida[1]

PRECIS

The subject of this article needs two immediate qualifications. First, it
concerns only a smaller unit, John 6, within a larger unit, the Gospel of
John, and thus it must be considered at best a *first probe*, to be corrected
by, even if also corrective of any fuller work on the larger text. Second,
the subtitle should be read in the light of the epigraph. The essay is "an
adventure of vision", an exercise in structuralist imagination rather than
the detailed application of a deductive method and the precise application
of a metatextual vocabulary. I have tried quite deliberately to keep the
metatextual terminology to an absolute minimum and to use or create
only what this present text seemed to demand.

What would one see if one took John 6 as a unity and officially omitted
any historical questioning of the text? What would happen if one
attempted by looking at *how* the text means to see *what* the text means?
An historical vision could legitimately explain disjunctions in terms of

---

* This article appeared in *Semeia* 26, 1983, pp. 3-21.

[1] Jacques Derrida, "Force et Signification", *Critique* 193-94 (June-July, 1963) was the
opening essay in his *L'écriture et la différence* (Paris: Seuil, 1967), a collection of essays all,
save one, published separately during 1963-1966. The collection has been translated by
Alan Bass as *Writing and Difference* (Chicago: University of Chicago Press, 1978), and this
opening essay, "Force and Signification," (pp. 3-30) has been reprinted in *Structuralist
Review* 1, 2 (Winter, 1978): 13-54. My quotation is that essay's opening sentences.

sources and redactions, of additions appended by an initial author, an intermediate redactor, or even a final editor. But a structuralist vision will want to know, even granting all that is true, how did such an appender add it here rather than there, now rather than earlier or later? The adventure of vision is to see John 6 as a whole and to study how it holds together as such.

I. UNITY

John 6 may be taken as an integrated whole for both external and internal reasons.

A. *External Indices of Unity*

John 6.1 contains the phrase "*After this Jesus* went to the other side of the Sea of *Galilee*" and John 7.1 repeats most of this with "*After this Jesus* went about in *Galilee*."

B. *Internal Indices of Unity*

There are three internal indications of unity, in terms of theme, frame, and structure.

(1) *Theme.* The general theme of "bread" appears as early as 6.5 and as late as 6.58 and thus dominates the chapter.

(2) *Frame.* There is a precise inclusion between the handling of the Disciples in 6.1-15 and the Twelve in 6.67-71:

The Disciples (6.1-15)	The Twelve (6.67-71)
The Disciples (6.3)	The Twelve (6.67)
Philip (6.5, 7)	Simon Peter (6.68)
Andrew (6.8)	Judas (6.71a)
The Disciples (6.12)	The Twelve (6,70, 71b)

Granted these general frames, one might also draw attention to (1) Jesus' foreknowledge in 6.6 and again in 6.64, 71; and (2) the mention of Simon Peter in 6.8 and 6.68.

(3) *Structure.* There is a general parallel structure within the chapter:

(a) Jesus and the Crowds	6.1-15	6.22-59
(b) Jesus and the Disciples	6.16-21	6.60-71

The first column of verses is primarily Jesus' deeds for the Crowds or Disciples while the second column is primarily his words to the Crowds or Disciples.

There is thus sufficient indication of unity within John 6 to render valid its study within the overall unity of the Gospel of John.

II. TIME

The text is broken up by several temporal indices. These may be distinguished as internal and external ones.

A. Internal Indices of Time

The internal indices differentiate the text into: (1) 6.1-15. The *first day* is specified directly by the following two indices. (2) 6.16-21. The *night* is specified directly by "when evening came" (6.16) and "it was now dark" (6.17). The *second day* is specified directly by "on the next day" (6.22).

B. External Indices of Time

There is also a single temporal index linking the text with an external situation. This is given directly and explicitly by, "Now the Passover, the feast of the Jews, was at hand" (6.4).

Three points may be noted immediately concerning the phrase. It is displaced, disconnected, and disassociated within its context.

(1) *Displacement*. It is quite common to start a narrative with a temporal and spatial index. The standard opening is: "Once upon a time in a land far away". In the present case, the order is spatial (6.1) followed by temporal (6.4). This is exactly the same sequence given in the external indices of inclusion for the text (see IA above), when one compares 6.1, 4 with 7.1-2: "After this Jesus went about in Galilee; he would not go about in Judea, because the Jews sought to kill him [*space*]. Now the Jews' feast of Tabernacles was at hand [*time*]."

My present point is not, however, the spatial and teporal sequence but rather the fact that the spatial index is given in full in 6.1, the story gets underway in 6.2-3, and only then, almost as an interruption, is the temporal index cited in 6.4. One expects its position to be immediately after 6.1 rather than after 6.3.

(2) *Disconnection*. The feast of Passover is said to be "at hand". Thereafter, throughout John 6, one waits in vain for some connection between this statement, vague as it is, and the feast of Passover itself. This is what happens in the three other places where John declares a feast to be "at hand": (a) 2.13 leads into 2.23; (b) 7.2 connects with 7.8, 10, 11, 14, 37; and (c) 11.55 continues with 12.1; 13.1, 29; 18.28, 39; 19. 14, 31, 42. After 6.4, however, there is no further mention of the Passover whose nearness has just been noted.

(3) *Disassociation*. The second half of the sentence in 6.4b, "the feast of the Jews", indicates that (a) the implied readers are "not-Jews" but (b) leaves open whether the implied writer is "Jew" or "not-Jew". (For

example: "It was thanksgiving, a holiday for Americans", is being said to non-Americans by either an American or non-American).

III. SPACE

The text is divided spatially by indices which are more complicated than the temporal ones. These may be designated as general and specific internal indices as well as external ones.

A. General Internal Indices of Space

The text is broken up as folows by these indices. It should be noted that the divisions are close to but not identical with the previous temporal divisions.

(1) 6.1-15. The *first land* is specified directly by "to the other side of the Sea of Galilee" (6.1).

(2) 6.16-24. The *sea* is specified directly by the repeated mentions of "sea" (6.1, 16, 17, 18, 19, 22, 25).

(3) 6.25-71. The *second land* is specified directly, first for Jesus and the Disciples by "at the land" (6.21), and then for the Crowds by "got into the boats and went to Capernaum" (6.24). In 6.22 there is a counterpoint to the same phrase in 6.1 ("the other side of the sea").

B. Specific Internal indices of Space

Each of the three spatial contexts has been organised or centred around a specific phenomenon, respectively, a mountain, a boat or boats, sand a synagogue.

(1) 6.1-15 (*first land, mountain*). This scene opens with Jesus located positively εἰς τὸ ὄρος (6.3). It concludes with Jesus located, again positively, in the same place, πάλιν εἰς τὸ ὄρος (6.15). It is only because of these positive frames that one presumes, negatively, that the central event takes place *not on the mountain*. There is thus a triple sequence of on (6.3), off (6.5-14), and on the mountain (6.15).

(2) 6.16-21 (*sea: single boat*). This unit receives a treatment somewhat similar to that of the mountain. There is again a triple sequence of inside (6.16-18), outside (6.19-20), and inside the boat (6.21).

(3) 6.22-24 (*sea: multiple boats*). This unit is simpler than the preceding one. It has a double sequence of being without (6.22) and then with boats (6.23-24). But this whole incident both separates absolutely what happens to Jesus and the Disciples in the between-time and the between-space of 6.16-21 from what happens to the Crowds on the same sea. they do not experience the combination of both outside-time (the night between the two days) and also outside-space (the sea between the

two lands) during which Jesus proclaims to the Disciples his outside-grammar revelation: "I AM" (6.20).

(4) 6.25-71 (*second land: synagogue*). Once again this unit is simpler than the initial two sections. There is only a double sequence and even this must be considered implicit and indirect. The dialogue of 6.25-58 concludes with, "This he said in the synagogue" (6.59a). The dialogue which then ensues in 6.60-71 is unspecified with regard to space but one presumes negatively that it is *not in the synagogue*. hence, presumably, a double sequence of inside (6.25-59) and outside the synagogue (6.60-71).

C. External Indices of Space

Those internal indices connect, to some extent, with these external ones.

The first land and its mountain are specified but negatively as being "on the other side of the Sea of Galilee, which is the Sea of Tiberias" (6.1). This also specifies, and positively, the sea between the two lands. But it is the second land and its synagogue which is specified most explicitly and positively. the scene is set in Capernaum (6.17, 231, 24) and is centred around "the synagogue, as he taught at Capernaum" (6.59b).

IV. NARRATIVE

The terms "Narrative" and "Discourse" distinguish between deeds and words within the text. The normal line between Narrative and Discourse is indicated by the quotation mark. I do not intend any other more profound differentiation at the moment.[1]

A second distinction is that between Actant and Action. Actants are the personae who cause certain effects, or Actions, within the text.

---

[1] I am aware that the terms "Narrative" (deeds) and "Discourse" (words) are not entirely satisfactory. They may cause confusion with the much more technical distinctions between Story (the content, the what) and Discourse (the expression, the how) suggested by Seymour Chatman, *Story and Discourse: Narrative Structure in Fiction and Film* (Ithaca, N.Y.: Cornell University Press, 1978). I have not been able to adapt Chatman's excellent categories to John 6 (although it may well be possible to do so with future study) primarily because of the very special relationship between what Jesus does (my "Narrative") and what Jesus says (my "Discourse") in John 6. But, for future reference, see Chatman's section on (his term) "Discourse" (pp. 146-262) and especially his comment that, "When we know more about textual and semantic analysis, it may be possible to develop viable taxonomies of dialogue types" (p. 177). He cites Maurice Blanchot's three-way distinction of dialogue, exemplified from Malraux, James and Kafka, and notes that "Kafka's characters, for their part, are doomed forever to talk at cross purposes, past each other" (p. 178). The application of that concept to the "non"-dialogue in John 6 is quite obvious.

A. Narrative Actants

(1) 6.1-15. Between the external index of space in 6.1 and the external index of time in 6.4, the three major Narrative Actants are introduced, separately and pointedly.

(a) Jesus is introduced first in 6.1, as if he was crossing the sea by himself ("Jesus went"), although, of course, the Disciples are with him. But the principal Narrative Actant may be appropriately introduced first and alone.

(b) Crowds are introduced in second place in 6.2, and they have "followed him".

(c) Disciples finally appear in 6.3 and they are simply "with" Jesus.

Later, with a deliberateness similar to their introduction in 6.1-3, the three Narrative Actants separate and go their different ways in 6.15-16.

(2) 6.16-21. Only two Narrative Actants reappear here; the Disciples alone (6.16-10), then Jesus and the Disciples (6.19-21).

(3) 6.22-24. Although the other two Narrative Actants are mentioned (6.22, 24) the Crowds are alone in this unit.

(4) 6.25-59. The Disciples are textually absent, with only Jesus and the Crowds explicitly mentioned. It is clear from 6.60, of course, that the Disciples were actually present throughout 6.25-59.

But there is a strange development between 6.25-40 and 6.41-59. Prior to 6.25-40 the Crowds have been frequently identified with various terms (6.2, 5, 10a, 10b, 14, 22, 24). That is, four times in 6.1-15 and twice in 6.22-24. Now, suddenly, they become nameless. Throughout the fairly long section in 6.25-40 they are identified only indirectly, remaining hidden behind such words as "they" or "them". But, again suddenly, they are termed "the Jews" in 6.41 and 6.52 and it is "the Jews" who speak with Jesus throughout 6.41-59. The Crowds of 6.1-40 become "the Jews" of 6.41-59.

(5) 6.60-71. Once again only two Narrative Actants are textually present, but now it is Jesus and the Disciples.

But a similar, strange development takes place between 6.60-66 and 6.67-71 as previously between 6.1-40 and 6.41-59. In 6.60-66 the Disciples are named three times (6.60, 61, 66). Then in 6.67-71 there appears a group not heretofore either distinguished or named. And as with the Disciples in 6.60-66, so now this new group, the Twelve, is named three times once they appear (6.67, 70, 71).

B. Narrative Actions

There are two main Narrative Actions to be considered in the text: Moving and Feeding.

(1) Narrative Moving

For Narrative Moving I wish to distinguish between Moving in terms of Space and Moving in terms of Narrative Actants.

(a) Narrative Moving and Space

In terms of Space the Moving is rather homogeneous. First, Jesus explicitly (6.1), the Disciples implicitly (6.3), and the Crowds explicitly (6.2, 5), "went to the other side of the Sea of Galilee" (6.1). So also, again with Jesus and the Disciples in first place (6.17, 21), and the Crowds in second place (6.24), there is a recrossing of the sea to Capernaum.

(b) Narrative Moving and Narrative Actants

But Moving is much more significant not just in terms of who is Moving to where but in terms of who is Moving to which other Narrative Actant.

Jesus and the Disciples

Coming. Jesus comes to the Disciples but the Disciples do not come to Jesus. Thus, Jesus comes to the Disciples in 6.16-21 and this advent is emphasised by the rather awkward comment in 6.17b. After having noted that the Disciples had embarked, it is then said that Jesus had not arrived. "When evening came, his disciples went down to the sea, got into a boat, and started across the sea to Capernaum. It was now dark, and Jesus had not yet come to them" (6.16-17). It should be noted that when Jesus comes to the Disciples in 6.21 they are immediately where they want to be. The Disciples, on the other hand, never come to Jesus; they are always simply there (6.3). Compare, in contrast, Mark 6.35 with John 6.5.

Going. Jesus leaves the Disciples in 6.15. Although the primary withdrawal here is from the Crowds, the terminal presence of Jesus on the mountain alone (6.15) reflects back on the initial one on the mountain with his disciples (6.3). So also do the Disciples leave Jesus in 6.16 (compare, in contrast, Mark 6.45), and (some of) the Disciples leave him in 6.66.

Jesus and the Crowds

Coming. Jesus never comes to the Crowds. It is twice stressed, most emphatically, that they come after him. They move after him, first in 6.2 ("a multitude followed him") and 6.5 ("a multitude was coming to him"), and again later in 6.22-25 ("seeking" in 6.24, "found" in 6.25). Thus, once on each day and once on each land, the Crowds move after Jesus. Compare, for contrast, Mark 6.33-34 with John 6.2, 5, and note that the Crowds precede Jesus in Mark so that he comes to them.

Going. Jesus, of course, leaves the Crowds in 6.15. It would also seem
that he is leaving them, textually, in 6.59. But nowhere in the text are the
Crowds explicitly described as Moving away from Jesus.

In summary: Jesus never comes to the Crowds but they always come to
him; Jesus comes to the Disciples and they never come to him; Jesus
leaves them both but the Disciples and not the Crowds leave him.

(2) Narrative Feeding

The Narrative Action of Feeding in 6.1-15 is totally dominated by Jesus.
In terms of Action, he himself distributes the food in 6.11, in contrast,
for example, with Mark 6. 41 where the Disciples do this.

(3) Narrative Moving and Narrative Feeding

The twin Narrative Actions are closely linked together in that the Crowds
come to Jesus, the Feeding ensues, then Jesus and the Disciples leave, and
the Crowds follow. Thus the feeding is at the centre of the Moving and
the Moving is to and from the Feeding.

V. DISCOURSE

The simplest reading of the text reveals how the predominance of
Narrative in 6.1-21 gives way to the predominance of Discourse in 6.22-
71. But before turning attention to that situation, it will be useful to study
the interaction of Narrative and Discourse in 6.1-24.

(1) 6.1-15. In this unit there is a section of Discourse (6. 5-10) framed
by two Narrative sections (6.1-4, 11-15). The Narrative is quite
conceivable by itself, as if one read from 6.1-4 into 6.11-15. But the
interaction of Narrative and Discourse in this small unit of 6.1-15 effects
certain very significant results.

(a) The Discourse in 6.5 stresses, just as did the Narrative in 6.11, the
complete dominance of Jesus over this entire event. Compare, in contrast,
Mark 6.35, where the Disciples initiate the Discourse.

(b) The Discourse here establishes the pattern of (i) a dialogue
composed of (ii) questions which (iii) are not really answered. This will
be much more important in 6.25-71.

(c) The predominance of Narrative over Discourse in 6.1-15 prepares
the way for the opposite situation in 6.25-71.

(d) In 6.5-10 the three Narrative Actants become Discourse Actants
that is, they talk about themselves. Thus in 6.5 Jesus asks the Disciples
about the Crowds: "How are *we* to buy bread, so that *these* people may
eat?" This will also be of future importance.

(e) The Discourse between Jesus and the Disciples in 6.5-10 contains a
single Discourse Actant who, unlike the preceding case, is never a
Narrative Actant. Yet this Discourse Actant is the necessary basis for the

continuance of both Narrative and Discourse. In 6.8 Andrew says, "There is a lad here who has five barley loaves and two fish." When one notices that this Discourse Actant is absent in Mark 6.30, one might well wonder if it has a function here in John. At very least, it is a first alert to the possibility of Discourse Actants who are not Narrative Actants, who appear only in the Discourse and yet on whom the whole Narrative and Discourse may depend.

(2) 6.16-21. In this unit there is again Discourse (unanswered dialogue) in 6.20 within Narrative frames in 6.16-19 and 6.21. Once again the Narrative is conceivable without the Discourse and once again Narrative Actants cross the quotation marks to become Discourse Actants. Jesus talks about himself to the Disciples and about them to themselves.

But now, in contrast to 6.1-15, the Discourse is extremely important. In Mark 6.49-50 the frightened disciples "thought it was a ghost, and cried out; for they all saw him, and were terrified". In such a situation the phrase *ego eimi* may well be translated by the reassuring, "It is I." But not so in John where there is no mention of non-recognition. There is, of course, fear which is the proper response of numinous awe. In such a context, then, the phrase must be given full transcendental value. Given absolutely, without any qualification or addition, it breaks the rules of grammar and must be taken precisely as such a breach. Jesus says: I AM.

B. Narrative Actants And Discourse Actants

A distinction was noted above between Narrative-Discourse Actants and pure Discourse Actants, between Actants appearing in both Narrative and Discourse and those appearing only in Discourse. These latter now require further study.

(1) The Presence Of Discourse Actants
The following are the major Discourse Actants to be noted in 6. 25-71.

(a) Jesus introduces God under various titles. The first mention is of "God the Father" (6.27) and thereafter one finds "God" (6.29, 33, 46), "my Father" (6.32, 40), "the Father" (6. 37, 44, 45, 46 twice, 57, 65), "the living Father" (6.57), and "Him Who Sent Me" (6.38, 39).

The Crowds refer to God, once as "God" (6.28) and once as "He" (6.31).

The Disciples do not mention any Discourse Actant but the Twelve mention God in addressing Jesus as "the Holy One of God" (6.69).

(b) Jesus speaks of the "Son of Man", once to the Crowds, once to "the Jews", and once to the Disciples (6.27, 53, 62). He also refers to "Him Whom He Has Sent" (6.29), and to "the Son" (6.40).

There are no such references for either Crowds or Disciples, but the Twelve address Jesus as "the Holy One of God" (6.69).

(c) Jesus refers to "Moses" (6.32), "the prophets" (6.45), and "your fathers" (6.49). The Crowds also refer to "our fathers " (6.31) .

The Crowds refer to the parents of Jesus: "Jesus, the son of Joseph, whose father and mother we know" (6.42).

(d) Finally and most importantly, there is a group designated repeatedly by Jesus, and nobody else, with such expressions as (i) "he who..." (6.35, 47), or (ii) "all who..." (6.37, 39, 40, 45), or (iii) "anyone who..." (6.50, 51), or "no one... unless..." (6.44, 65).

(2) The Dominance of Discourse Actants

There are two facets to this domination. First, once certain Discourse Actants appear they dominate not only the succeeding Discourse but even the preceding Narrative as well. These Discourse Actants *absorb* and *consume* (the verbs are not innocently chosen) the Narrative Actants themselves. Second, the apparent exception to that generality is Jesus. In this case all the mediator Discourse Actants are absorbed along with the Narrative Actant Jesus into the Narrative-Discourse Actant, the "I" of Jesus. Here it is this Narrative-Discourse Actant which continues to dominate the text and which absorbs and consumes the Narrative Actant Jesus himself.

(a) *God.* The domination of this Discourse Actant over the entire text, both Narrative and Discourse, will be discussed below under C.

(b) *Jesus.* After the supreme and unqualified revelation of "I AM" in 6.20, it is not very surprising that the "I" of Jesus should dominate the Discourse. This is effected in two ways. First, of course, only Jesus uses "I" within the Discourse. The Disciples/Twelve (6.68-69) and the Crowds (6.28, 30, 34, 52) use "we". Second, and more important, all other mediating Discourse Actants are absorbed into this "I" of Jesus. Thus, anything said of Discourse Actants such as "Son of Man", or "Son", or "Him Whom He Has Sent" is repeated also in terms of the "I" of Jesus, with one very important exception:

Son of Man. In 6.27 it is the "Son of Man" who "will give" them "the food which endures for eternal life". But in 6.50-51, "I shall give" (51) this bread "that a man may eat of it and not die" (50). Again, what is said of the "Son of Man" in 6.53 is repeated of the "I" of Jesus in 6.54: "unless you eat the flesh of the Son of man and drink his blood, you have no life in you; he who eats my flesh and drinks my blood has eternal life".

Son. In 6.40 it is a question of "every one who sees the Son and believes in him...". But in 6.36, "you have seen me and yet do not believe".

The Sent One. In 6.29 Jesus refers to "him whom he has sent"; but, in 6.30 it is a case of "him who sent me".

Finally, there is the statement in 6.62, "What if you were to see the Son of man ascending where he was before?" Nowhere in John 6 is there any mention of the "I" of Jesus ascending to heaven. This leaves an unfulfilled expectation reminding us that John 6 is part of a wider unity and 6.62 will be repeated in terms of the "I" of Jesus only much later in 20.17. "I am ascending to my Father."

In summary, then, the Narrative Actant Jesus and also the mediator Discourse Actants such as "Son of Man", "Son", and "Sent One", are absorbed into and consumed by the Narrative Discourse Actant, the "I" of Jesus.

(c) *The Crowds & "The Jews"*. One could imagine three types of pronominal interaction within Discourse:

1. "I-You": speaker and hearer interact as reciprocating "I" and "You" in their mutual Discourse.

2. "I-He": speaker interacts reciprocally with another than the hearer in his own Discourse.

3. "You-He": speaker has the hearer ("you") and another ("he") interact reciprocally in his own Discourse.

In the light of these possibilities, there is a very strange change between Jesus' dialogue with the unspecified Crowds in 6.25-34 and the specified "Jews" in 6.35-38.

In dialogue with the Crowds (1) there is not a single instance of "I-He" Discourse but (2) "I-You" (6.26, 30, 32a, 34) and (3) "You-He" (6.27, 29, 32 twice) are about evenly distributed. Note, for example, how 6.26 ("I-You") shifts to 6.27 ("You-He"), or again how 6.32a ("I-You") moves to 6.32b ("You-He").

But in dialogue with "the Jews" all of this changes completely. (1) Now "I-He" dominates completely (6.35b, 37, 38, 39, 40, 44, 45b, 54, 56, 57) so that (2) only three uses of "I-You" (6.36, 47a, 53a) and (3) only one use of "You-He" appear (6.53b). Note, for example, how 6.53-54 move from "I-You" (53a) to "You-He" (53b) to "I-He" (54).

This means, in summary, that the "You" of the Crowds/"Jews" disappears almost completely. It is displaced and absorbed by the reiterated mentions of the new Discourse Actant, "He who..." (see B(l)(d) above).

(d) *The Disciples*. There is a rather similar development in the case of the Disciples. Although there is no such sheer numerical predominance of "I-He" as previously in 6.25-59 for the Crowds and "the Jews", it is clear, in 6.60-66, that (1) "I-He" gets the last word in 6.65b ("no one can come to me unless it is granted him by the Father") despite about even usage of (2) "I-You" (6.63, 65a) and (3) "You-He" (6.62).

Like the Crowds and "the Jews", the departing Disciples lose their "You" into "He who..." ("no one...unless...").

(e) *The Twelve.* In 6.67-71 the dialogue is exclusively I-You with nothing of either "I-He" or "You-He". But I am not inclined to read this as a terminal exaltation of "I-You" over the other forms of dialogue in John 6. First, there is the evident and supreme approbation contained in the reiterated "I-He" expressions noted above. Second, there is the fact that 6.67-71 is very deliberately open to the future of the Gospel as a whole. This derives not only from the instability effected by the positive and negative poles of "*Simon* Peter" in 6.60 and "Judas the son of *Simon* Iscariot" in 6.71, but also from the fact that, at this stage, we do not know what it might mean "to betray him".

In conclusion, then, the Narrative-Discourse Actant, the I of Jesus has taken over the Discourse completely; but, the most important recipient of this dialogue is "I-He", so that it is the "He who..." that is the counterpart of the "I" of Jesus.

C. Narrative Actions and Discourse Actions

A very similar process takes place between Narrative and Discourse Actions as that just seen for Narrative and Discourse Actants.

(1) The Presence of Discourse Actions

There were two Narrative Actions considered earlier: Moving and Feeding. In the Discourse two new Discourse Actions are introduced. But these are not new in the way that the added Discourse Actants (God, Son of Man, etc.) were new, that is, not previously mentioned in the Narrative. They are new because they are the transcendental equivalents of the earlier Narrative Actions of Moving and Feeding. The Discourse Actions are transcendental Moving and transcendental Feeding. But, as with the Discourse Actants, once these Discourse Actions are introduced they dominate both the Narrative and the Discourse by absorbing and consuming the Narrative Actions within themselves.

(a) Narrative Moving and Discourse Moving

In discussing the Narrative Action of Moving above, I distinguished between Moving in Space and Moving between Actants. So also here with Discourse Moving.

1. Discourse Moving in Space

Narrative Moving in Space was rather uniform: Jesus and the Disciples (6.1-3), and then the Crowds (6.2,5) crossed the sea; the Disciples and Jesus (6.16-21), and the Crowds (6.22-25) crossed it back again.

But the new Discourse Moving separates Jesus from all the others, intersecting, as it were, all such horizontal movements with its own radical verticality. This Discourse Moving involves Jesus' descending and reascending back to heaven:

descending: 6.33, 38, 41, 42, 50, 51, 58 (see also 46)

reascending: 6.62

This then becomes the primary Moving and it overshadows completely any geographical movements by Jesus or the others.

2. Discourse Moving among Actants

In similar fashion another and superior Moving subsumes the movements of either Crowds to Jesus or of Jesus to the Disciples. Any Moving to Jesus must be a "coming" (6.35-37, 44, 65) which is "given" (6.37, 39) or "drawn" (6.44) or "granted" (6.65) by God. Only one who has "heard and learned from the Father comes to me" (6.45). Even more significantly, not even a choice by Jesus himself precludes this imperative: "Did I not choose you, the twelve, and one of you is a devil" (6.70). Neither the Crowds' coming to Jesus nor Jesus' coming to the Disciples is what counts since all such Narrative Moving is controlled absolutely by a far more profound and transcendental Discourse Moving.

(b) Narrative Feeding and Discourse Feeding

The second major Narrative Action was Feeding. As one moves into Discourse one is prepared for a rather obvious parallel between feeding and teaching, between bread and revelation. This would be an obvious development of 6.1-15 (feeding, bread) and 6.16-21 (teaching, revelation). One is quite prepared for a relationship between Narrative and Discourse along the following lines. In Narrative: (1) Source of Food, (2) Feeder, (3) Feeding, (4) Food, (5) Consumption of Food, (6) Consumer, (7) Bodily Life, will beget a parallelism in Discourse of (1') Source of Revelation, (2') Revealer, (3') Revealing, (4') Revelation, (5') Belief, (6') Believer, (7') Eternal Life. But this is not all that happens. Still, what does happen is in complete continuity with the fundamental process whereby Discourse has been steadily absorbing and consuming the Narrative and where the only Narrative element (Actants and Actions) not already thus consumed is the Narrative-Discourse Actant, the "I" of Jesus. But it would be impossible to emphasise too much the paradoxical nature of this final consumption since it is the "I" of Jesus that demands that the "I" be consumed. Thus even, or especially, here the absolute and unqualified "I AM" of 6.20 is still dominant, even over "I AM to be consumed" in 6.51-58.

The steps of the process whereby the Feeder becomes the Food are both deliberate and obvious:

1. The first step is 6.25-34 and the message is soothingly acceptable. God will give you the true bread from heaven which ensures eternal life. What can anyone respond but: "Lord, give us this bread always" (6.34).

2. The second step is 6.35-48 (in a giant chiasm between 6.35a and 6.48 with the centre at 6.42a) and now the Discourse turns problematic but not yet as problematic as it will be later. This bread is now identified with the "I" of Jesus. Feeder and Food are equated. The response now is murmuring and questioning (6.41-42). But the situation is not yet desperate. At this point it is still possible to hear Jesus metaphorically. If he is heavenly bread, one could see it as a metaphorical expression that he is not only Revealer (Feeder) but Revelation (Food). The call for *consumption* would still be metaphorical and would mean *acceptance* of the Revealer as the Revelation.

3. The third step is in 6.49-58 and it may be summarised as follows:

6.49-50	Bread/Eat	
6.51-52	I/Bread/Eat/My Flesh	
6.53-56		Eat/Flesh//Drink/Blood [four times]
6.57	I/	/Eat/Me
6.58	Bread/Eat	

The outer frames of 6.49-50 and 6.58 do not really go beyond the development of the second step in 6.35-48. The next inner frames of 6.51-52 and 6.57 already go beyond this by insisting outside metaphorical tolerances that the bread, which is Jesus, must be *eaten*. But it is the inner core of 6.53-56 that makes it clear that something beyond metaphor is happening.

In a formulaic, hypnotic, and almost rhapsodic repetition the phrases, Eat/Flesh//Drink/Blood, move the Discourse beyond any interpretation in terms of merely *accepting (eating)* the Revealer.

I would summarise the total development so far as follows:

6.25-34	Bread
6.35-48	I/Bread
6.49-58	I/Bread/Eat Me
	Eat/My Flesh//Drink/My Blood

Two questions must now be asked. First, what is the meaning of this fourfold repetition of Eat/Flesh//Drink/Blood? Second, why is it placed precisely here in John 6?

The language of 6.49-58 is explicable only in terms of eucharistic formulae known from outside this chapter but it is even more startling than the similar formulaic repetitions in I Cor. 11.27-29 (eat/bread// drink/cup). This furnishes four main points: it is formulaic, eucharistic language; it is extremely more *realistic* than is usual elsewhere for such formulae; it is addressed to the murmuring and debating Crowds/ "Jews"; it is not reacted to by them but by the Disciples among whom it causes a division (6.60-66).

It is the reaction of the Disciples that must come first in interpretation since John omits here any reaction from the Crowds/"Jews". To the murmuring Disciples Jesus says: "'Do you take offence at this? Then what if you were to see the Son of man ascending where he was before?'" (6.61b-62). At first glance the logic of this question is not very compelling. If one presumes that *ascension* means some sort of great triumphant manifestation, then belief would be rendered easier rather than harder by witnessing it. But if ascension means crucifixion, then the logic is clarified. So also is the basic meaning of 6.51-58. Jesus is announcing there that to accept him is to accept the one who must die, who must die by the violent separation of body and blood, that is, as we shall only know later, by crucifixion. But it is also to insist that such acceptance is the only way that acceptance will ever after be possible. In other words: I am always the one to be consumed. Hence, of course, the double mention of betrayal (6.64, 70-71) follows the mention of crucifixion-ascension (6.62).

Thus the primary function of the eucharistic language is to indicate a split in eucharistic understanding, that is, in the permanent acceptance of crucifixion, among the Disciples. Jesus must always be accepted as the Crucified One. What the alternative to crucifixion-eucharist might be is not indicated within this chapter (parousia-eucharist?).

But the unit in 6.51-58 is expressly addressed to the Crowds/"Jews" who do not react to it after 6.59 while the Disciples to whom it is not specifically addressed are the ones who respond to it, both negatively and positively. For John "the Jews" are those who will deny and reject the divine necessity of this crucifixional destiny and by so doing render it inevitable. *The supreme irony is that, for John, those who reject crucifixion theoretically will thereby effect it politically.* Hence, although addressed to "the Jews", their final reaction is not recorded yet. But it is reacted to immediately by some of the Disciples now because even though they will not effect the crucifixion, they will deny its permanent and enduring, that is, its eucharistic necessity.

VI. SCRIPT

This final section will, first, sum up what has happened so far, and, second, draw attention to what is the most obvious facet of the text and therefore is almost always overlooked: *it is written.*

A. *Time, Space Narrative, Discourse*

John 6 is not just composed of a simple balance of Narrative (6.1-24) whose physicality symbolises what the succeeding Discourse (6.25-71) renders spiritual and transcendental. It is characterised by layers of text whose successive levels dominate and absorb the previous ones. In view of the text's dominant motif of eating it seems necessary to characterise this process as *consumption*.

There exists first of all the consumption of the Time, Space, Narrative and Discourse of the Jewish Passover experience by the Time, Space, Narrative and Discourse of a universal "Passover" phenomenon. Thus the Time of 6.4 is universalised into day-night-day and the Space sequence of crossing the sea, ascending and descending the mountain, and entering the synagogue is negated by having the sea recrossed, the mountain reascended, and the synagogue exited. The narrative of the Feeding in 6.1-15 transcendes the Exodus feeding stories as the Dialogue makes explicit in 6.31-33, 49, 58. And now the murmurings of the Crowds or Disciples is not about the narrative on Feeding as it was during the Exodus but about the very Discourse itself (6.41, 52, 60-61).

There is also, however, the consumption of the Time, Space, and Narrative of this universalised "Passover" by the Discourse which accompanies them.

Most specifically there is the consumption of the text's receiver within the collectivity of the "He Who..."

Finally, and most importantly, there is the consumption *by* the text's receiver (as "He Who...") *of* the "I" of Jesus, whose absolute "I AM" (6.20) will nevertheless transcent both "I am the bread" (6.35, 48, 51a) and "I am to be consumed" (6.51b-57).

B. *It Is Written*

The Crowds, representing the Jewish Passover experience, and Jesus, advocating its transcendence, both invoke the biblical writings as support. In 6.31 the Crowds, talking of physical feeding, say: "It is written, 'He gave them bread from heaven to eat.'" And in 6.45, Jesus, speaking of spiritual feeding, says: "*It is written* in the prophets, 'And they shall all be taught by God.'" Thus the twin poles of the Discourse alike appeal to "it is written".

This central and double appeal to Scripture, and thus to *script*, force us to face what we are carefully avoiding in studying this "oral{ Discourse, namely, the most obvious and invisible fact about the Narrative and Discourse in John 6: *it is written*. Peter is absolutely correct in saying to Jesus: "'You have the words of eternal life'" (6.68b) but we, the readers, know them only as written, as script, and we know even Peter's oral confession only as written, as script.

At this point I am beginning to glimpse a question which renders the laborious structural analysis at least personally worthwhile because it has unearthed a hermeneutical issue which historical analysis did not and presumably could not uncover.

Is it of any significance that we read John 6 as *script* rather than see and hear "it' happen as event? When John 1.14 says that "the Word became flesh" and John 6.63 adds that "the flesh is of no avail," should we conclude that the Word of God became flesh and voice in order finally to become script: "the Word became script"? There, presumably, is the hermeneutical heart: is the Word of God oral or scribal or both, and, if both, are there differences and heirarchies to be maintained within that answer? Or does the Word of God have a history wherein it was originally oral and thence became scribal and what differences and heirarchies exist between such stages: oral (lost forever?), oral-scribal, and pure scribal? And is that the end of such an historical development? At this point we can sense the questions reaching out to envelope our contemporary selves. Does it make any difference that I am asking these questions in script and that you are reading them from script and how can we either ask or answer them without inevitable paradox? How could we proclaim in script the primacy of orality?

But in raising these questions I recognise that I am far from being alone. For this precise problem there is already

> a community of the question, therefore, within that fragile moment when the question is not yet determined enough for the hypocrisy of an answer already for an answer to have initiated itself beneath the mask of the question, and not yet determined enough for its vice to have been already and fraudulently articulated within the very syntax of the question. A community of decision, of initiative, of absolute initiality, but also a threatened community, in which the question has not yet found the language it has decided to seek, is not yet sure of its own possibility within the community. A community of the question about the possibility of the question.[1]

The brilliant polarities of the community of this question are represented by the writings of Walter Ong[2] and Jacques Derrida.[3] Ong

---

[1] Jacques Derrida, *Writing and Difference*, p. 80.

[2] Walter J. Ong, *The Presence of the Word*, (New Haven, CT: Yale University Press, 1967); *Rhetoric, Romance and Technology*, (Ithaca, NY: Cornell University Press, 1971); *Interfaces with the Word*, (Ithaca, NY: Cornell University Press, 1977). A magnificent section of that last book, pp. 230-71, has been reprinted as "Maranatha: Death and Life in the Text of the Book", *JAAR*, 45 (December 1977), pp, 419-49.

[3] Besides the collection noted in the first footnote above, see also, "White Mythology: Metaphor in the Text of Philosophy", *New Literary History*, 6 (1974), pp. 5-74; and *Of*

argues for the primacy of oral over scribal communication basing himself primarily on the historical primordiality of speech over script in both the species and the child. This is, however, a very dangerous argument since logically it would give an even more elevated and primordial value to the gurgle and the grunt. It is also anomalous that Ong never seems at all self-conscious in *writing* about the primacy of orality or even in citing the Scriptures in support of this primordiality. Derrida, who has the advantage of a single word, *écriture*, meaning both writing and Scripture, argues for the philosophic primordiality of *écriture* since script reveals more fully, openly and honestly the absence and deferment at the heart of the sign, of all signs of course, but which the presence of the speaker disguises in oral conversation while the absence of the writer proclaims it in scribal dialogue.

Holding, for here and now, the discussion exclusively to oral and scribal communication and bracketing the far more compelling problem of electronic communication (of Derrida one must ask: does the videotape of a dead lover reveal presence or absence, or does it, by intensifying the illusion of presence, intensify even more devastatingly the experience of absence?), I find that John 6 seems more adequately understood through Derrida than through Ong, and for two reasons.

First, if the "words" of Jesus are a mystery of spirit and life (6.63b, 68), wherein what must always be consumed must always be there to be consumed anew, does this not apply more to the scribal than the oral Word of God?

Second, the discourse in John 6 is in dialogue format and the dialogue is one of question and answer. What could be more oral than question and answer since questioner and answerer must be mutually present to one another? But these questions in John 6 seem to receive non-answers or pseudo-answers. I think this is empirically verifiable since if one lined up all the questions in one column and all their answers in another, juggled a column, one could hardly line them up properly without prior knowledge of John 6. Here is a list of questions and "answers" in John 6:

Grammatology, trans. by Gayatri Chakravorty Spivak (Baltimore, MD: The Johns Hopkins University Press, 1976).

Question	Answer	Non-Answer	Counter-Question
6.5		6.7	
6.9		6.10	
6.25		6.26	
6.28	6.29		
6.30 (two)		6.30-33(?)	
6.42 (two)		6.43	
6.52		6.53	
6.60			6.61-62 (two)
6.67			6.68a
6.70			

There are twelve questions of which only two receive real answers; eight receive non-answers; two receive counter-questions; and one, the final word of Jesus, is a question which, in receiving no answer, terminates the Discourse. In authentic aural dialogue such "answers" would soon generate protest and demand for real answers.

Thus John 6 creates the illusion of orality and the entire Discourse proceeds through questions and pseudo-answers. The one exception is, of course, the "I AM; do not be afraid" of 6.20, but that is an exception to everything, and even that is now script and only script. Tentatively, then, John 6 moves towards this: the Word of God is script.

C. Script and Eternal Life

Throughout 6.25-71 Jesus promises both eternal life and a raising up on the last day. "Life" is mentioned in 6.33, 35, 48, 51, 53, 57, 63; "eternal life" in 6.27, 47, 51, 58, 68; "raising up" in 6.39, 44; and the last two terms are combined together in 6.40, 54. Read together the promise is of eternal life here and now immediately as well as the promise that death will not affect the individual believer who will be raised up on the individual's last day. As used in John 6, it does not seem possible that "the last day" could refer specifically to a cosmic eschaton, else the believer would have to be "dead" for the period before its advent. But that, of course, would require further discussion in the light of the entire gospel.

But the far more important point to be noted is how the Discourse Actants are reflected in this promise. It is *never* said to anyone in John 6 by Jesus: "if *you* believe, eat, drink, etc... I will give *you* eternal life and I will raise *you* up on the last day." As noted before, the discourse "I" of Jesus subsumes all other titles and even Jesus himself, but the recipients of eternal life are not a "you" but a "he who".

And all of this endures only in script, for us here and now it endures only in script. In script, then, the Discourse "I" of Jesus remains eternally but the believer, even in script, obtains eternal life not as a personal "you"

but within the community of a "he who..." In the words of the script, "As
te Father sent *me*, and *I* live because of the Father, so *he who* eats me will
live because of me" (6.57).

D. Gathering the Fragments

I have held until last one unit of text not previously discussed but
singularly striking in its emphasis. "And when they had eaten their fill, he
told his disciples, 'Gather up the fragments left over, that nothing may be
lost.' So they gathered them up and filled twelve baskets with fragments
from the five barley loaves, left by those who had eaten" (6.12-13). It is
useful at this point, as so often throughout this paper, to keep an eye on
Mark, not in terms of sources but simply as a variation on the same story.
Mark 6.41b-43 says: "and he divided the two fish among them all. And
they all ate and were satisfied. And *they* took up twelve baskets full of
broken pieces and of the fish." Note the vagueness of Mark's *they*. Thus
John is very different from Mark, in that he has: (1) an explicit command
from Jesus to gather the fragments; (2) the command is explicitly to his
disciples; (3) the reason is also given by Jesus: "that nothing may be lost";
(4) the disciples explicitly gather only the bread and not the fish. But
there is something even more striking in John and that is the way these
"twelve baskets" at the start of the chapter in 6.13 force a linkage with the
previously unmentioned "twelve" disciples at the end of the text in 6.67-
71. One therefore presumes that there is one basket for each of the twelve
disciples who stay with Jesus after the others depart.

It is impossible to read the text of John in terms of respect for either
the pastoral site or the divine gift. The former would demand even
greater concern for the fish fragments and the latter would demand at
least equal care for both. It is only of the bread that nothing must be lost,
and the bread, with the fish quietly forgotten, becomes the discourse "I"
of Jesus. It is, then, the fragments of Jesus which must be gathered so that
nothing may be lost.

THE WOOING OF THE WOMAN AT THE WELL:
JESUS, THE READER AND READER-RESPONSE CRITICISM*

LYLE ESLINGER

The history of the critical study of the Bible shows a time-honoured tradition of methodological borrowing and cross-fertilisation from other disciplines. From historians biblical scholars have learned about history and they have adapted the tools of historical analysis to study events in the Bible. From folklorists they have learned about traditional stories and the means by which such stories are created, adapted, and transmitted from generation to generation. Classicists' studies of the Homeric sagas have been profitably turned to the study of the patriarchal cycles in Genesis. And from literary theory and criticism especially, biblicists' understanding of the whole range of biblical literature has been improved.

Contemporary study of European and English literature has gone through at least three distinct phases: Historical Criticism, in which the text is examined as a representative product of specific social, political, and historical contexts; a "New Critical" or Formalist phase, both reactionary movements devoted to the study of the text as an independent artistic object, comprehensible in and of itself; and recently, among other things, Reader-Response Criticism which shifts the focus of attention to the reader and the question of how the text creates and/or is created by reading activity. In biblical studies we are beginning to see a shift from strictly historical concerns to those of the New Critics. Major concern for the reader's influence on interpretation remains largely over the horizon.

Yet the fact that the Bible has a long history of use as Scripture—normative literature—argues for an awareness of the demands it makes on its readers, the literary devices it uses to make such demands, and the possible response(s) that any given piece of Scripture may give rise to.[1] Especially in the New Testament we see an effort to persuade the reader to do or desist from this or that, to believe this or reject that. In the

---

* This article appeared in *Literature and Theology* 1/1 (1987), pp. 167-83.
[1] Cf. J. Faur, "Some General Observations on the Character of Classical Jewish Literature: A Functional Approach", *Journal of Jewish Studies* 27 (1977), p. 32.

gospels the reader is a privileged onlooker, guest of an external, unconditioned narrator—a so-called "omniscient" narrator—watching characters within the story. As the reader observes, the characters are exhorted, usually by Jesus, to do or believe this or that. Alternatively, and here we approach the topic of reader-response, the characters are presented as believing or knowing something, or as failing to believe or know something. The reader, who usually knows the truth of the matter thanks to the narrator, is consequently led to evaluate the characters. That evaluation is the reader's response. The literary means used to guide such response are what I would like to look at, using the story in John 4 as an example.

Modern readers of the story about the woman at the well have called attention to three features: first, the story seems to be modelled on a recurring Old Testament story about a meeting between a man and a woman at a well (Gen 24; 29; Exod 2; cf. 1 Sam 9); second, there are a number of double entendres in the vocabulary used by Jesus and the woman; and third, there seems to be a gap in the logic and topic of conversation beginning with v. 16, where the conversation switches from water and drinking to the Messiah and Jewish religion. In order to understand reader response in John 4 one must first understand the meaning of these three features, since they are the literary means that shape that response.

I. THE BETROTHAL TYPE-SCENE

In the Old Testament there are at least three instances of a scene in which a man and a woman meet at a well, resulting in their betrothal.[1] Though each instance of the type-scene has its own contextual peculiarities there is a pattern of similarities and the scene in John 4 shapes these likenesses.[2] By modelling the story on a type-scene familiar to his readers from scripture, the author of chapter 4 is able to draw on the meaning of prior instances to guide his reader's understanding of the meeting between Jesus and the Samaritan woman. Because the previous occurrences of such a meeting always result in the betrothal of the two characters, the reader is

---

[1] So described by R. Alter, *The Art of Biblical Narrative* (London: George Allen & Unwin, 1981), pp. 50-51.

[2] See J. Bligh, "Jesus in Samaria", *Heythrop Journal* 3 (1962), p. 332; A. Jaubert, "La Symbolique du Puits de Jacob Jean 4.12", *L'Homme devant Dieu. Mélanges offerts au Père Henri de Lubac. Théologie* 56 (Paris, 1963), pp. 70-71; M.-E. Boismard, "Aenon, Près de Salem", *Révue Biblique* 80 (1973), pp. 223-26; N. R. Bonneau, "The Woman at the Well, John 4 and Genesis 24", *Bible Today* 67 (1973), pp. 1252-59; J.H. Neyrey, "Jacob Traditions and the Interpretation of John 4.10-26", *CBQ* 41 (1979), pp. 425-26; C.M. Carmichael, "Marriage and the Samaritan Woman", *NTS* 26 (1980), pp. 336-38; P.J. Cahill, "Narrative Art in John IV", *Religious Studies Bulletin* 2 (1982), pp. 45-46.

led to believe that this fourth instance will have the same result. The narrator need only allude to a single item or pattern to evoke the entire configuration of associations attached to the type-scene. Such allusions may take the form of vocabulary links, parallels in phrasing sequence, in sequence of events or conversational patterns, in geographical settings, or parallels in itineraries.[1]

The betrothal type-scene, with the relevant verses from John 4 in brackets, is:

i.   The future bridegroom (or surrogate) journeys to a foreign land (vv. 1-6).

ii. There he meets a girl, usually described as a "maiden" (na'arâ) at a well (vv. 6-7).

iii. Someone, the man or the maiden, draws water from the well (vv. 7-15).

iv. The maiden rushes home to bring news of the stranger (vv. 28-30, 39-42).

v.   A betrothal is arranged, usually after the prospective groom has been invited to a betrothal meal (vv. 31-38).[2]

In the gospel version parts 3 and 5 are radically altered. No water is drawn. There is no betrothal, nor is there a betrothal meal. These differences are keys to an understanding of how the author is manipulating this literary convention and with it his reader's response.

In addition to the overall pattern of the type-scene the author also alludes to specific items from each of the three Old Testament instances:

i.   Vv. 1, 3, 6 (Exod 2.14-15): like Moses, Jesus believes that the Pharisees (cf. Pharaoh) have heard about his actions and he leaves his country to avoid them. On his journey in a foreign land he sits down by a well and there meets a girl.

ii. V. 6b (Gen 29.7)[3] Both Jacob and Jesus come to the well at noon.

iii. Vv. 7, 9 (Gen 24.17-18). Like Eliezer, Jesus says give me a drink. Unlike Rebekah, the Samaritan woman does not immediately comply.

---

[1] Cf. Alter op. cit. 51. R. Culley has tabulated the parallels between the Old Testament instances of the type-scene in *Studies in the Structure of Hebrew Narrative* (Philadelphia/Missoula: Scholars Press, 1976), p. 42. The case for the inclusion of John 4.1-30 alongside the others is presented in tabular form by Boismard *op. cit.*, pp. 223-24, and Bonneau *op. cit.,* p. 1254.

[2] Alter, *op. cit.,* p. 52.

[3] Though the actual time of day signified by ὥρα ἦν ὡς ἕκτη is uncertain, it is probable that "the sixth hour" refers to noon. Cf. C.K. Barrett, *The Gospel According to St John* (London: SPCK, 1955), 194; R. Bultmann, *The Gospel of John* (Philadelphia: Westminster, 1971), p. 178.

The type-scene in John 4 functions exclusively on the level of communication between the author and the reader; the characters are not addressed by it. The type-scene is a device that the author uses to guide the reader's perception of what is happening in the story. The reader is intended to believe that Jesus and the Samaritan are moving towards betrothal.[1]

II. DOUBLE ENTENDRE

Supplementing the influence of the type-scene are a number of double entendres made by the two characters in conversation. The reader's recognition of the double entendres, all of which have sexual overtones, leads to the belief that both characters are engaging in a bit of covert verbal coquetry. The formal suggestiveness of the betrothal type-scene is supported from within the story by the characters, whose interaction seems to have an implicit sexual orientation. Because of the nature of a double entendre—a word that conveys an indelicate meaning under cover of an innocent one—the responsibility for perceiving a sexual undertone rests solely with the beholder. Neither the reader nor the characters can be certain that what they hear is what was meant. For the reader this ambiguity means that he may wrongly attribute carnal interests to one or both characters and that his perception may reflect his concerns and values, not the characters'. But given the authorial encouragement by means of the type-scene (contextual suitability), the apparent confirmation in the responses within the conversation (sexual overtones being answered in kind), and the initial lack of any sexual interest disclaimers from either character, the reader is free to entertain a reading that incorporates the sexual overtones and implications of the double entendres.

As with the type-scene, the reader's understanding of the double entendres comes from the Old Testament:

1. To Drink Water from a Cistern or Well

With a strong, euphemistic sense, the expression appears in a warning against promiscuity in Proverbs 5.15-18.

15. Drink water from your own cistern, flowing water (πηγῆς) from your own well (φρεάτων).
16. Should your springs (ὕδατα ἐκ τῆς σῆς πηγῆς) be dispersed abroad, streams of water in the streets?
17. Let them be yours alone, and not for strangers with you.

---

[1] Cf. Carmichael, *op. cit.*, p. 338.

18. Let your fountain (ἡ πηγή σου) be blessed, and rejoice in the wife of
your youth .

To drink water from a well or cistern obviously refers to sexual
relations; the reader is exhorted to conjugate only with his wife (cf. vv.
18-19).[1] The "springs" of v. 16 seem to refer to the male's semen; the
"well" of v. 15 and the "fountain" of v. 18, on the other hand, seem to
refer to physical features of the female (cf. πηγή in Lev 12:7; 20:18).

2. Living Water

In the Old Testament this expression is used in two separate ways, a
situation inviting double entendre. "Living water" can refer to spring
water (Gen 26.19) and is best translated "flowing water" (cf. LXX Gen
21.19). A derivative metaphoric usage equates God (Ps 36.9; Jer 2:13),
the mouth of the righteous (Prov 10.11), the fear of the Lord (Prov
14.27), and so on with the fountain of life, a source of refreshment to
righteous humanity.

On the other hand, living water has sexual connotations in Jer 2.13 .
The water imagery of this verse parallels that of Proverbs 5.15-18 and
Canticles 4.12, 15.[2] The immediate context is one of condemnation of
Israel's unfaithfulness to its spouse, Yahweh (e.g. 2.2, 24, 32; 3.1-5, 20).
In 2.13 Jeremiah accuses Israel of sexual promiscuity using the
euphemistic claim that it has "hewn its own cisterns" (cf. Prov 5.15)
instead of drinking water from Yahweh, the fountain of living water.
Israel has done what Proverbs 5.15-18 advises against.

In Canticles 4.12 the writer describes his sister as a locked garden, a
sealed fountain—she is a virgin.[3] In v. 15 the writer continues in the same
vein; the female is a garden fountain (πηγὴ κῆπον) a well (φρέαρ) of
living water. The literary device here is double entendre; the expressions
can be taken as euphemisms and metaphors. The terms for a water supply

---

[1] W. McKane, *Proverbs* (Philadelphia: Westminster, 1970), p. 318.
[2] Cf. M. DeRoche, "Israel's 'Two Evils' in Jeremiah 11.13", *Vetus Testamentum* 31
(1981), pp. 369-72 and the gloss in Proverbs 9.17-18d (LXX), which follows an admonition
against association with loose women:
17. Bread secretly eaten is sweet, and purloined water delightful.
18. But he does not know that mortals are undone by it, and meet the gates of Hades.
18a. Turn away; do not linger in the area; do not let your eye gaze at her.
18b. Step across another man's water; and pass by another's river.
18c. Abstain from someone else's water and do not drink from another's fountain.
18d. So you may live long and add more life to yourself.
The fact that the *LXX* glossator chooses to explain the subject of "stolen water" with
euphemistic hydrological admonitions shows that the euphemism was known and
understood even in a non-Israelite cultural context.
[3] M. Pope, *Song of Songs* (New York: Doubleday, 1977), p. 488; cf. E. Ullendorff, "The
Bawdy Bible", *Bulletin: School of Oriental and African Studies* 42 (1979), pp. 449-50.

are used in the same way as in Prov 5: 5-18.[1] The fountain of living water differs from the simple fountain of water in its intimations of fecundity, an aspect of female sexuality celebrated throughout the book of Canticles (e.g. 4.13-14).

3. Springs, Wells, and Fountains

Further demonstration of euphemistic usage is unnecessary. For πηγή (spring, fountain) see Lev 12.7; 20.18; Prov 5.15, 16, 18; 9.18c (LXX); Canticles 4.12, 15; Jer 2.13; for φρέαρ (cistern, well) see Proverbs 5.15; 23.27; Canticles 4.15. Though fountain or well usually refers to female sexuality it can also be applied to males (Prov 5.16; Jer 2.13).[2] Literary devices such as euphemism and double entendre are suggestive, not explicit, and demand flexibility from the reader in reception of the suggestion.

III. DISCOURSE STRUCTURE

Readers have frequently remarked on the intricate literary artistry of John 4,[3] but descriptions have been limited to large, thematically based categorisations of the entire chapter.[4] The narrator himself offers a more detailed analysis of the conversation in the form of the introductory tags that he attaches to each character's statements.

---

[1] Pope (ibid., p. 489) summarises a number of traditional interpretations that find euphemism in v. 12. Oddly, Pope fails to recognise the double entendre in "living water" despite his erotic interpretation of the immediate context and his awareness of the euphemistic use of "fountain" in v. 12.

[2] More detailed discussion of the exact anatomical features alluded to is provided by McKane (op cit., p. 318-19), who surveys various suggestions.

[3] E.g. Bligh op. cit.; M.P. Hogan, "The Woman at the Well (John 4.1-42)", *Bible Today* p. 82 (1976); Cahill op. cit.

[4] F. Roustang, "Les moments de l'acte de foi et ses conditions de possibilité", *Recherches de Science Religieuse*, p. 46 (1958), 345; Bligh op. cit., pp. 329-31; Hogan op. cit., pp. 665-66.

	7b.	λέγει αὐτῇ ὁ Ἰησοῦς
	9.	λέγει οὖν αὐτῷ ἡ γυνὴ ἡ Σαμαρεῖτις
	10.	ἀπεκρίθη Ἰησοῦς καὶ εἶπεν αὐτῇ
	11.	λέγει αὐτῷ ἡ γυνὴ
	13.	ἀπεκρίθη Ἰησοῦς καὶ εἶπεν αὐτῇ
	15.	λέγει πρὸς αὐτὸν ἡ γυνή
	16.	λέγει αὐτῇ
	17a.	ἀπεκρίθη ἡ γυνὴ καὶ εἶπεν αὐτῷ
	17b.	λέγει αὐτῇ ὁ Ἰησοῦς
	19.	λέγει αὐτῷ ἡ γυνὴ
	21.	λέγει αὐτῇ ὁ Ἰησοῦς
	25.	λέγει αὐτῷ ἡ γυνὴ
	26.	λέγει αὐτῇ ὁ Ἰησοῦς

Jesus opens and closes each half of the conversation. The first segment is devoted to the topic of wells, water, and drinking; here we find the exchange of double entendres. Jesus's directive in v. 16 seems off topic and creates the disruption that divides the conversation in half.[1] It is, nevertheless, an excellent riposte to the woman's coquettish double entendres. The subsequent change to the topic of worship is a result of Jesus' bringing the implicit sexuality of the first topic to the surface. The woman tries to rescue herself from embarrassment (v. 17a) but when Jesus persists (v. 17b) she changes the topic altogether. The major division in the conversation is thus a meaningful development that can only be understood in the light of the sexual content implicit in vv. 7-15.

But how do all of these literary devices work to affect the reader? Before that question can be answered the reader's preparation through John 1-3 must be reviewed. The reader comes to the story of the woman at the well already educated by chapters 1-3. In the prologue (1.1-18) the narrator introduces the divine, eternal Logos who comes down to the level of phenomena—"the Logos became flesh and dwelt among us" (v. 14)—and is announced to humanity by John, a man sent from God (vv. 6, 15). Then the narrator identifies the incarnate Logos as Jesus, the Christ

---

[1] Many readers have tried to resolve the abrupt disjunction that they see in v. 16 by suggesting that Jesus (or the author) was attempting to expose, allegorically speaking, the religious infidelity of the Samaritans as symbolised by the woman's promiscuity. "Jesus is not simply exposing the woman's individual matrimonial maladjustment; he is exhibiting...the religious situation of the Samaritan people" (J Marsh, *Saint John*. (Harmondsworth: Penguin, 1968)), p. 214; cf. C.H. Dodd, *The Interpretation of the Fourth Gospel* (Cambridge: CUP 1953), p. 313; Bligh op. cit., pp. 335-36; Boismard op. cit., p. 225; Bonneau op. cit., p. 1258. The allegorical explanation is rejected by Bultmann (op. cit., p. 187) who explains that Jesus switches subjects simply to demonstrate his own omniscience (cf. Neyrey op. cit., p. 426 n. 29). Roustang (op. cit., pp. 360-61) provides a third perspective with a psychological explanation in terms of Jesus's efforts to convert the woman.

(v. 17). The prologue is the external, unconditioned narrator's definition, addressed to the reader alone, of Jesus' identity. It also explains how a more limited knowledge about him comes into the world through John.

In 1.19-28 we see an encounter between John, the man from God, and religious officials of the Jews, who are confused about his identity and mission. John declares that he is only a messenger announcing the advent of one, greater than himself, who is as yet unknown to them (v. 26).

In 1.29-34 John sees Jesus, recognises him only because God reveals to John that Jesus is the one he was sent to announce, and proclaims that Jesus is the hitherto unknown one (v. 30), the Son of God (v. 34).

The results of the proclamation follow (1.35-51). Hearing John's inspired testimony, two of his own disciples follow Jesus and address him as Rabbi (v. 38). One of these two then tells his brother that they have found the Messiah (Christ, v. 41). John's testimony has produced its first correct, second generation identification of Jesus. In v. 43 Jesus calls Philip to follow him, but he does not identify himself. Philip then tells Nathanael that they have found Jesus of Nazareth, of whom Moses and the Prophets wrote (v. 45). Philip's own failure to identify Jesus results in an unspecific testimony to Nathanael, who consequently questions the possibility of any good coming from Nazareth (v. 46). But Nathanael's misunderstanding about Jesus is removed when Jesus demonstrates his supernatural power. Nathanael then addresses Jesus as "Rabbi" and correctly identifies him as Son of God and king of Israel (v. 49).

Without the inspired testimony of John it takes a miracle for Nathanael to know who Jesus is; this is the first of several incidents that reveal the human characters' inability to understand who Jesus is, or what he means when he speaks, or what his interests and goals are.

In chapter 2 the reader views two more instances of such misunderstanding, once on the part of Jesus's own mother and once more on the part of "the Jews" (v. 18). These repeated misconceptions are examples of the theme announced by the narrator in the prologue, "He was in the world... and the world knew him not" (v. 10; cf. vv. 5, 11). When Jesus' mother tells him at a wedding that they have run out of wine, a simple observation, he snaps back that his hour has not yet come (v. 4). Though the reader does not yet know what hour it is that Jesus refers to (cf. 7:6, 8, 30; 8:20), it is clear that Jesus' reading of his mother's statement is made from a different conceptual context.[1] Instead of

---

[1] A retrospective Christian reader would, of course, immediately recognise that Jesus refers to his hour of death and perceives the request for wine as a request for his atoning blood, which is symbolised by the wine at the last supper. The disguised allusion even continues through to v. 10. Jesus uses the waterpots used for Jewish purification (from sin), has them filled with water, and then turns it into wine. The head waiter's remark that the best

explaining the communication gap the narrator focuses the reader's attention on the simple fact that there is a conceptual gap, even between Jesus and his own mother. Human characters do not see as Jesus; and the gospel reiterates an old theme from the prophet Isaiah but applies it to Jesus:

> For my thoughts are not your thoughts,
> And your ways are not my ways. (Isa 55.8)

In the second instance Jesus, following a confrontation with the Jews over the correct use of the Temple, says that he could raise the Temple in three days if it were destroyed (v. 19). The Jews naturally think he refers to the Temple building but the narrator advises the reader that Jesus was actually referring to his own body and his future resurrection (vv. 20-22). This time the reader sees the communication gap and knows why it is there. The human characters think and speak in terms of the mundane; Jesus thinks and speaks in terms of his divine origin and mission.

In chapter 3 the reader sees one more instance of this problematic gap and then John is brought back to deliver a little explanation and to prepare the reader for a first hand experience of the gap as he reads chapter 4. In chapter 4 the reading experience becomes an actual experience of the communication gap that the reader has already observed several times between the human characters in the story and Jesus.

Nicodemus, though a ruler (3:1) of the Jews, has as much difficulty understanding Jesus as all the rest. When Jesus talks about the necessity of being reborn Nicodemus is naturally incredulous. "How can a man be born when he is old? Can he enter the second time into his mother's womb, and be born?" (v. 4). Jesus explains that rebirth is necessary to

---

wine has been kept for last is a thinly veiled evaluation of the superiority of Jesus's "wine" to the waters of Jewish purification (cf. 1.17).

But in this experiment of following the course of a reader through the Gospel, I am presuming to follow a first-time reader, not already well-versed in the story or Christian theology. If one might allow, for a moment, that the gospel of John was not written with a specifically Christian audience in mind, this first-time reader would not be such an implausible intended audience for "the good news". Nevertheless, it is possible for even a jaded Christian reader with a modicum of self-awareness to follow the logic of such a reading and to receive a similar impress from it as I am suggesting for the first-time reader.

Moreover, Wayne A. Meeks has gone so far as to suggest that even educated readers of the Johannine community might be taken in by the ambiguities, ironies, and other occasions for reader response. *"The reader cannot understand any part of the Fourth Gospel until he understands the whole* [my emphasis]. Thus the reader has an experience rather like that of the dialogue partners of Jesus... *The book functions for its readers in precisely the same way that the epiphany of its hero functions within its narratives and dialogues* [Meeks' emphasis]" ("The Man from Heaven in Johannine Sectarianism", *Journal of Biblical Literature* 91 (1972), pp. 68-69). Regardless of the reader's background, says Meeks, it is designed to involve the reader in sharing some of the same confusions and misunderstandings as the characters within it.

bridge the communication gap (vv. 3, 8), which is a product of the separation between two different levels of existence, that of flesh and that of the spirit (vv. 6, 11-12). Even though he is a teacher of Israel Nicodemus's carnal understanding does not allow him to leap out of his own conceptual world (cf. 8: 23). Though Jesus does not speak in carnal terms ("we speak that which we know and bear witness of that which we have seen", v. 11), Nicodemus can understand only in such a register.

Next, the reader hears a conversation between John and his disciples in which John makes two essential points. First, John states that Jesus is drawing all the followers away from himself because Jesus is the divinely ordained bridegroom, whose followers—the bride—rightly belong to him. John himself is only the friend of the bridegroom (vv. 27-30). John's analogy encourages the reader to think about Jesus in a matrimonial manner.[1] Remembering that John is the man sent by God to announce Jesus's arrival, the reader who is guided by the typology of the betrothal scene in chapter 4 will take John's description in chapter 3 as strong support for his suspicion that Jesus might marry or have relations with the Samaritan. Second, John re-emphasises the distinction between the mind of Jesus and the mind of man. Jesus, coming from above, is above all and speaks from that context. His human audience, being of the earth, are bound to speak and understand in earthly terms—"no man receives his witness" (3.32). Moving into chapter 4 the reader will learn, at first hand, the truth of that statement.

Shifting from John at Aenon (3.23) to Jesus in Judea, a new scene opens in chapter 4. Jesus' departure from Judea to avoid confrontation with the Pharisees is modelled on Moses's flight from Egypt to escape the Pharaoh's wrath (Exod 2.14-21). Both escapees have challenged the authorities— Jesus by baptising and making converts (3.22, 26; 4.1), Moses by acting as though he were Israel's prince or judge (Exod 2.11-14)—and both subsequently sit down by a well in a foreign land where they meet a girl (Jn 4.6; Exod 2.15).[2] The outcome of Moses's flight and meeting at the well was betrothal followed by marriage. Because Jesus's movement and encounter are patterned after Moses's, the reader is led to believe that Jesus will follow the same course. The narrator's analogical description supplies the reader with information that leads the latter to entertain an idea about Jesus that is at odds with prior narratorial characterisation, but in keeping with the fallible human characters' understanding of Jesus. By allowing the reader to cross over, from an all-seeing narrative perspective to a limited human perspective on Jesus, the

---

[1] Carmichael, *op. cit.*, p. 335.

[2] Bultmann (*op. cit.*, p. 175) and Marsh (*op. cit.*, p. 203) are incorrect when they say that the itinerarian note in 4.1-3 serves merely to shuffle Jesus on to the next set in Samaria.

narrative uses reader response to involve the reader in a real experience that is much the same as that of human characters in the preceding context. To what end? Perhaps to elicit a Job-like experience of the real difference between reading about how other humans—poor fallible creatures—failed to appreciate Jesus for what he was, and an actual experiential grasp of how one, as reader, shares the same shortcomings and misunderstanding of Jesus as the Gospel characters. The reading experience moves the reader from ersatz, second-hand understanding of human failure to comprehend Jesus, to a culpable, direct share in that same failure.

> I have heard of thee by the hearing of the ear; but now mine eye seeth thee.
> Wherefore I abhor *myself*, and repent in dust and ashes (Job 42:5-6).

The allusion to the betrothal type-scene introduces the possibility that Jesus may become involved with a woman—perhaps all his treasures are not in heaven after all. The allusion, however, is a trap. The reader is baited to entertain carnal thoughts about Jesus' motives and later his meanings. But such thoughts depend on the reader's own suppositions, abetted though they may be. As a reader, he supplies the literary competence that recognises and understands the allusion; as a human being with a carnal mind he knows that marriage implies carnal knowledge and he attributes carnal interests to Jesus so long as the text allows and encourages him to do so. Reader response is thus a product of the reader's conceptual horizons—he who is of the earth speaks (and thinks) of the earth (3.31)—and the possibilities and constraints that lie in the text.

The allusion to the type-scene with reference to Moses is reinforced in v. 6 by the mention of the well of Jacob. This allusion prods the reader to recollect the associations between Jacob and a well in the Old Testament. Only one incident focuses on such an association and, not surprisingly, it is the betrothal type-scene in Gen 29. The allusion is strengthened by the narrator's statement that it was about the sixth hour when Jesus sat down at Jacob's well. A parallel temporal notice in Gen 29:7 places Jacob at the well at the same time.[1] These multiple allusions make it easy for the reader to view this scene as another incidence of the type-scene.[2]

The reader's expectations are rewarded by the entry of the Samaritan woman into the scene. The literarily predestined crossing of paths is

---

[1] Cf. J.H. Bernard, *St.John* (Edinburgh: T. & T. Clark, 1928), p. 136, who also notes that this description of Jesus, tired and resting by a well, is parallel to that of Moses resting by the Midianite well, especially in Josephus's account.

[2] As, indeed, many readers have; see Ref. 3.

foregrounded by the vocabulary and structural links between vv. 5-6 and v. 7:

vv. 5-6   ἔρχεται οὖν εἰς πόλιν τῆς Σαμαρίας...ἐαθελέζετο οὕτως
v. 7   ἔρχεται γυνὴ ἐκ τῆς Σαμαρίας...ἀντλῆσαι ὕδωρ.[1]

Events proceed as the type-scene leads the reader to expect. Jesus begins the familiar sequence with his request for a drink, just as Eliezer did when he saw Rebekah coming to the well to draw water (Gen 24.17). Jesus seems to take an active, complicit role in the unfolding of the pattern, more encouragement to the carnal mind.

In v. 8 the narrator follows Jesus's request with a comment (indicated by the conjunction γάρ) on the request. But this clarification about why Jesus asked the woman for a drink is itself ambiguous. Does he ask her for a drink because his disciples are unavailable or because he and the woman are alone and he can make free with her without damaging his reputation? The ambiguity makes the reader responsible for his own interpretation, which is, nevertheless, influenced toward the less innocent by the constant allusions to the type-scene and by Jesus's forwardness itself.[2]

Introducing the woman's reply (v. 9), the narrator draws attention to her nationality, which explains her response. She points to two facts, one political, one sexual, that make the request surprising. Jesus is a Jew, she a Samaritan; he is a man, she a woman.[3]

The woman makes her meaning clearer in her subsequent explanation.[4] She says Jews do not συνχρῶνται with Samaritans. The word

---

[1] The same structural pattern is used by the narrator of 1 Sam 9.14, who uses it to describe the meeting of Samuel and Saul in an Old Testament allusion to the betrothal type-scene. Cf. Alter *op. cit.*, pp. 60-61.

[2] The note that the disciples have gone to town to buy food also makes room for their return with food and their request that Jesus eat (v. 34). At that point in the episode, when any uncertainty has vanished about Jesus's intentions towards the woman, the return of the disciples provides Jesus with an opportunity to express his true concerns and desires as opposed to mundane wants or needs. When Jesus asks the woman for a drink because his disciples have gone to buy food, the reader is allowed, even encouraged, to entertain carnal suspicion. When the disciples return with food and ask Jesus to eat, he says his food is his divinely ordained work (v. 34). The contrast between the reader's suspicions about what the request for a drink signifies and Jesus' explicit refusal of food, which reveals his actual attitude to the appetites of the flesh, is highlighted by the disciples. They disappear at drinking time and reappear at eating time, both regulated stages in the betrothal type-scene. With their return it becomes clear that the type-scene and its manipulation have been a trap.

[3] Had she not wanted to draw attention to their different genders and the consequent sexual possibilities of Jesus's request—given the Old Testament traditions about meetings at wells—she need not have contrasted herself as a woman (γυναικός), the feminine form Σαμαρίτιδος being grammatically sufficient for the political contrast.

[4] Though commentators regularly attribute v. 9b to a redactor or glossator, there is no grammatical warrant in favour of such a reading (against e.g. Bernard *op. cit.*, p. 138;

συγχρῶνται is a double entendre. With a personal dative object it can mean "to associate with", "to be intimate with", or "to have sexual intercourse with".[1] Her superficially innocent statement that Jews are not normally friendly with Samaritans has a sexual overtone that explains why she contrasts herself as a "woman" with Jesus, obviously a man. She seems to have read Jesus's request for a drink as more than a simple request for water, a plausible reading in view of the Old Testament evidence about the plurisignation of "drinking water". The reader, who may have already wondered about the possibility of sexual connotations in Jesus' request,[2] takes the woman's suggestions as partial confirmation of his own suspicions about Jesus's intention. But the reader must wait for further statements from Jesus himself to confirm his carnal comprehension.

The first part of Jesus's reply deals with knowledge and identity (v. 10). The woman, representing the flesh and carnally limited knowledge, does not or rather cannot know what this gift is, nor can she know Jesus's true identity as the Logos of chapter 1. In contrast the reader knows what the gift of God is because he was privileged to overhear Jesus tell Nicodemus what it is (3.16) and he also knows who Jesus is from chapter 1. Consequently when he hears Jesus telling the woman that he would have given her 'living water' he is prevented by his privileged textual knowledge from giving free rein to a carnal reading of the double entendre 'living water'. Had Jesus not recalled this information from the

---

Bultmann *op. cit.,* p. 178; Barrett *op. cit.,* p. 194). Normally a reader will understand consecutive statements in a written record of conversation to be from the speaker last introduced unless the text will not sustain this reading strategy as, for example, in the untagged transition between v. 7 and v. 8. Since v. 9b presents no such difficulty, the label 'gloss' is superfluous; at best one might argue for a narratorial comment.

[1] Most recent discussion of the verb follows D. Daube's treatment in "Jesus and the Samaritan Woman: The Meaning of συγχράομαι", *Journal of Biblical Literature* 69 (1950), pp. 137-47, understanding the verb to mean 'to use vessels together with'. Grammatical objections to Daube's suggestion have been raised by D.R. Hall ("The Meaning of συγχράομαι in John 4.9", *Expository Times* 83 [1971/72], pp. 56-57), who correctly notes that in compound verbs such as συγχράομαι it is the verb itself that governs the dative; the prefixed preposition only intensifies (cf. W.W. Goodwin, *Greek Grammar* rev. ed. by C. B. Gulick [New York: Caratzas Brothers, 1981, p. 194]).The meaning of συγ-χράομαι must therefore be derived from χράομαι. When χράομαι is used to describe actions between persons it can refer generally to emotionally coloured interaction—to treat someone as a friend or an enemy or to associations and intimacies, but its most particular reference is to sexual intercourse (H.G. Liddell, R. Scott, H.S. Jones, *A Greek-English Lexicon* Oxford; Clarendon Press, 1968, p. 2002 IV 2). Given the characteristic sexual orientation of the word's usage, and given the specific narrative context in John 4 with its numerous double entendres, its sexual imagery, and its allusions to the Old Testament instances of the betrothal type-scene, the onus of proof lies on those who would disallow the perception of sexual overtones to the woman's statement about relations between Jews and Samaritans.

[2] E.g. Carmichael *op. cit.,* p. 336 n. 16.

preceding context, the reader would have had sufficient contextual warrant to support an unambiguous carnal reading.

As a result the reader cannot be certain about how to interpret the double, or rather triple entendre in v. 10. Underlying the apparent meaning of 'living water', that is flowing or fresh water are two possibilities: either Jesus, the divine Word, offers the woman something like wisdom (Prov 13.14; 14.27; 16.22) and relationship with God (Ps 36.9) or he, as the Word become flesh, responds to her coquetry with a sexually suggestive offer of his own 'living water' (cf. Prov 5.15-18; Canticles 4:12, 15). The ambiguity places the reader in an interpretational bind, granting him a vivid experiential grasp of the problem faced by the human characters in the narrative. In fact if he did not have chapters 1-3 to rely on the reader would see only sexual undertones in 'living water' in accordance with the multiple allusions and the type-scene in chapter 4.

To the woman, who has no knowledge of chapters 1-3, Jesus's offer seems to indicate his willingness to be 'friendly' (συνχρῶνται, v. 9) with her. The feigned politeness of her response—she addresses him as "Sir" (Κύριε, v. 11)—is ironic. She has properly addressed Jesus as "Lord" (cf. Jn 13.13) yet her address is only false modesty, a sham embarrassment at the sexual undertones she hears in Jesus's offer. Her provocative intention unfolds in what follows.

Certain that Jesus was not referring to the physical water in Jacob's well, she coyly points out that Jesus has no bucket to draw water out of the deep well. The word she uses for "well" (φρέαν) is another double entendre. She is really talking about her own 'well' but conceals her lasciviousness under the guise of an innocent reference to Jacob's well. Her curiosity about the location of Jesus's living water is even more revealing; she asks not how or where he will get it, but where he has it, implying that she thinks he has it on his person. Her question is provocative; she has just "exposed" her "well" by mentioning it, now she wants Jesus to reveal the source of his "living water".

The woman's comparison of Jesus to Jacob serves several purposes. First, she quickly covers her brazenness by returning, apparently, to the topic of Jacob's well. Second, her comparison is a challenge. She wants Jesus to prove his superiority to Jacob and his well by showing her where he has his living water and, by implication, giving it to her. Can Jesus with his living water give as much satisfaction as Jacob, whose well has watered so many? Third, her comparison alludes to the story of Jacob's adventures in Genesis 29-30. Jacob married Rachel and Leah after he rolled away the stone from the well (φρέαρ, Gen 29.10) and watered Laban's flocks. He fathered eleven sons (Gen 29.32—30.24) and husbanded many animals (Gen 30.35-43). The Samaritan woman has mentioned the well, sons, and flocks in the same sequence as Genesis does: after Jacob drank from the well progeny multiplied. The woman's allusion questions whether Jesus can equal Jacob's performance with his own living water. The woman's carnal interpretation of Jesus's answer reinforces the reader's own appreciation of such a reading, yet he cannot completely identify with it because she interprets in ignorance of information that he has. His privilege puts him in a quandary, the experience of which gives him a direct perception of the basic problem in the gospel of John, man's misconception of Jesus and misunderstanding of what Jesus says.

Jesus responds to the woman's challenge (vv. 13-14). He points out that those who drink the 'water' of Jacob's well do not quench their desire for water. The woman (who has had at least five husbands [v.18]), Jacob, his sons, and his flocks (cf. Gen 30.38, 41) have all returned many times to drink water from the 'well'. Jesus claims that those who drink the water he gives will not thirst again. His living water will satisfy desire. And though the drinking of Jacob's well produced a long succession of eleven sons, and many animals, Jesus claims that his water will create a fountain (another symbolic double entendre) that springs up into eternal life from the one who drinks it.

Again Jesus's words are open to two very different interpretations. To the reader the mention of eternal life will recall 3.15-16, where Jesus says that whoever believes in him will have eternal life. The connection leaves little doubt about the sphere in which Jesus's thoughts are moving. No longer able to entertain the twofold reading of Jesus's statements himself, the reader now understands how the woman can continue to do so—how he would do so in her place—since she does not share the reader's privileged access to Jesus's conversation with Nicodemus. The reader now knows how it is possible to be so wrong about Jesus and there is, henceforth, sympathy for the failings in understanding of the characters in the Gospel.

It is no coincidence that the numerous allusions to previous incidences of the type-scene cease with the woman's remarks about Jacob in v. 12. When Jesus is allowed to resolve the ambiguity about his intentions in vv. 13-14 the narrator ceases to support the reader's carnal interpretation. The allusions have served their purpose and they are now retired, allowing the reader to concentrate on the continuing story of the woman's misconceptions, which are also soon to be corrected. And when the woman receives her correction, the reader also receives his, perhaps to a greater degree: "for unto whomsoever much is given, of him shall much be required: and to whom men have committed much, of him they will ask the more" (Lk 12.48).

To the woman Jesus's positive response to her challenging comparison signals his readiness to prove his superiority to Jacob. Once more with provocatively feigned propriety (cf. v. 11) she says, "Sir, give me this water." Her request forces Jesus to take action, but she does not get the expected response.

Jesus's reply to the woman's request reveals that he too was aware of the sexual implications of the meeting and the overtones in the conversation (v. 16). His directive to go call her husband is the exact opposite of what the woman expected him to do. At the point where she expected to get his 'living water' Jesus's command comes as a rebuke to her carnal misconceptions. Had she not been making sexual advances, had Jesus not understood them, and had the reader not understood both the woman and Jesus, his command to go call her husband would make no sense here. Jesus tells her to get her husband exactly when she expected to commit adultery against the man.

Surprised by Jesus's response, the woman first tries to deny that she is attached (v. 17), perhaps thinking that Jesus will go ahead once he believes she is single. The fact that she does not ask why he should suddenly change topics from 'living water' to her husband indicates that she is aware of the connection.

Jesus, in total control of the conversation, now openly reveals his disinterest in her charms by demonstrating his supernatural knowledge of her past (v. 17). To the reader this demonstration completely destroys any misunderstanding he might have had about Jesus, but the woman is not so easily convicted. She is, however, convinced that she misread Jesus's intentions, so she tries to extricate herself from her embarrassing predicament. Her changed demeanour is highlighted by her third, modified use of the polite address, "Sir".[1] No longer feigned, her politeness expresses her respect for Jesus, whom she now regards as a holy prophet. Her show of respect is intended to restore her own appearance of respectability. Further towards that end, she completely changes the topic from 'wells', 'water', and husbands to the more decent topic of the proper place to worship. The change in the lady's manner is also highlighted by the parallel between her discussion of worship (v. 20), and her reflections on Jacob (v. 12), which share the same respective position in each half of the conversation. In v. 12 she compared what the patriarch had done with what Jesus proposed to do, her aim being provocation. In v. 20 she compares the place of worship suggested by the patriarchs' behaviour with the place of worship that Jesus and the Jews

---

[1] Cf. Barrett *op. cit.,* p. 197.

propose. Now she is a pious lady having a nice religious conversation with a prophet—all very proper indeed.

Undeterred by this evasion, Jesus brushes aside the woman's evasions as meaningless in the light of his perceptions of worship (vv. 21-24). He evaluates her comparison of places of worship just as he did her comparison of Jacob and himself (vv. 13-14). Her religious comparisons are ultimately on the same plane as her previous sexually oriented comparison of Jesus and Jacob. Even the woman's conscious intention to elevate herself and her thoughts to the level on which Jesus converses brings her no nearer to the matters of which he speaks. His message, which she has refused to hear so far, is beyond comparisons of the type she wishes to make.

In a last ditch effort to maintain her respectability, which Jesus has not shown even the slightest concern to attack, the woman digresses again. In response to Jesus's remark about Samaritan ignorance (οὐκ οἴδατε, v. 22) she says that she knows (οἴδα, v. 25) that the Messiah is coming and will tell the Samaritans everything. Jesus cuts off this evasion with a simple self-identification. "I am he."

The narrator wraps up his rendition of the betrothal type-scene with his own version of the betrothal meal to celebrate the non-union. In this instance, what we have is a description of Jesus's refusal to eat the food brought by his disciples, underscoring his lack of interest in such earthly affairs (vv. 31-34). Instead of eating a betrothal meal to celebrate his engagement to the willing Samaritan, Jesus tells his disciples, "My food is to do the will of him who sent me" (v. 34).

This final twist in the adaptation of the betrothal type-scene is aimed directly at the sole witness to its employment, the reader. A last reminder of his folly, which was far worse than that of the Samaritan woman because it was an error in judgement, not one of ignorance, the 'non-betrothal meal' ensures that the reader will remember the lesson.

For John 4, then, the focus of reader-response criticism is able to shed new light on the literary devices such as the type-scene and the double entendres that are employed in the text. Commentators who have observed the presence of the type-scene in John 4 have sometimes misunderstood it as a statement made by the author rather than a strategy used by him to lead the reader to a particular experience. Thus the type-scene is understood to suggest that the Samaritan woman (or people) is united in a spiritual or symbolic marriage with Jesus.[1] Yet the narrative itself nowhere describes or even hints at a consummation between Jesus and the woman. Jesus' refusal of the 'betrothal meal' points in the exact

---

[1] E.g. Boismard *op. cit.*, p. 225; Neyrey *op. cit.*, p. 426; Carmichael *op. cit.*, pp. 341-46.

opposite direction. When, on the other hand, the type-scene is understood as a strategy designed to mislead the reader so that he may gain an actual experience of the gap between Jesus and his human auditors the absence of a consummation makes good sense.[1] "What makes problematic sense as a statement makes perfect sense as a strategy, as an action made upon a reader rather than as a container from which a reader extracts a message."[2]

---

[1] Cf. Cahill *op. cit.,* p. 47.

[2] Stanley Fish, "Literature in the Reader: Affective Stylistics", *Is There a Text in This Class?* (Cambridge, Mass.: Harvard UP, 1980), p. 23.

After the completion of this essay (written and presented as a public lecture sponsored under a fellowship with the Calgary Institute for the Humanities in 1982) a similar approach to John 4 has come to my notice, too late for an integrated response. Gail R. O'Day has now published her study, "Narrative Mode and Theological Claim: A Study in the Fourth Gospel" *(Journal of Biblical Literature* 105 (1986), pp. 657-68), also advocating a reader-response reading of John 4 (pp. 665-68). Because O'Day does not perceive the use of the type-scene or the multiple double entendres and because she takes the woman's question at the end of v. 9 as a narratorial comment, her reading is quite different from that offered here. There is, nevertheless, a remarkable methodological agreement about the potential of a reader-response approach to illuminate both John 4 and the literature of the Fourth Gospel in general.

JOHN 4.16: A DIFFICULT TEXT
SPEECH ACT THEORETICALLY REVISITED*

EUGENE BOTHA

1. INTRODUCTION

The dialogue between the protagonist of John's story, Jesus, and the woman of Samaria has intrigued scholars for many centuries, because of the subject matter, the way in which the incident is depicted and the occurrence of irony in the text. In general it can perhaps be stated that this story does not present exegetes with insurmountable problems. However, the same cannot be said of the very sudden and abrupt change of topic in the conversation between Jesus and the Samaritan woman in John 4.16. The problematic nature of this break in the text is clearly reflected by the comments of various scholars, who differ markedly in their interpretations of this verse. A few examples will illustrate this: Carmichael (1980:338) and Eslinger (1987:178), who both contend that the scene at the well is loaded with sexual and marital overtones, state that this abrupt change would be inexplicable, were it not for the underlying marital theme. Olsson (1974:184) refers to a number of interpretations and concludes that most scholars read this utterance as a sort of "leading" of the woman in which her faith is tested, her conscience awakened, and her loose living criticised. Bernard (1928:143) states that the abruptness is caused by the fact that we have only fragments of the original conversation and not the full conversation. O'Day (1986:66) suggests that the introduction of the woman's marital status is intended to shed further light on Jesus' person as revealer. Boers (1988:170) also sees this as a transition to prepare the woman for Jesus' miraculous abilities. Lindars (1972:185) contends that Jesus' command indicates that he wants her to understand that he is not speaking about real water, while Morris (1981:264) and Hendriksen (1976:164) find the logic behind the utterance in the fact that the woman is a sinful person and that her sins must first be revealed before the dialogue can continue. Schnackenburg (1968:432)

---

* This article appeared in *Scriptura* 35, 1990, pp. 1-9.

argues against this view and aligns himself more with the position that the introduction of this topic serves to illuminate Jesus' role as revealer.

From the above it is significant to note that while the interpreters have all tried to explain the logic of the introduction of the new theme, there have been no real explanations offered as to the manner in which the new topic is introduced. It is clear that a new topic is introduced in 4.16, but the fact remains that it is done in an extraordinary manner, which commentators have so far not been able to explain adequately. The abruptness and the sudden nature of this change of topic has been noted, but explanations seldom focus on the question of why the change is made in such a blunt manner, and not more gradually, despite the fact that this blunt manner immediately attracts attention. The problem regarding 4.16 is best illustrated if the prior dialogue is scrutinised.

> 4.7 Jesus opens the discussion and asks for a drink of water.
>
> 4.8 The implied author explains the absence of Jesus' disciples.
>
> 4.9 The woman reacts negatively and points out the socio-cultural problems.
>
> 4.10 Jesus retaliates and suggests that if she had adequate knowledge, she would ask him for water, living water.
>
> 4.11f The woman questions Jesus' ability and his authority to provide her with this water, misunderstanding his reference to 'living water'.
>
> 4.13f Jesus explains fully what he means by living water by referring, inter alia, to eternal life.
>
> 4.15 The woman accepts that Jesus can provide her with this water, and indeed asks him to give this to her.
>
> 4.16 At this stage, while the question of water/living water has been debated since 4.7, the character Jesus suddenly commands the woman to fetch her husband. It is precisely this abrupt break in the text that creates the problems, since this command seems to be totally out of context.

In this article we will argue that the application of speech act theory to this particular text can possibly supply explanations of this difficult text, which up till now were not available to New Testament exegetes. What makes the solution that we offer here attractive is that it is a relatively simple explanation, but one which inherently also allows for the possibilities mentioned by previous exegetes.

2. SOME GENERAL PRINCIPLES

The application of speech act theory to biblical texts is, of course, not a new endeavour. Westland (1985), Aurelio (1977), Arens (1982) and Du Plessis (1985) have all attempted this. More recently volume 41 of *Semeia* was devoted to speech act theory and biblical criticism. We will not offer a full discussion of the theory here, but only explain some relevant principles and continue to apply the theory to our present text. (For an elaborate discussion of speech act theory see Pratt 1977, White 1988:1-24 and Botha 1989:68-90).

When a conversation takes place between two participants, it is assumed that both parties share certain knowledge or beliefs which make communication possible. Bach and Harnish (1979:5-6) called these beliefs MCBs or "mutual contextual beliefs" which include knowledge of the specific speech situation, knowledge about their relative positions, cultural and social rules and traditions, presuppositions and so on. In addition, the following three assumptions must be shared by participants engaged in a verbal exchange in order to make the communication successful. The "linguistic assumption" (Bach and Harnish 1974:7) which means that the author of an utterance and the hearer are both able to handle the language used adequately. The "communicative assumption" (Bach and Harnish 1979:7) is the assumption that requires that the intention of the author of an utterance is that his utterance would be understood, and the "presumption of literalness" (Bach and Harnish 1979:61) is the presumption which postulates that if the speaker can be taken literally, he should be taken as speaking literally. Furthermore, any conversation is also governed by rules, which both parties in any exchange take to be in force. These rules to be observed are called in speech act theory appropriateness conditions or felicity conditions that must be met in order to make any communication effective and successful. Depending on the context, each speech situation has its own specific appropriateness conditions, but there are also more general and universal conditions which speakers must also observe in order to make communication possible. The general principle was called by Grice (1975:45) the "co-operation principle" or CP, which is "a rough general principle which participants will be expected ... to observe, viz.: make your conversation contribution such as it is required, at the stage at which it occurs, by the accepted purpose or direction of the talk-exchange in which you are engaged."

Under the general principle Grice (1975:45-49) proposed four categories of maxims, or large general appropriateness conditions that are

normally assumed to be in force in a normal conversation. The maxim of
quantity which requires that a contribution is as economical as required—
not more or less informative than is needed should be given; the maxim
of quality in which sincerity is the key—the contribution should not be
intentionally false; the maxim of relation which requires that the
contribution must be relevant to the talk-exchange; and the maxim of
manner which requires that the utterance must be perspicuous. Bach and
Harnish (1979:63) follow Grice in this, but also add a maxim of
sequencing, which requires that a contribution should be "appropriate to
the stage of the talk-exchange". Participants in conversation normally
assume that these principles/maxims are being observed mutually, and that
the speech behaviour is governed by these rules.

However, it should be noted that these maxims can deliberately or
unintentionally not be observed. In severe cases this non-fulfilment of a
maxim can lead to the ultimate breakdown of the communication between
the participants. However, in a literary speech situation this is not the
case, and we can agree with Pratt (1977:163) that whenever some maxim
is intentionally not observed, by characters or the narrator, the particular
maxim is merely flouted by the implied author. Grice (1975:49) describes
flouting and argues that this results in conversational implicature. In
discussing this concept of conversational implicature McLaughlin
(1984:32) states:

> Conversational behaviour that appears to violate or blatantly flout the
> maxims ordinarily gives rise to speculation as to why the co-operative
> principle does not appear to be in force, and this state of affairs invites
> conversational implicature-broadly construed, the engagement of a set
> of interpretative procedures designed to figure out just what the
> speaker is up to.

In a literary speech situation flouting is always valid for the
communication between implicit author/narrator and implied
reader/narratee. Whenever flouting has taken place the resultant
problematic situation must be resolved by means of implicature on this
level. However, it is possible that in literature the fictional character or
speaker is failing to fulfil the CP in a fictional (re)construction of a
verbal exchange. This failure of a character can result in the breaking off
or failure of a conversation on the level on which the characters are
interacting. But the CP between implied author and readers is of course
not violated and the readers can also assume that it is not, and "it is this
assumption which determines the implicatures by which we resolve the
fictional speaker's violations at the level of our dealings with the author"
(Pratt 1977:178). This invites the readers to calculate the implicatures

arising from the character's deviant behaviour, and thus ensures enhanced communication between implied author and implied reader (see also Du Plessis (1988:311-324) regarding implicature in Luke).

The flouting of these above-mentioned maxims results in a number of so-called figures of speech such as metaphor, hyperbole, meiosis, and irony. In this respect speech act theory provides a novel way of looking at these phenomena and identifying them. In John, where we find a large number of ironies, insights of speech act theory can be of special significance in identifying and understanding this figure of speech (see Amante 1981; Schiffrin 1981, 1984; and Botha 1989:143-155).

3. A SPEECH ACT READING OF JOHN 4.16

Keeping these general principles in mind, we can now turn to John 4.16. Whenever we refer to either Jesus or the Samaritan woman, we are referring not to the flesh and blood persons, but we refer to them as characters (personages) in John's story. For the sake of clarity we have in some instances added the term 'character' to the participants in John's account. An analysis of the conversation between Jesus and the woman in 4.7-15 reveals that the following principles can be seen to govern this particular exchange:

* They both share enough and appropriate MCBs to make the conversation possible.

* They approach and deal with one another respectfully and politely (Botha 1989:106-155).

* Both give signals that they are willing to keep up continued participation in the conversation, by, inter alia, turn taking, observation of CP and maxims, and so on.

* The CP and maxims (relevancy, clarity, quantity, quality, sequencing, etc.) have been observed in the dialogue leading up to 4.16.

* The conversational position or status of the two participants has been determined by the conversation so far, and it seems that they treat each other as equals. The implied reader is aware, of course, that Jesus is more than a mere Jew, but the character of the woman does not know it, and only later in the conversation allows Jesus to assume a superior position.

Keeping the above in mind, by applying some of the principles of speech act theory to this scene, we can perhaps explain why the utterance of Jesus is so remarkable and conspicuous. In addition, we can perhaps also explain the dynamics of the conversation which led to this abrupt change in topic. To approach an explanation, it would perhaps be advisable to use a parallel conversation to elucidate some of the aspects involved.

Take for example two conversationalists who are engaged for some time in a discussion of a mutual colleague, who suddenly approaches A from the back and A says: "Don't you think Fred sometimes acts like an idiot?" to which B replies: "I planted some shrubs yesterday." In order to make sense of B's utterance A must, on the basis of assumptions about rules and principles of conversation which they both share, make a number of inferences. This is, of course, done automatically and subconsciously, but could perhaps be explained in the words of A as: "B violated the maxim of relevance, but so far in the conversation he was very co-operative. For some reason B has chosen to flout the maxim, and therefore indicated that he does not want to pursue the topic any further. He is telling me he does not want to talk any more about this particular subject, and that I should follow his example." If A turns round and sees Fred, the reason for B's flouting of the maxim will become clear to him.

It seems that Jesus' utterance in 4.16 can be explained in much the same way. So far the woman had shown that, despite the social and cultural difficulties, she is prepared to continue to interact with Jesus, especially in 4.15 where she grants Jesus a position of relative superiority and asks for the water he has to offer. She is willing to pursue the topic of the water. However, the situation and Jesus' full explanation in 4.13f make it quite clear that she is completely on the wrong track. Jesus is talking about spiritual matters, while she misunderstands him and thinks that the reference is on the natural level to real water. This is clear from the reason she gives for wanting this: so that she does not need to come back again to fetch real water. As far as the character Jesus is concerned, the discussion so far is a failure—and he intends to terminate this specific line of discussion. However, the appropriateness conditions established for the discussion so far dictate that he should observe the politeness principle and keep the CP intact. Thus he can hardly criticise her openly for not understanding, or terminate the conversation, without transgressing accepted conversational rules and appear extremely rude, and perhaps losing her continued participation. The character Jesus therefore has to follow another strategy and flouts the maxim of relevancy ('be relevant'), manner ('be perspicuous') and sequencing ('be appropriate to that stage of conversational behaviour'). It is exactly this flouting of three maxims that makes this utterance so conspicuous for readers and commentators.

The character Jesus does not want to pursue this issue (which the woman is clearly not understanding) any further and indicates this to her in a way which forces her to arrive at this by means of implicature. This 'break' created by the flouting of maxims, indicates to the other character that the current line of discussion should be terminated, and it gives Jesus the opportunity of continuing the conversation and introducing a new programme or topic. Because of the relative status granted to him by the woman in 4.15 he is able to take the initiative in introducing a new topic.

That the intended perlocution (to stop the woman pursuing the misunderstanding and direct her to a new topic) does indeed become a realised perlocution is clear from her reply in 4.17 where she does not press Jesus again to provide her with the water, but rather acknowledges his refusal to continue the subject of water, reacts to his newly introduced topic, and agrees to discuss the question of her husband(s). By flouting the maxims, the character Jesus has ensured that she realises that he is unwilling to continue the conversation on this level, and that he intends changing the topic. She is not severely criticised or affronted and thus it is ensured that the CP remains intact. This guarantees the continuation of the dialogue and ensures her (positive) participation.

On the level of the conversation between the implied author and implied readers (see Staley 1968:47-85, Culpepper 1987:15-44 and Botha 1989:97-105), this utterance where the maxims of relevance, manner and sequence were violated, confronts the implied readers with the same problems as the character of the woman. They also have to explain the violation of certain conversational rules by means of implicature. The only difference is that they are informed readers, knowledgeable about Jesus, his work and position, able to grasp subtle ironies and misunderstandings by characters (Culpepper 1987:161-165; Duke 1984:88-90: O'Day 1986). The effect of Jesus' utterance in 4:16 on the implied readers is slightly more extensive than on the effect on the character of the woman, in the sense that it is a clear indication to them that her understanding so far is inadequate. The character of the woman is merely induced to change the topic, while the same speech act induces the readers, because of their knowledge of Jesus, to also provide a reason for the change in topic. The advantage for the communication between implied author and implied readers, in structuring the utterance in this way is, of course, to keep the readers involved in the narrative by forcing them into conversational implicatures. Their continual involvement and attention is necessary since from 4.16-26 on the crux of the dialogue with the woman is discussed and here their attention needs to be ensured. The fact that the woman understands Jesus wrongly is also evident for the implied readers, since in 4.13f the implied author gave a very clear explanation of what he/she is talking about by indicating to the readers, via the utterance of Jesus in 4.16, that the woman made the wrong deductions. The implied author is thus ensuring that the readers do not make the same mistakes. If the protagonist Jesus, with whom the implied readers are identifying strongly, is not satisfied with her response in 4.15, it is a way of indicating to the implied readers that they should avoid a similar understanding and their pre-knowledge about Jesus should help them to arrive at the right conclusions. They are actually called upon by the implied author to firmly establish the exact status of the dialogue so far, and to interpret Jesus' words correctly, before the next, very significant part of the dialogue develops. It is a most effective transitional technique of the implied author to enable the readers to correctly interpret information so far supplied and to ensure their continued participation of the implied readers, as the nature of the changed topic is not too clear. They can only be sure that the woman's interpretation is wrong and that they should not follow it, but to what exact topic the change is made, is not yet clear. This also invites continued attention, since the story is not yet finished and a more satisfactory ending must still be anticipated.

CONCLUSION

From the above it is clear that the simple application of speech act theory to the text of Jn 4.16 can indeed help to clarify both why this utterance is so significant and why the change of topic is so abrupt. If one takes the two levels of conversation in the text into account it becomes clear how the speech acts on the level of the character serve to enhance the communication on the level of the interaction between implied author and implied readers. The explanation on the level of the character is simple and logical, since it is a universal way in which conversationalists deal with language. On the level of the communication between the implied author and the implied readers, this utterance is also very functional and facilitates the participation and evaluation of the implied readers in a way a simple change in topic could never achieve.

We can conclude that it seems that speech act theory is a very promising development in the study of language and language function, and can definitely contribute much to supplement traditional exegesis in arriving at a better understanding of the dynamics of the text of the Bible, as this example from John 4 clearly shows.

BIBLIOGRAPHY

Amante, D. J. "The Theory of Ironic Speech Acts" *Poetics Today* 2, (1981) pp. 77-96.

Arens, E. *Kommunikative Handlungen: Die paradigmatische Bedeutung der Gleichnisse Jesu für eine Handlungstheorie.* (Düsseldorf: Patmos, 1982).

Aurelio, T. *Disclosures in den Gleichnissen Jesu. Eine Anwendung der Disclosure-Theorie von I.T. Ramsey, der modernen Metaphorik und der Sprechakte auf die Gleichnisse Jesu.* (Frankfurt/M: Lang, 1977) (Regensburger Studien zur Theologie 8).

Bach, K. & Harnish L.M. *Linguistic Communication and Speech Acts.* (Cambridge: MIT, 1979).

Barrett, C.K. *The Gospel According to St. John: An Introduction with Commentary and Notes on the Greek Text.* 2nd ed. (London: SPCK, 1978).

Bernard, J.H. *A Critical and Exegetical Commentary on the Gospel According to St. John.* 2 vols. (New York: Charles Scribner's Sons, 1929).

Boers, H. *Neither on this Mountain nor in Jerusalem. A Study of John 4.* (Atlanta: Scholars, 1988) (SBL Monograph series 35).

Botha, J.E. *A Study in Johannine Style: History, Theory, and Practice.* D Th Dissertation. (Pretoria: University of South Africa, 1989).

Carmichael, C.M. "Marriage and the Samaritan Woman." *NTS* 26 (1980), pp. 332-346.

Cole, P. & Morgan, J.L. (eds) *Syntax and semantics, vol. 3: Speech Acts.* (New York: Academic, 1975).

Culpepper, R.A. *Anatomy of the Fourth Gospel: A Study in Literary Design.* 2nd ed. (Philadelphia: Fortress, 1987).

Du Plessis, J.G. "Why did Peter ask his question and how did Jesus answer him? or: Implicature in Luke 12:35-48." *Neotestamentica* 22, (1988) pp. 311-324.

Duke, P.D. *Irony in the Fourth Gospel: the shape and function of a literary device.* (Ann Arbor: University Microfilms International, 1984).

Eslinger, L. "The Wooing of the Woman at the Well: Jesus, the Reader and Reader-response Criticism." *Journal of Literature and theology* 1, (1987) pp. 167-183. [Reprinted in the present volume]

Grice, H.P. *Logic and Conversation* (1975) in Cole & Morgan 1975: pp. 41-58.

Hendriksen, W. *The Gospel of John.* (Edinburgh: Banner of Truth, 1976). (New Testament Commentary.)

Lindars, B. *The Gospel of John.* (London: Oliphant, 1972). (New Century Bible.)

McLaughlin, M.L. *Conversation: How Talk is Organised.* (Beverly Hills: Sage, 1984).

Morris, L. *The Gospel According to John: The English Text with Introduction, Exposition and Notes.* (Grand Rapids: Eerdmans, 1981). (New International Commentary on the New Testament.)

O'Day, G.R. *Revelation in the Fourth Gospel: Narrative Mode and Theological Claim.* (Philadelphia: Fortress, 1986).

Olsson, B. *Structure and Meaning in the Fourth Gospel.* (Lund: Gleerup, 1974). (Coniectanea Biblica, New Testament Series 6.)

Pratt, M.L. *Towards a Speech Act Theory of Literary Discourse.* (Bloomington: Indiana University, 1977).

Schiffrin, D. "Tense Variation in Narrative." *Language* 57 (1981), pp. 45-62.

Schiffrin, D. "How a Story Says what it Means and Does." *Text* 4, (1984) pp. 313-346.

Schnackenburg, R. *The Gospel According to St. John, vol. 1.* (New York: Herder, 1968). (Herders Theological Commentary to the New Testament.)

Staley, J.L. *The Print's First Kiss: A Rhetorical Investigation of the Implied Reader in the Fourth Gospel.* (Ann Arbor: University Microfilms International, 1986).

Wendland, E.R. *Language, society and Bible translation. With special reference to the style and structure of segments of direct speech in the Scriptures.* (Cape Town: Bible Society of South Africa, 1985).

White, H.C. "Speech Act Theory and Literary Criticism." *Semeia* 41 (1988), pp. 1-24.

JOHN 5.1-18
A SAMPLE OF NARRATIVE CRITICAL COMMENTARY*

R. ALAN CULPEPPER

Just as the test of any recipe is how tasty a meal one can prepare when using it, so the test of any critical method must be whether it can bring to light fresh perspectives on a text. Since narrative criticism is still a recent development, few samples of its application to specific passages have been published. The way is open for exploration of new procedures and formats. What follows, therefore, is a merely an effort to demonstrate one way in which one might approach a passage like Jn 5.1-18.

At the outset we might do well to note briefly the "état du recherche." A 1985 article by L.Th. Witkamp addresses "The Use of Traditions in John 5.1-18."[1] The article reflects both the continuing preoccupation with separating sources and redaction in the Gospel of John and the impasse to which we have come in source criticism in Johannine studies. As Witkamp demonstrates, it is widely agreed that the core of Jn 5.1-18 once belonged to the signs source (SQ). In support of this consensus Witkamp cites Bultmann, Becker, Fortna, Martyn, Nicol, Schnackenburg, Schultz, and Teeple.[2]

When one examines the matter more closely, however, the differences among these scholars over which verses can be assigned to the source reveals the limitations of source criticism. Jn 5.3b-4 is generally recognised as a later gloss because it does not appear in $\mathfrak{P}^{66}$, $\mathfrak{P}^{75}$, or B.[3] Jn

---

* This article appeared in *La communauté johannique et son histoire*, ed. J.-D. Kaestli J.M. Poffet & J. Zumstein (Geneva: Labor et Fides, 1990) pp. 131-151. It has been translated from the French by J.-D. Kaestli.

[1] L.Th. Witkamp, "The Use of Traditions in John 5.1-18", *JSNT*, 25 (1985), 19-47.

[2] Ibid., p. 19.

[3] Zane C. Hodges, "Problem Passages in the Gospel of John. Part 5: The Angel at Bethesda-John 5.4", *Bibliotheca Sacra*, 136 (1979), 25-39, argued for the authenticity of these verses, but his argument is convincingly rebuffed by Gordon D. Fee, "On the Inauthenticity of John 5.3b-4", *Evangelical Quarterly*, 54 (1982), 207-218. Michael Mees, "Die Heilung des Kranken von Bethesdateich aus Joh. 5.1-18 in frühchristlicher Sicht", *NTS*, 32 (1986), 696-608, has collected all the references to John 5.1-18 in early Christian literature. Both Tertullian and Tatian knew of this verse, so the text containing John 5.4 may be just as ancient as $\mathfrak{P}^{66}$ and $\mathfrak{P}^{75}$.

5.3b-4 is therefore not assigned to the source by any of the scholars mentioned in the following discussion.

Bultmann assigned vv. 2-16 to the SQ.[1] While Becker agrees in attributing vv. 9b-16 to the source,[2] most others break the narrative at v. 9a, identifying vv. 2-9a as source material and vv. 9b ff. as the evangelist's addition to the traditional healing story. Nicol argues that vv. 1-9 contain few elements characteristic of Johannine style while vv. 10-18 are thoroughly Johannine in style.[3] Fortna accepts Haenchen's suggestion that the story originally concluded with v. 14b.[4] C.H. Dodd, who did not subscribe to the theory of a SQ, nevertheless recognised the traditional character of vv. 2-9a.[5] Rudolf Schnackenburg agrees with this consensus but identifies the note in v. 6 that Jesus knew how long the man had been lying there as an insertion by the evangelist.[6] Raymond E. Brown maintains that the Sabbath motif was an integral part of the pericope from the beginning, but he concedes that vv. 9b-13 may be a secondary expansion of the Sabbath motif.[7] The variations we have just noted show that although one may still speak of a consensus regarding the traditional character of vv. 2-9a and possibly v. 14b there has been little agreement as to the precise identification of the source material.

Barnabas Lindars proposed that even the original core to the story betrays evidences of the conflation of two sources. The sign, he contended, is the product of "the fusion of a non-Synoptic Jerusalem Tradition and the well-known Galilean story in Mk 2.1-12," which John used with a minimum of rewriting.[8] Witkamp builds on Lindars' thesis, arguing that the evangelist's literary technique of introducing dialogue and

---

[1] Rudolf Bultmann, *The Gospel of John: A Commentary*, trans. G. R. Beasley-Murray, et al. (Philadelphia: Westminster Press, 1971), pp. 237-247; D. Moody Smith, Jr., *The Composition and Order of the Fourth Gospel: Bultmann's Literary Theory* (New Haven: Yale University Press, 1965), pp. 41-42, 130-134.

[2] Jürgen Becker, *Das Evangelium nach Johannes I*, Ökumenischer Taschenbuch-kommentar zum Neuen Testament, 4/1 (Gütersloh: Gütersloher Verlaghaus Gerd Mohn, 1979), pp. 229-230.

[3] W. Nicol, *The Semeia in the Fourth Gospel: Tradition and Redaction* (Leiden: E.J. Brill, 1972), p. 32.

[4] Robert T. Fortna, *The Gospel of Signs: A Reconstruction of the Narrative Source Underlying the Fourth Gospel*, SNTS Monograph Series 11 (Cambridge: Cambridge University Press, 1970), pp. 48-54; Ernst Haenchen, "Johanneische Probleme", *Zeitschrift für Theologie und Kirche*, 56 (1959), 48-49.

[5] C.H. Dodd, *Historical Tradition in the Fourth Gospel* (Cambridge: Cambridge University Press, 1963), p. 178.

[6] Rudolf Schnackenburg, *The Gospel according to John*, vol. 2 (New York: Seabury Press, 1980), p. 95.

[7] Raymond E. Brown, *The Gospel according to John*, Anchor Bible, 29 (Garden City, N.Y.: Doubleday, 1966), p. 210.

[8] Barnabas Lindars, *The Gospel of John*, New Century Bible (London: Oliphants, 1972), p. 52; cf. pp. 209-210.

misunderstanding can be seen in this pericope.[1] Witkamp concludes that "the widely accepted opinion that Jn 5.2-9a (+ 14b) once existed as a self-contained miracle story has little to recommend it because the narrative contains several indications of John's hand redacting and fusing his sources."[2] For a full representation of the basis for this conclusion, I refer you to Witkamp's fine article.

This rapid survey is sufficient to establish two observations: (1) parts of Jn 5.1-18 are based on traditional material, possibly a sign found in the signs source, and (2) identification of precisely what that source contained has proved to be extraordinarily difficult. Fortunately, the meaning of the story in its present setting does not depend on distinguishing the source from the evangelist's redaction. This survey also reveals the degree to which scholarship on these verses has been preoccupied with the issue of their origin and formation. Far less attention has been paid to their literary form and function in their present setting, though one finds perceptive insights in the course of commentaries which were primarily concerned with the text's composition history.

The question I raise, therefore, is a simple one: What do we see in Jn 5.1-18 when we turn from source and redaction-critical analysis to analysis of its form and function as a narrative segment in the larger narrative of the Gospel?

THE NARRATIVE SETTING

Several factors call attention to the prominent position of Jn 5.1-18. I am aware that there are significant reasons for reversing the order of chapters 5 and 6 and that several modern commentaries have followed Bultmann's thesis at this point (e.g., Becker and Schnackenburg),[3] but I am primarily concerned with the logic of the present state of the text. One could, of course, do narrative criticism of a reconstructed earlier stage of the Gospel text, but that is not my purpose.

Jn 2-4 is generally recognised as a unit of material beginning at Cana with the first, numbered sign and ending at Cana with the second, numbered sign (see esp. 4.46, 54). The progression of scenes in this section parallels the movement in Acts from Jerusalem to the Gentiles. Jn 2-4 begins at a Jewish wedding, then moves to the temple in Jerusalem, a Pharisee (Nicodemus), John the Baptist in Aenon near Salim, the

---

[1] Witkamp, "The Use of Traditions in John 5.1-18", pp. 24-25.
[2] Ibid., p. 29.
[3] See Bultmann, *John*, pp. 209-210; Schnackenburg, *John*, 2.5-9; Smith, *Composition and Order*, pp. 128-130.

Samaritan woman at Sychar, and ends with the royal officer (possibly a Gentile) in Galilee.

As a unit Jn 2-4 prepares us for Jn 5.1-18 by the various ways in which water functions in this section: At Cana Jesus replaces the water of cleansing with good wine (2.7-9), he instructs Nicodemus that in order to enter the kingdom of God one must be born of water and spirit (3.5, 8), the baptism of John and of Jesus is a subject of discussion among the disciples of John and the Jews (3.22-23, 25; 4.2), and Jesus offers the Samaritan woman living water (4.10-15). Jn 5.1-18 then shows that the true power of healing comes not from water but from Jesus. His word alone accomplishes what the man had been denied in thirty-eight years of waiting for the waters to stir.

Jn 5.1 marks a transition to a new section of the Gospel, using three markers that appear at significant junctures elsewhere in John: the phrase μετὰ ταῦτα, a reference to a Jewish festival, and a change of location.[1] The phrase μετὰ ταῦτα appears frequently at transitions: Jn 2.12 (μετὰ τοῦτο); 3.22; 4.43 (μετὰ δὲ τὰς δύο ἡμέρας); 6.1; 7.1; see also 13.27; 19.28; and 21.1. The phrase appears again in our passage at 5.14. Supporting μετὰ ταῦτα as an introduction to a new section or episode is a reference to a Jewish festival, similar to the references in Jn 2.13 (where we find almost an exact parallel to Jn 5.1); 6.4; 7.2; 11.55; and 13.1. Jn 5.1 also notes a change of location (to Jerusalem) that prepares the reader for the introduction of a new scene and a new set of characters (the man at the pool and the Jews). Notation of a change of location at the beginning of a new episode occurs also in Jn 2.12 and 13; 3.22, where Jesus and the disciples travel to a location in Judea; 4.3-4, where they journey to Sychar; 4.46, where they travel to Cana of Galilee; 6.1, where Jesus crosses the Sea of Galilee; 7.1, where Jesus goes to Galilee and eventually returns to Jerusalem; and 11.1ff. which prepares for Jesus' return to Bethany (see also 12.1). Individually, these three markers may not be important, but when they occur together—as they do in Jn 5.1—we may be confident that they signal the beginning of a new episode.

In fact, Jn 5.1-18 is closely tied to two larger units, Jn 5.1-47, which I would call an episode, and Jn 5-10, which I would call a section. I am using *episode* to indicate a series of related scenes, and *section* to indicate a series of related episodes. Moving from smaller to larger narrative units, therefore, we may speak of scenes, episodes, and sections.

The section Jn 5-10 is marked by cycles of increasing hostility against Jesus set in the context of Jewish festivals. It begins with a healing at the

[1] See R. Alan Culpepper, "The Gospel of John and the Jews", *Review and Expositor*, 84 (1987), pp. 276-277.

Pool of Bethesda (5.1-18), followed by a discourse in response to the Jews (5.19-47), and ends with a similar healing at the Pool of Siloam (9.1-7), followed by a series of dialogues (9.8-41) and discourses (10.1-38) and Jesus' withdrawal from Jerusalem (10.39-42). The rising hostility is introduced by the explanation in Jn 5.16, "and this was why the Jews persecuted Jesus, because he did this on the sabbath," and 5.18, "This was why the Jews sought all the more to kill him, because he not only broke the sabbath, but also called God his Father, making himself equal to God." These statements introduce and foreshadow the role of the Jews in the rest of the Gospel. The remainder of the discourse charges the Jews not having accepted the witnesses to Jesus (5.19-47).

In the next episode (Jn 6) the Jews murmur against Jesus (6.41) and then fight with one another (6.52). At the beginning of the following episode (Jn 7-8) the reader is warned that the Jews were seeking to kill Jesus (7.1). The level of hostility escalates in the ensuing debate. The authorities seek to arrest Jesus. There is a division (σχίσμα) among the people (7.43). Jn 8 contains the most hostile exchange between Jesus and the Jews, with Jesus finally declaring that their father was the devil (8.44). The Jews respond that Jesus is a Samaritan and has a demon (8.48), and they attempt to stone him (8.59). In the final episode of this section (Jn 9-10) there is division (σχίσμα) among the Pharisees (9.16). The Jews take official action against Jesus' followers (9.22). A division (σχίσμα) among the Jews follows (10.19), with some saying that he is demonic and others defending him. The section ends with the Jews again taking up stones against Jesus (10.31, 33) and Jesus withdrawing from Jerusalem (10.40). The importance of Jn 5.1-18 in the development of the plot of the Gospel of John is therefore clear: it introduces the reasons for the Jews' hostility against Jesus and defines their role as his antagonists.

Jn 5.1-18 must also be read in close relation to the remainder of Jn 5.[1] The reference to the sabbath in vv. 9b-10, 16, and 18 raises the issue of Jesus' authority, which is the basis for the discourse in Jn 5.19-47. The Son's authority derives directly from the Father (vv. 19, 30). Because the Father is still working, it is right that the Son should do the works of the Father, even on the sabbath (vv. 17, 20). The healing was a sign pointing to the power of the Son to give life (v. 21), so the sign points ultimately to Jesus' role as the Son of God (v. 25) and Son of Man (v. 27) who will give life to all who believe and sit in judgement over all who will not believe (vv. 24-29). Jesus' authority is declared by John, the works that he does, the Father himself, the Scriptures, and even Moses; but still they do not

---

[1] See esp. J. Bernard, "La guérison de Bethesda. Harmoniques judéo-hellénistiques d'un récit de miracle un jour de sabbat", *Mélanges de Science Religieuse*, 33 (1976), pp. 3-34; 34 (1977), pp. 13-44.

believe (vv. 31-47). The issue is raised again in Jn 7, where in the context of further debate over Jesus' authority Jesus responds: "...are you angry with me because on the sabbath I made a man's whole body well?" (7.23). We see, therefore, that Jn 5.1-18 is not a self-contained unit artificially set in its context; it is an essential part of both the episode (Jn 5.1-47) and the larger section (Jn 5-10). We can trace a continuity of character, conflict, themes, and imagery from Jn 2-4, through Jn 5.1-18, and into Jn 5-10. Only when seen in this context can the pericope be interpreted adequately.

THE NARRATIVE STRUCTURE

We may now turn our attention to the narrative structure of the pericope itself.

Jn 5.1-18 is the third sign, the first that is not numbered. The pattern of the first two signs is fairly clear:[1]

(1) *A supplicant presents Jesus with a request:*
   implicit, "They have no wine" (2.3), or
   explicit, "he [the official] begged him to come down
      and heal his son" (4.47).
(2) *Jesus rebuffs the request:*
   to his mother: "O woman, what have you to do with me?
      My hour has not yet come" (2.4);
   to the official: "Unless you see signs and wonders you
      will not believe" (4.48).
(3) *The supplicant persists:*
   Jesus' mother (to the servants): "Do whatever he tells
      you" (2.5);
   The official: "Sir come down before my child dies"
      (4.49).
(4) *Jesus gives instructions that will grant the request:*
   to the servants: "Fill the jars with water"
      (2.7; see 2.8);
   to the official: "Go, your son will live" (4.50).
(5) *The other person complies with Jesus' order, and the sign is accomplished:*
   The servants fill the jars, draw from them and carry it
      to the chief steward (2.8-9);
   The official believes and goes home (4.50).
(6) *The sign is verified by a third party:*

---

[1] This sevenfold pattern was suggested to me by Paul D. Duke and H. Stephen Shoemaker, who picked it up in David Buttrick's preaching classes.

> The chief steward (who did not know the origin of the
> wine) calls the bridegroom and says: "Every man serves the
> good wine first...but you have kept the good wine until
> now" (2.10) [The irony is that the wine was not served by
> the bridegroom but by Jesus, and it had not been kept by
> any ἄνθρωπος but by the Lord.[1] Like good wine, good irony
> is delicious!]
> The official's servants met him and told him that his son was
> living. He asked them the hour when he began to get well.
> They said the seventh, and the father knew that that was
> the hour at which Jesus had said to him, "Your son will
> live" (4.51-53).
>
> (7) *There is a response of faith:*
> The disciples "believed in him" (2.11).
> The official "believed, and all his household" (4.53).

Following the reporting of the sign, in each of these cases, the sign is numbered (2.11; 4.54).

When compared with these first two signs, Jn 5.1-18 seems to be a deliberate variation on the form of a sign. Note the points of contrast:

(1) *A supplicant presents Jesus with a request.* But in Jn 5.1-18 the man at the pool asks nothing. It is Jesus who directs the question: "Do you want to be healed?" (5.6).

(2) *Jesus rebuffs the request.* In Jn 5, however, it is the cripple who is evasive: "Sir, I have no man (ἄνθρωπος) to put me into the pool when the water is troubled, and while I am going another steps down before me" (5.7). Again we note the irony: the cripple has no man to help; the incarnate logos stands before him ready to make him whole.

(3) *The supplicant persists.* Here, Jesus persists. Both the initial request and the response at this point in the first two signs are evidence of some degree of confidence in Jesus, but such openness to his power is missing in this story.

(4) *Jesus gives instructions that will grant the request:* "Rise, take up your pallet and walk" (5.8). At this point Jn 5.1-18 follows the form of the first two signs, except of course that the man had made no request. Jesus' authoritative word is central to the story.[2]

---

[1] On the ironic use of ἄνθρωπος in relation to Jesus in the Gospel of John, see: R. Alan Culpepper, *Anatomy of the Fourth Gospel: A Study in Literary Design* (Philadelphia: Fortress Press, 1983), pp. 171-172.

[2] See C.H. Dodd, *The Interpretation of the Fourth Gospel* (Cambridge: Cambridge University Press, 1953), pp. 319-320.

(5) *The other person complies with Jesus' order, and the sign is accomplished.* The healing is accomplished. The man took up his pallet and walked (5.9). In the first two signs the response of the servants and the official precedes the miracle; they act on Jesus' word and the miracle occurs. Here, however, the man became well and then took up his pallet and walked (5.9). The sequence is important: the miracle precedes his obedience, not vice versa as in the first two stories.

(6) *The sign is verified by a third party.* The Jews reprimand the one who had been healed for carrying his pallet on the sabbath, unwittingly verifying that the healing had been accomplished. Their role is similar to that of the chief steward at the wedding at Cana and the official's servants in the second story.

(7) *There is a response of faith.* In contrast to the first two signs, there is no response of faith. The man who had been healed reports Jesus to the Jews. They respond not with faith, but by persecuting Jesus (5.16, 18).

This comparison is illuminating. It shows how the evangelist plays with the form of a sign story once that form is set—and analysis of the subsequent signs would reveal further variations on this pattern. Jesus' word remains central to the sign, but the points of contrast between Jn 5.1-18 and the first two signs invite further attention to structure and characterisation in this third sign story.

Three characters appear in Jn 5.1-18: Jesus, the man at the pool, and the Jews. The disciples are never mentioned. Moreover, the story focuses on only two of the characters at time:

1. Jesus and the man at the pool (5.5-9a)
2. the Jews and the man who had been healed (5.10-13),
3. Jesus and the man (5.14),
4. the man and the Jews (5.15), and
5. Jesus and the Jews (5.16-18).

Observing this technique of pairing the characters off against each other helps us to divide the pericope into five scenes. We see immediately that while the story begins with an exchange between Jesus and the man at the pool, it ends with the confrontation between Jesus and the Jews that sets up the discourse in 5.19-47. The man at the pool features in the first four scenes and then disappears. In these four scenes he is with Jesus twice and with the Jews twice. Jesus appears in the first, the third, and the climactic fifth scene. The story, therefore, is like a dance in which the dancers exchange partners until the intended match is achieved.

The first three verses serve as a detailed introduction to the story. As we have seen, v. 1 serves as a transitional marker in the larger narrative, placing the action in the context of a Jewish festival and moving Jesus and the reader to Jerusalem. The narrator carries the reader into the story by moving from the general to the specific: Jerusalem; a pool; a multitude of invalids, blind, lame, paralysed; one man. Like a zoom lens on a camera this introduction brings the reader's attention to focus on the man at the pool.

The scene itself, of course, has been the subject of a great deal of discussion. The name of the pool is given variously in the manuscripts as Bethesda, Bethzatha, Bethsaida, and Belzetha. The Nestle 26th ed. persists in printing Bethzatha in the text, but Jeremias,[1] David J. Wieand,[2] Barrett,[3] Schnackenburg,[4] and others support the originality of the reading Bethesda. This reading receives further support from the Copper Scroll (3Q15 XI 12f.). Josephus refers to a place in Jerusalem called Bezetha (Jewish Wars 2.328, 530; 6.149-151), so Bethesda itself may be a corruption of an even earlier form.[5]

Let us return to our narrative-critical analysis. Once the stage has been set, the new character, the man at the pool, is introduced. We are given only a minimal description of the man because only his response to Jesus matters in this story. The action begins in the mind of Jesus, and the narrator provides us a brief "inside view," reporting that Jesus saw this man and knew that he had been there for a long time. Only then does a character speak.

Note the handling of time in this introduction to the story. The narrator races across Jesus' journey to Jerusalem, describes the setting at the pool, briefly takes note of the man's thirty-eight years of suffering, slows the tempo dramatically to tell us what Jesus knew at that time, and then finally reports direct speech, Jesus' question to the man. The introduction therefore contains both spatial and temporal changes in point of view. While zooming in on one man at a pool in Jerusalem, the pace of the narration slows from summary, to description, to dialogue. In the same verses there is a shift in verb tenses from the imperfect and aorist tenses in v. 1 to the present tense in the description of the setting, then from the imperfect verbs in vv. 3 and 5 to the present tense ($\lambda \acute{\epsilon} \gamma \epsilon \iota$) in v. 6. By this

---

[1] Joachim Jeremias, *Die Wiederentdeckung von Bethesda. Joh. 5,2,* FRLANT, 41 (Göttingen: Vandenhoeck und Ruprecht, 1949), pp. 6-8.

[2] David J. Wieand, "John V. 2 and the Pool of Bethesda," *NTS,* 12 (1966), pp. 392-404, esp. pp. 394-395.

[3] C.K. Barrett, *The Gospel according to St. John,* 2nd ed. (Philadelphia: Westminster Press, 1978), pp. 251-253.

[4] Schnackenburg, *John,* 2.94.

[5] For a summary and critique of the theses of Jeremias and Antoine Duprez, see W.D. Davies, *The Gospel and the Land: Early Christianity and Jewish Territorial Doctrine* (Berkeley: University of California Press, 1974), pp. 302-313.

change of spatial and temporal point of view the reader is brought right into the scene.

Similarly, at the end of the story the narrator provides a transition to the following discourse and the rest of the gospel narrative. The action is reported in present tense in v. 14 (εὑρίσκει), then in the aorist tense in v. 15. Verse 16 is the narrator's comment reflecting on the significance of the event as a completed action and pointing ahead to events that have not yet been reported in the narrative: "And this was why the Jews persecuted Jesus, because he did this on the sabbath." Verse 17 consequently seems detached from the story. We are not told where or when Jesus said this to the Jews, but v. 17 provides the point of transition for the discourse that follows in 5.19-47. Finally, v. 18 is a concluding comment from the narrator that repeats the substance of v. 16, emphasising its importance by repetition and driving home the significance of this story.

The beginning and ending of this story are clearly marked, therefore. By means of skilful narrative framing, involving changing spatial and temporal points of view, the reader is progressively drawn into and then removed from the scene of the action.[1]

THE CHARACTERS

Since most of the action is focused on the characters, and since they are paired off in the various scenes, I will organise my remaining comments around the three characters.

Jesus

The reader brings to Jn 5.1-18 at least the characterisation of Jesus that has emerged from the prologue and Jn 1-4. Those of us who have read these passages many times read with the full character of the Johannine Jesus in mind. I will refrain from entering into discussion of the merits of analysis from the perspective of a first time reader or an informed reader.[2] My own approach favours the perspectives and sensitivities of a reader familiar with the Johannine tradition since I believe the original, intended readers were probably familiar with the traditions of the Johannine community. It will not be possible here to trace fully the characterisation of Jesus in the Gospel. For a more complete discussion, please see the relevant sections of *Anatomy of the Fourth Gospel*.

---

[1] Cf. Culpepper, *Anatomy of the Fourth Gospel*, p. 31; Boris Uspensky, *A Poetics of Composition: The Structure of the Artistic Text and Typology of a Compositional Form*, trans. V. Zavarin and S. Wittig (Berkeley: University of California Press, 1973), pp. 71-75.

[2] See Stephen D. Moore, "Narrative Commentaries on the Bible", *Foundations and Facets Forum*, 3, 3 (September 1987), 44-47.

Here we will limit our attention to the verses at hand. The characterisation of Jesus is extended primarily through indirect means. That is, the narrator gives us a report of what Jesus did and said and how the other characters respond to him. From these reports we as readers test and extend the picture of Jesus that we have formed from reading the first four chapters of the Gospel. At three points, however, the narrator provides an "inside view" of what Jesus thought or knew, or an explanatory comment about the action being narrated. These comments are especially significant. We find them in verses 6, 16, and 18:

> "When Jesus saw him and knew that he had been lying there a
> long time..." (v. 6).
> "And this was why the Jews persecuted Jesus, because he did
> this on the sabbath" (v. 16.).
> "This was why the Jews sought all the more to kill him,
> because he not only broke the sabbath but also called God his
> Father, making himself equal with God" (v. 18).

The last two comments, of course, characterise the Jews as much or more than they do Jesus.

From what Jesus says and does we gain a distinct impression of his sovereign manner and his concern for the physical and spiritual needs of the man at the pool. Jesus initiates the exchange with the question, "Do you want to be healed?" He heals the man with an authoritative command. Jesus is not bound by religious law, even the sabbath law. Jesus then finds the man in the temple and warns him about the terrible consequences of sin. Parenthetically, we may note that while Jesus' warning in v. 14 may be interpreted as contradictory to his later pronouncement in Jn 9.2,[1] it is not necessary to understand from v. 15 an implication that the man's infirmity had been caused by his sin. Jesus may just as well be using the man's release from his infirmity as an occasion to warn him that he needs release from the power of sin even more.

Jesus' final pronouncement in v. 17 provides a lens through which to view the entire story. What Jesus has done, healing the man on the sabbath and then warning him about the awful consequences of sin, he has done because of his unique relationship to God as Father. Indeed, because Jesus does "what he sees the Father doing" (5.19) and the works the Father gives

---

[1] Haenchen reads the verse as affirming that illness is retribution for sin, and therefore assigns the verse to the Evangelist's source: *John 1*, ed. Ulrich Busse, trans. Robert W. Funk, Hermeneia (Philadelphia: Fortress Press, 1984), p. 247. See also Becker, *Das Evangelium nach Johannes*, p. 232.

him to do (5.36), we may understand that what Jesus has done is the work of the Father.

In this brief passage, therefore, we have a remarkable picture of Jesus as the one who mediates the power of God to human suffering. He frees the man at the pool from his physical brokenness and points him in the direction of spiritual health. He gives life. By his presence and his word he replaces holy places, festivals, and laws.[1] What Jesus does, moreover, he does as the Son of the Father, bound to the Father's will and authority. Because Jesus' role as Son involves violation of the religious laws pertaining to the sabbath and blasphemy, the Jews seek to kill him. This basis for the conflict between Jesus and the Jews is set both by Jesus' actions and by the narrator's concluding, interpretative comments.

The Man at the Pool

The cripple is one of the least defined characters in the Gospel. He appears only in these verses. All we are told about him is that he had been ill for thirty-eight years (v. 5), and he had been lying there a long time (v. 6). The rest we must gather from what he says and does.

The man at the pool is passive. Jesus approaches him, and he approaches him with a question about his will to be whole: "Do you want to be healed?" Although Haenchen disagrees, Dodd and Brown are probably right in inferring that the implication of Jesus' question is that the man at the pool lacked the will to be well.[2] Jesus is an authoritative figure, and we have just been told of his knowledge of the man's condition.

The man blames his continued infirmity on others. It is their fault that he could not get into the pool when the waters stirred. This character trait is reinforced when the man later answers the Jews by saying that it was not his fault that he was carrying his pallet on the sabbath. The one who had healed him had told him to do so.

The most puzzling aspect of his character concerns his final act, telling the Jews that it was Jesus who had healed him. Some interpreters have suggested that this act might be viewed as a positive witness for Jesus. Four factors seem to me to point in the direction of interpreting this act in a more negative way, as reporting Jesus to the Jewish authorities: (1) The man's earlier responses have established the trait of seeking to pass responsibility from himself to others; (2) Jesus' warning in v. 14 underlines that he is a sinner; (3) we have seen formal contrasts between

---

[1] See esp. Davies, *The Gospel and the Land*, p. 313: "God's creative activity in Christ is not tied to 'place' or 'time.'"

[2] Contrast Haenchen, *John 1*, pp. 245-246; Dodd, *Historical Tradition*, pp. 178-179; and Brown, *John*, p. 209.

this passage and the first two signs, where individuals come to believe in Jesus; and (4) this pericope functions to establish the opposition to Jesus and explain some of the reasons for it. Jesus, and later the preaching of the Gospel, encounters both active hostility and the obtuseness or self-centred blindness of individuals. The companion sign in Jn 9 shows a very different outcome from a similar healing.

The man at the pool is bound to his infirmity. Even when Jesus heals him, he remains a crippled person bound to himself and to sin because he will not open himself and respond with faith in Jesus.

The Jews

The characterisation of the Jews in the Gospel of John is greatly advanced by Jn 5.1-18. It should no longer be necessary to emphasise that we are concerned about the characterisation of the Jews in the Gospel of John, and that the characterisation in this Gospel should have no bearing on Christian-Jewish relations today. In this article I am no more concerned about the historical role of the Jews in the ministry of Jesus than I am with the historical Jesus. We are treating both Jesus and the Jews as characters in the gospel narrative. If we allow our interpretation of the Gospel to foster persecution of Jews, then we have betrayed both our Lord and the Christian faith.[1]

Jesus has encountered little opposition or conflict through the first four chapters of the Gospel. At most this conflict is foreshadowed in the interrogation of John the Baptist by those sent from the Jews and by Jesus' exchange with the Jews in the temple. With Jn 5.1-18, however, the conflict between Jesus and the Jews is established, and this conflict will build throughout the rest of the Gospel.

The Jews have only one concern in these verses: care that the law is obeyed, that the sabbath is honoured. Mishnah Yom Tob 6.2 declares that "Any act that is culpable on the Sabbath, whether by virtue of the rules concerning Sabbath rest or acts of choice or concerning pious duties, is culpable also on a Festival-day."[2] But this festival day was also the sabbath, and sabbath law forbade carrying a burden and healing when life is not threatened (m. Shabbath 7.2; m. Yoma 8.6).

The Jews appear in v. 10, just after the narrator has reported that the healing took place on the sabbath. By withholding this information and supplying it just at this point, the narrator forces the reader to review the healing from a new perspective which catches the reader by surprise. The Jews confirm the significance of this new information: "It is the sabbath, it

---

[1] See further my article, "The Gospel of John and the Jews", *Review and Expositor*, 84 (1987), 273-288.

[2] Herbert Danby, *The Mishnah* (Oxford: Oxford University Press, 1933), pp. 186-187.

is not lawful for you to carry your pallet" (v. 10). When the man blames his transgression of the law on his healer, the Jews naturally inquire as to the identity of the healer. When they learn from the man that it was Jesus, they begin to persecute him for this transgression of the sabbath law. Their opposition to Jesus because of his violation of the law is emphasised by the narrator's concluding comments in vv. 16 and 18. These comments at the end have the effect of telling us why this is an important story; it explains the origin of the conflict between Jesus and the Jews.

The characterisation of the Jews will be developed more fully in the following chapters, but Jn 5.1-18 is its foundation. They persecute Jesus and seek to kill him because he broke the law of Moses. They see in this sign not the healing, liberating power of God at work in Jesus but the sin of one who has broken the law. The Jews are presented here as bound to the law. Because they cannot see beyond the law, they oppose Jesus.

Perhaps it is not too subtle to say that each of the three characters in Jn 5.1-18 is bound: Jesus is bound to the will of the Father, the man at the pool is bound to his infirmity (and perhaps also to the power of sin), and the Jews are bound to the law. The action that takes place, therefore is the result of the bondage, or primary allegiance of each of these characters. Nor should we miss the importance of Bultmann's observation that when Jesus frees the man from his bondage he brings him in conflict with the law.[1] When one receives the revelation of the Son who is bound only to the Father, that one will invariably be brought into conflict with all other powers. The question is whether we will choose to live under the sovereignty of the Son or give in to the other powers with which we are put in conflict. Like the man at the pool, whose life was touched by the Son, the reader must choose whether he or she will walk with Jesus or with the human powers that oppose him.

RETROSPECT

So much has been written about the Gospel of John that it would be foolish to think that a new method would provide a radically new interpretation of a passage like Jn 5.1-18. Nevertheless, this exercise has been productive. By focusing attention on the story in the light of its features as narrative we have seen more clearly the importance of its contrast with the pattern set by the first two signs, the skill with which changing spatial and temporal point of view is handled in the beginning and end of the story, the importance of noting the role of the narrator throughout the story, and the skilful depiction of the three characters. By paying attention to the

---

[1] Bultmann, *John*, p. 247.

narrative features of the text we have gained a fresh appreciation for its artistry and power.

THE BIRTH OF A BEGINNING: JOHN 1.1-18*

WERNER H. KELBER

Henceforth, it was necessary to begin thinking that there was no centre, that the centre could not be thought in the form of present-being, that the centre had no natural site, that it was not a fixed locus but a function, a sort of nonlocus in which an infinite number of sign-substitutions came into play. This was the moment when language invaded the universal problematic, the moment when, in the absence of a centre or origin, everything became discourse.

Jacques Derrida

The beginning is the most important part of the work.

Plato

Look with favour upon a bold beginning.

Virgil

The beginnings and endings of all human undertakings are untidy...

John Galsworthy

0. INTRODUCTION

In John's gospel narrative as in any other literary work there is a need for commencement, for "without at least a sense of a beginning, nothing can really be done, much less ended" (Said: 49-50). Each author must make a commitment to a point of departure from which the work is to take its initiative. In John's case, the beginning is consciously constructed in the so-called prologue to the gospel (Jn 1.1-18). It signals a prefatory gesture which prepares the way for what is to come. The beginning of the Λόγος ("Word") in and with God, his coming as life and light into the darkness of the world, the baptiser's witness to him, the rejection by his own, the calling forth of the children of God, the Λόγος incarnational mission and the radiance of his glory, his superiority over Moses, and his implied

---

* This article appeared in *Semeia* 52 (1990), pp. 120-144.

seeing of God—these are the dramatic and thematic directives which guide the reading of what follows.

What distinguishes the Johannine prologue is that its ambitions go far beyond the need to introduce the gospel narrative. It accomplishes more than any conventional function of beginning. For in writing a beginning to his narrative the author harks back to the transcendental beginning of the world. This designation of the primordial, divine ἀρχή ("beginning") involves the writer in one of the intrinsic paradoxes of beginnings. For ὁ Λόγος ἐν ἀρχῇ ("the Word in the beginning"), while insinuating foundational stability, can in his logocentric self-centredness engender neither world nor text. A disestablishment of the ἀρχή is required to get the narrative under way. Indeed, the decentring of the Λόγος provides the very rationale for the narrative. And thus the prologue in preparing for what is to come already seeks to overcome the Λόγος ἐν ἀρχῇ even as it inscribes him ἐν ἀρχῇ. From this perspective, the crucial issue raised by the prologue is the issue of beginning itself.

1. WISDOM'S MYTH

Among the countless models invoked as ideological prototype for John's pre-existent Λόγος, Jewish Wisdom can at present be regarded as the favourite candidate. Coming forth from the mouth of the Most High, Wisdom existed at the beginning before the world was created (Wis 9.1-2; Prov 8.22-23). Subsequent to her participation in the work of divine creation (Prov 8.27-31), she was sent down from the heavenly abode to make a dwelling place on earth (Wis 9.1-2; Sir 24.8ff). Whoever finds her, will find life (Prov 8.35), for she is like a tree spreading forth its branches of glory and grace (Sir 24.16). But she cannot herself find a resting place on earth, because all foolish men reject her (En 42.2). This Wisdom presentation in the canonical and apocryphal books of the Hebrew Bible offers "good parallels for almost every detail of the Prologue's description of the Word" (Brown: 523). It clearly provides us with a key to the principal operations of the Λόγος.

Undoubtedly, history of religion parallels and the comparative method can serve as heuristic aids in interpretation. But all too often paradigms such as Wisdom, or the earlier gnostic redeemer myth (Colpe; Johnson: 91-126) were developed into synthetic reconstructions taking on a life of their own which they never enjoyed in actual religious history. Even if it is granted that there existed an identifiable Wisdom myth, the prologue still does not live up to it in all its aspects. The baptiser's witness, the contradictory juxtaposition of flesh and glory, the contrast between Christ and Moses, and the issue of the visibility versus the invisibility of God are not recognisable as distinctive Wisdom features. What seems to be required, therefore, is a determination not simply of the paradigm embraced by John, but of the use made of it, a process which inevitably entails transformations (Kee: 99-125).

Comparative recourse to history of religion models can also prevent us from asking more probing questions. If John's beginning is as deeply informed by Wisdom as many interpreters are inclined to suggest, why is it that neither σοφία ("wisdom") nor σοφός ("wise man") are featured in prologue or gospel narrative? If one assumes that Jesus could not be identified with the female σοφία, it must be pointed out that both Q (Matt 11.19b/Luke 7.35) and Paul (1 Cor 2.24) were doing just that. The very existence of Wisdom features in the prologue forces the question why John's Jesus is introduced as Λόγος, and not as Σοφία . Reference to the interchangeability of σοφία with λόγος in hellenistic Judaism, and to Philo's transference of σοφία attributes upon the λόγος (Mack: 96-107,141-54) is but another recourse to the history of religious ideas which leaves the basic question unanswered. Why does the Johannine prologue perceive Jesus as entering the darkness of the world not as Wisdom, but in fact as Λόγος?

To rely on Wisdom as *the* explanatory model is to content ourselves with surface answers, and to sustain our belief in the beginning of the Λόγος as a theological commonplace. Recourse to an analogous intellectual model hardly does justice to the historical and philosophical questions raised by the genesis of the logocentric ἀρχή. Here as elsewhere we have prematurely grown satisfied with results obtained by the comparative method, results so eminently plausible as to distract us from a genuinely critical interrogation. For in the history of ideas little is genuinely understood by appeal to external influences on a text. "In order for an 'influence' of alien concepts to be absorbed, a situation must have previously emerged within which these concepts could be greeted as an aid for the expression of a problem already present" (Pannenberg: 153). Indeed, the appropriation of a Λόγος christology in completely detached fashion seems all the more unlikely in view of Martyn's recent demonstration of John's narrative engagement in and response to his contemporary situation. What was it in the tradition from which the gospel emerged that inspired the evangelist to postulate the beginning of Jesus as Λόγος ἐν ἀρχῇ? In philosophical, postmodern terms, the apotheosis of the Λόγος signifies the quintessential logocentric gesture (Derrida, 1976, 1978, 1981). Installed in privileged position, the Λόγος presents himself as foundational stability, a force outside of time and prior to world. He constitutes transparency and transcendence in full regalia. In thus elevating Jesus to the position of transcendental signified, the prologue has accomplished what postmodernism fears most about logocentrism: a fundamental immobility which seeks to stall the flux of life and to conceal the permutations and transformations that give birth to all elements, including that of the Λόγος himself. World and language are reduced to the primordial reference point which delimits play and consummates desire. Viewed from this angle, the Λόγος proves himself to be a child of the archaeology of the human spirit which always places an ἀρχή (as well as a τέλος) above the flux of discourse.

The postmodern polemic toward logocentrism has the minimal advantage of teaching us that Wisdom's myth hardly exhausts the way we can think about the Λόγος. This transcendental Λόγος who acts as preexistent referent, who does not submit to any external tribunal, and who touches base with none other but himself in Divinity and with Divinity in himself...this Λόγος claims absolute authoritative privileges. Precisely because scholarship has safely tucked him away in Wisdom's myth and has made him look so natural, so innocent, he merits closer scrutiny. Precisely because John's prologue raised the issue of beginning to its transcendental outer limits, it deserves critical examination.

All writings strive to constitute authority for themselves and for their readers, and one of the principal functions of a written beginnings is to install authority "by allowing it to be set forth as clearly and in as much detail as possible" (Said:16). Concealed in the Λόγος posture of underived origin and transcendental presence is a strong will to power, and we must ask him who claims these categorical privileges: Whence did you acquire this privileged position? Is there no prior otherness that you are dependent on and which is concealed by your imperial gesture?

2. THE ΛΟΓΟΙ AND THE ΛΟΓΟΣ

To obtain a fresh perspective on the Johannine Λόγος we turn to Polycarp's letter to the Philippians which records the following outburst:

> Everyone who does not confess that Jesus Christ has come in the flesh is an antichrist: and whoever shall not confess the testimony of the cross, is of the devil; and whoever perverts *the words* of the Lord...and says there is neither resurrection nor a judgement, that man is the firstborn of Satan. Therefore let us abandon the foolishness of the great majority and the false teachings, and let us return to *the Word* which was transmitted to us from the beginning (7.1-2).

Writing at the beginning of the second century, Polycarp addressed "the great majority" of heretics among the Philippian Christians with a polemical shrillness which appears excessive even when measured against the customary agonistic tone of ancient rhetoric. Highly offensive as the statement is for us, it does give us insight into the heart of the bishop's anxiety. Apparently a majority of the Christians at Philippi availed itself of "the words of the Lord" in ways which prompted a denial of incarnation, the cross, individual resurrection and future judgement. How is it that the dominical λόγοι ("words") could become the centre of so grave a controversy?

Without immediately invoking the ill-definable concept of gnosis or gnosticism, it can be plausibly argued that what Polycarp condemned as a "perversion of the words of the Lord" constituted a language world which was marked by distinctly oral attributes. For what he denounced as a heretical distortion of the sayings describes rather well their efficacy in an oral, life-giving sense. Words when spoken are bound to present time and in a sense advertise presentness (Ong: 101, 167-69, passim). The oral performance of the λόγοι of the Lord likewise manifests presence. If, moreover, in the early Christian milieu the words were spoken prophetically, e.g., in the name and on the authority of the living Lord, they could be understood as effecting both the presence of Christ and communion with him. But whenever the dominical λόγοι were experienced as a presently realised authority grounded in the living Jesus, then the past of Jesus' earthly existence and his death, and also a future resurrection of the believers and eschatology in general had lost their meaning. If the words of the Lord conveyed present life, why bother about his past life or an alleged future life? We have no way of knowing whether Polycarp had a sayings or discourse gospel in mind, a genre which despite writing's countervailing force retained the speaking fiction of the "living Jesus" or the "risen Christ." But the problem he addressed and the "heresy" he repudiated was that of a metaphysics of presence which thrived on an oral apperception of the dominical sayings.

In view of the Philippians' heresy it is instructive to observe the strategy Polycarp used to cut the ground from under the "perversion" of the dominical sayings. The bishop who in the spirit of emergent orthodoxy insisted on redemption grounded in Jesus' past and consummated only as eschatological experience, appears to have questioned at least by implication a full soteriological efficacy of the oral proclamation of the "words of the Lord." The same concern must have motivated his counsel to return to the Word as it was in the beginning. His invocation of the Λόγος ἐν ἀρχῇ comes in the face of the λόγοι whose administration has proven problematic. In this sense the Λόγος ("Word") is constituted as authority over the heretical application of the λόγοι ("words"). The Λόγος asserts control over the λόγοι.

In view of John's own preponderance of sayings and discourses, is it believable that his elevation of Jesus to Λόγος was as disinterested in the problematics of these λόγοι as it appears from studies on the prologue? Could one not in analogy to Polycarp's regressive move from the λόγοι to the Λόγος postulate a similar motivation for the Johannine installation of the transcendental Λόγος? In different words, we are inclined to assume an intra-Johannine dynamic between the λόγοι and the Λόγος which illuminates John's predilection for the authoritative singular. This is not to dismiss the influence of Wisdom altogether. But it is to postulate *both* external *and* internal dynamics in the formation of the Johannine Λόγος.

In distinction to the other three canonical gospels, the fourth gospel has availed itself of a sayings tradition of massive proportions. The Farewell Discourse alone (Jn 13.31-17.26), a vast repertoire of speech materials, comprises approximately one-fifth of the gospel. If we discount chapter 21 as a later redactional addition, three-fourths of chapters 1-20 consist of sayings, dialogues, and monologues. And if one disregards the narratologically more densely composed passion-resurrection story, approximately four-fifths of the preceding chapters 1-17 appear to consist of sayings (Sneller). So impressive is the sheer quantity of sayings in John that the question has been raised whether the gospel, or at least its sayings tradition, could have arisen out of anthological, clustering processes (Dewey).

As a result of the inscription of so large a mass of λόγοι, John's Jesus is by far "the most communicative" of the four protagonists dramatised in the canonical gospels (Kermode: 453). In his capacity as the incarnate Λόγος he delivers a preponderance of λόγοι. These are shaped into discourses which either stand by themselves or emanate from narrative segments. Most discourses aspire to the scenario of dialogues between Jesus and various interlocutors, but many in effect end up as monologues. In the most general sense the gospel is thus characterised by a sequence of narrative scenes and speech complexes with the focus frequently falling on the latter.

The tradition-historical provenance of the gospel's sayings tradition has long been an issue in Johannine scholarship. Perhaps the most prominent thesis developed in this regard was that of the *history-of-religions school* which flourished in the first four decades of this century. In genre, style, and conceptualisation the bulk of the gospel's sayings was said to have been drawn from a "book of revelation discourses" (Bultmann, 1971:17, n. 5, passim) which was gnostic in general outlook. It was assumed to have its closest parallels in Mandaean texts, and to have been related to Manichaean literature and to the Odes of Solomon as well. The Mandaean texts were traced back to the first century and assumed to have originated among the followers of John the Baptist. In sum, therefore, the *history-of-religions school* postulated a revelation discourse of gnostic, baptismal origin which John demythologised in the interest of his own christological project. The redeemer who enters the flesh belies the cosmic dualism of gnostic persuasion. As Bultmann understood the matter, however, John's revisionist project did not go so far as to erase the gnostic disposition of the source altogether: "Jesus [in John] is the perfect Gnostic, who knows his origin and his goal" (1971: 487).

Kloppenborg's recent work on Q has reminded us once again of the international character of sayings traditions, which range from Egyptian and Near Eastern Wisdom collections and Hellenistic gnomologia all the way to Cynic and rabbinic chriae arrangements. On the matter of sayings collections, early Christianity was thus a participant in widely practised cultural activities. Given the Christians' proven ability to make environmental genres and myths their own, the assumption of direct dependencies on a non-Christian source may oversimplify and unnecessarily rigidify more complex interactive processes. The proposition of an intrinsic Johannine sayings tradition worked out in creative adaptation to surrounding models has been strengthened by the discovery of the Nag Hammadi codices (Robinson, 1977). At least nine of the fifty-two Nag Hammadi tractates are either in part or *in toto* structured around the model of the sayings or discourse genre. A growing body of largely North American scholarship influenced by the work of Robinson and Koester has increasingly alerted us to the manifold analogies that exist between the Johannine sayings arrangements and the genre of sayings or discourse gospel at Nag Hammadi. Specifically Koester's studies of notable parallels between Johannine sayings and those in the Nag Hammadi sayings genre (1980a, 1980b, 1982:178-85), and Robinson's demonstration of a Johannine (and Markan) revision of Jesus' speech ἐν παραβολαῖς ("in parables"), or ἐν παροιμίαις ("in figures") versus his speaking ἐν παρρησίᾳ ("in plain speech; openly")—distinct genre designations of the sayings or discourse gospel—have made it ever more likely that John drew on and recontextualised an intrinsically Christian sayings genre.

At times the genre consists of discrete and identifiable sayings or parables of the Lord, as for example in Thomas, but more frequently sayings and parables are developed into running dialogues and discourses, as with the *Apocryphon of James*. What characterises all forms of the genre is a communication of the "living Jesus" or "risen Lord" to a privileged group of recipients, usually some trusted male and oftentimes female disciples. Both the exclusivity of audience and the "living" authority of the speaker suggest the theological category of "revelation discourses," the very category which had long been suspected of having formed the centre of generic identity for the Johannine sayings tradition. John's Farewell Speech in particular has many of the hallmarks of just such a revelation discourse. Its heavy concentration of speech materials consisting of sayings, clusters of sayings and dialogues, the exclusivity of audience which is limited to certain of the disciples, the ambiguity of Jesus' authority which far from being fully earthbound appears at times to be that of the "living" Lord (Jn 16.4; 17.11-12), use of the technical designations of speaking ἐν παροιμίαις ("in figures") versus ἐν παρρησίᾳ ("in plain speech; openly") (Jn 16.25, 29), as well as proven parallels between Johannine sayings and those in the discourse gospels— these are all indications of certain affinities between the Johannine Farewell Discourse and the genre of the revelation discourse.

Jesus' identity as the "living" or "risen" Lord suggests an authority that is operative in the present. His communication to an exclusive group of recipients, moreover, seeks to prevent dissemination among the many, and to assure self-disclosure among the privileged few. The virtual absence of a narrative framework further contributes to the open and direct address character of the discourses. Despite the fact that the revelation discourse is already a written product, it is motivated by the desire to overcome a sense of pastness that comes with all writing. In different words, the genre still seeks to cling to a metaphysics of presence.

That there could exist a connection between the λόγοι and the Λόγος in John has recently been suggested in what is the most exhaustive treatment of the prologue in modern exegetical history:

> The fact that it [the body of the gospel] recognises that Jesus' significance lies in his faultless articulation as reliable messenger of the words of God by virtue of his own personal engagement, is sufficient ground to call him the Word himself, the exegesis of God. In this way, the central significance of the theology of the Word in the body of the gospel corresponds to the citation of the Λόγος in the prologue (Theobald: 301-02).

In accounting for a link between the λόγοι and the Λόγος, Theobald appealed in general terms to a Johannine theology of the Word, while barely touching on the issue of the revelation discourse. And yet, the Johannine Jesus appears to have been promoted to the status of transcendental Word not merely because he was known as speaker of words, but more specifically because the genre of his many words had become an issue for the writer of the narrative gospel. John who espoused incarnation, death and futurity, could not allow the revelation discourse to remain on its own generic cognisance, for that genre's sympathies with a metaphysics of presence conflicted with the genius of narrativity to retrieve the past of Jesus' life and death. For John the dominical words were not those of the "living Jesus," a strangely disembodied figure, but almost always those of a historicised person. And even in those instances where the risen Lord speaks in John, his authority is grounded in an antecedent incarnational life and tested by a victorious death. Not unlike Polycarp, John grappled with the operation of the dominical λόγοι, but unlike the bishop he proceeded to incarnate the discourses in a narration of Jesus' life and death.

Recognition that John grappled with a revelation discourse model still does not explain the intra-Johannine logic that inspired the transcendentality of the preexistent Λόγος. What characterises the relation of the λόγοι with the Λόγος *is* plurality versus singularity, an issue in evidence elsewhere in the Johannine narrative. F.-M. Braun (40-67) has observed a Johannine tendency to refocus attention from the plural to the singular. The plural "commandments" (αἱ ἐντολαί) culminate in the "new commandment" (Jn 13.34: ἐντολῆ καινῆ); Jesus' "many works" (τὰ ἔργα) are accomplished in his "work" of glorification (Jn 17.4: τὸ ἔργον); the sign of the "loaves" of bread (οἱ ἄρτοι) gives rise to Jesus' self-identification as "the Bread" (Jn 6.48: ὅς ἄρτος); the "disciples" (οἱ μαθηταί) find ideal representation in the "Beloved Disciple" (Jn 19.26: ὁ μαθητὴς ὃν ἠγάπα ὁ Ἰησοῦς); the "sheep" (τὰ πρόβατα) shall become "one flock" and even "one shepherd" (Jn 10.16: μία ποίμνη, εἰς ποιμήν). A movement from the plural to the singular is thus an intrinsic feature of the Johannine narrative.

On this showing it is tempting to suspect a similar motivation for John's predisposition toward the metaphysical elevation of the Λόγος. A passage from the λόγοι to the Λόγος seems all the more plausible since the ownership of and authority over the λόγοι is indeed an issue for John. To be sure, the assumed movement from the λόγοι to the Λόγος grew out of composition-theological deliberations, whereas the above-mentioned examples are intrinsic to the narrative. We are dealing with two different, though not unrelated, spheres of hermeneutical activity. We shall in the concluding section probe a further motive for the constitution of Jesus Christ as transcendental authority vis-à-vis a competing authority. The point to be made here is that John's penchant for singularity in the face of plurality always entails the creation of authority. Just as authority is created by the new commandment, the work of glorification, the bread of life, the Beloved Disciple, the one flock or the one shepherd, so does in like manner the apotheosis of the single Λόγος constitute authority, and authority first and foremost over the plural λόγοι. In thus reaching beyond λόγοι and discourses of λόγοι toward the Λόγος ἐν ἀρχῆ, an authority is created which encompasses all the λόγοι, clusters of λόγοι, and the genre of revelation discourse itself. But whereas the "living Jesus" of the revelation discourse had been operative in the present, the Johannine Λόγος is lodged at the furthermost end of time, in the ultimate temporal anteriority of origin. In John, therefore, the beginning of writing initiates origin, and the textual creation of origin constitutes absolute authority.

Undoubtedly John's preexistent Word epitomises primary, oral utterance and not textualised verbalisation. The Λόγος constitutes personalised speech, or in mere traditional theological, but thoroughly oral terms, "a Person, God like the Father, but a different Person from the Father" (Ong: 185). And yet, the Λόγος cannot be verified as a child of oral interests and dynamics. For orality traffics in a plurality of λόγοι each of which presents itself as the *Urwort*. At best, therefore, there exists a plurality of original λόγοι, hence not the Johannine concept of the single Λόγος (Lord). This leads us to conclude that the privileging of the Λόγος, this logocentric reduction of the λόγοι to the Λόγος, was inspired by écriture. Once we concede a Johannine move from the λόγοι to the Λόγος, the latter stands exposed as a textually reinvented, monumentalised authority. Once we recognise an intra-Johannine dynamic between the λόγοι and the Λόγος, the latter shows itself as individualised, fantasised orality which has grown out of a process of metaphorical displacements and deferrals. In this sense the Λόγος ἐν ἀρχῇ reveals itself as being dependent on a prior otherness which was always already there.

3. DECENTRING AND INCARNATION

The beginning of John's prologue signals authority in view of what is to follow. It points forward to a continuity for which it has itself paved the way. In this sense, the Johannine constitution of a beginning and the inauguration of narrative seem rationally and unproblematically related to each other. "And yet we cannot forget that the authority limits as much as it enables" (Said: 34), and the more distant and transcendental it gives itself out to be, the greater the complications in what is to follow. Philosophically, how is the absolute Λόγος who has given himself to God and God to him, become the life and light of men? How does absolute Being transform itself into Becoming? Pragmatically, how is the metaphysical Λόγος ever going to engender linguistic or historical consecutiveness unless he somehow sets himself apart from his own totalising origin? In thus postulating a metaphysical fixed point behind the scenes, the prologue has created a problem for what is to follow, and the subsequent narrative is not simply the authorised product of the central authority, but also a way of coming to terms with the problems created by transcendental originality.

The fourth gospel, no less than Nietzsche, Freud, Heidegger or Derrida, affirms a decentring, and it does so in dramatic and ostentatious fashion. Apart from installing the Λόγος, the most important function of the prologue is to engineer his decentring from ἀρχή What it announces as the "coming into the world" (Jn 1.9c ἐρχόμενον εἰς τὸν κόσμον) amounts to a surrender of his privileged position in the interest of the human condition. The Λόγος was installed ἐν ἀρχῇ only to be dislodged from it. In applying the incision at the most decisive point, namely at the origin, the prologue administers decentring, a deconstruction of its own ontotheological foundation. Centring as much as decentring, and logocentrism no less than antilogocentrism are enacted in the prologue's programme.

The centring and decentring operations of the prologue have a direct bearing on the materiality of the gospel text and on the nature of its narrative project. An unremitting fixation on the metaphysical self-realisation of the Λόγος would not emanate into textuality. If a text was to assert itself and to survive its own logocentric origin, it had to strive to differ. This was the more desirable as ruptures with centres of self-reference have a way of engendering new modes of representation. Having predicated the absolute authority of the Λόγος as well as his decentring, John's gospel made the consequences of the Λόγος' displacement its prime objective. Indeed, it owes its existence not to the Λόγος' transcendental posture *per se*, but rather to his dislodgement from central place. The gospel justifies itself by narrating the self-effacement of the Λόγος, and it creates the *raison d'être* of its own written existence by tracing the Λόγος across the flux of human life.

Linguistically one is tempted to concur with Derrida that as a result of the rupture with primordiality "everything became [narrative] discourse," and that the decentring from the transcendental signified "extends the domain and the play of signification infinitely" (1978: 280). And theologically one is inclined to think that incarnation obliges readers to understand themselves not in relation to transcendentality, but to the worldly existence and crucifixion of the Λόγος. But it remains to be seen whether primordial authority is absorbed into narrative discourse, or if it strives to loom above narrative life.

In all, the centring and decentring operations of the prologue narrate three beginnings: the beginning of the Λόγος who is grounded in the preexistent ἀρχή (Jn 1.1), the beginning of John (the baptiser) whose witness introduces Jesus' ministry (Jn 1.6-8,15), and Jesus' own earthly beginning which sets the stage for his incarnational mission (John 1.14).

John's threefold beginnings signify three stages of Jesus' ἀρχή: the transcendental origin, his historical inauguration, and his own incarnational commencement (Theobald, 210). The making of a beginning has a way of begetting more beginnings, and the more distanced the primary beginning, e.g. the origin, the greater the need for decentring and successive beginnings.

The Λόγος' "coming into the world" raises the problem of his own earthly beginning. Where is his point of earthly inception to be located, and what is his mode of commencement? His primordial, logocentric beginnings, far from answering these questions, merely intensify the problems surrounding his incarnational appearance. The prologue addresses the issue by introducing John (the baptiser) in place of the expected Λόγος ἐν σαρκος ("Word incarnate"). Authorised by God (Jn 1.6: ἄνθρωπος ἀπεσταλμένος παρὰ θεού ["a man sent from God"]), the baptiser bears witness to Jesus, the light, so as to engender the faith of all in him. What clearly matters is John's witness, and not his apocalyptic proclamation or his baptismal activity. By witnessing to Jesus, the baptiser both inaugurates and legitimates him as the light come into the world. In that sense he addresses the problem of the Logos' earthly beginning.

There are, however, deeper complications lodged in the beginnings of John and Jesus. Although the baptiser proclaims the arrival of Jesus, the former is not strictly cast into the role of precursor, and although John is primarily witnessing to Jesus, it is his emphatic subordination to Jesus which typifies his narrative role and personal witness. When, for example, the narrator stipulates that John's witness precludes the latter's identification with light and life (Jn 1.8: οὐκ ἦν ἐκεῖνος τὸ φῶς, ἀλλ' ἵνα μαρτυρήσῃ περι τοῦ φωτός ["he was not the light, but came to bear witness to the light"]), he is thereby advising readers not to confuse John with Jesus himself. And when at a later point John himself insists on his inferior status vis-à-vis Jesus' transcendent priority (Jn 1.15: Ὁ ὀπίσω μου ἐρχόμενος ἔμπροσθέν μου γέγονεν, ὅτι πρῶτός μου ἦν ["He who comes after me ranks before me, for he was before me"]), his witness to Jesus amounts to a confession of subordination. It is entirely in accord with this subordinationist witness when outside the prologue the baptiser proclaims himself not to be the Christ (Jn 1.20, 3.28: Ἐγὼ οὐκ εἰμὶ ὁ Χριστός ["I am not the Christ"]). Clearly, the beginnings of Jesus and John are fraught with complications.

It has long been recognised that John (the baptiser's) defensive posture betokens a tradition which viewed him as a messianic personality of singular prominence (Baldensperger; Cullmann: 33-34; Smith: 26-27). This need not cause us to register full agreement with Bultmann's well-known thesis according to which the prologue was based on "a hymn of the Baptist community" (1971:18; cf. 108,174) which regarded John as the Revealer sent by God (84-97), and which provided the source for what came to be the Mandaean texts (1925). But it is undeniable that the prologue addresses the issue of competing allegiances to John and Jesus. The presence of a beginning has a way not only of begetting additional beginnings, but also of provoking rival beginnings. John's beginning has entered into conflict with Jesus' earthly beginning. Who is the authentic messianic inaugurator? This is the issue taken up in John's witness and resolved in the language of belatedness versus temporal priority (Foster: 113-14). Despite his belated appearance Jesus remains prior in time and hence superior in authority. The logical implications of anteriority and posteriority are thereby reversed. And if we inquire into the rationale for this reversal, we are led back to logocentric originality. Jesus' metaphysical protology enabled him to overcome his earthly belatedness.

Following the constitution of the Λόγος' transcendental ἀρχῇ and John's inaugural witness, Jesus' own incarnational mission marks the third beginning. The prologue enacts it with the memorable words: "...the Word became flesh...and we beheld His glory" (Jn 1.14: ὁ λόγος σὰρξ ἐγένετο...καὶ ἐθεασάμεθα τὴν δόξαν αὐτοῦ). This third beginning which sets the logical and theological premise for the subsequent narrative creates a dilemma of perplexing proportions. The assertions that "the Word became flesh" and that "we beheld his glory" generate a tension between what has conventionally been called an incarnational versus an epiphanic christology, two virtually unnegotiable concepts. In less traditional terms, the σάρξ/δόξα ("flesh/glory") dichotomy articulates the problematics of contingency and transparency, and of the signifier versus the signified. In the words of the prologue, "the light shines in the darkness" (Jn 1.5: τὸ φῶς ἐν τῇ σκοτίᾳ φαίνει), which suggests that the Incarnate somehow embodies transcendence in worldly contingency. The very narrative which grew out of the displacement of the metaphysical Λόγος seeks to retain his metaphysical profile.

Bultmann has explicated this dilemma as a theologically inescapable predicament intrinsically lodged in the Johannine concept of revelation. In his view, the gospel's main theme is incarnation. "It is in his sheer humanity that [the Λόγος] is the Revealer". But unless the δόξα were intelligible and indeed visible, "there would be no grounds for speaking of revelation". On the issue of the relation between σάρξ and δόξα Bultmann claims that "the δόξα is not to be seen *alongside* the σάρξ, nor through the σάρξ as through a window," but "in the σάρξ and nowhere else". This does suggest to him that "revelation is present in a peculiar hiddenness" (Bultmann 1971: 63). Understood in this sense, "revelation is a question, is an offence," and "the paradox which runs through the whole gospel" (1971: 62-63). Precisely speaking, therefore, Bultmann has *"aufgehoben"* (both suspended and preserved) the conflict between the incarnational and the epiphanic christology in the paradox of revelation.

Käsemann's provocative response to the Bultmannian position is well known. Already in his early study on the Johannine prologue (1969 [1957]) he stated emphatically: "This theme [of δόξα] is at the same time that of the whole Gospel which is concerned exclusively throughout with the presence of God in Christ" (159). His account with Bultmann is finally settled in his monograph on the high-priestly prayer the principal purpose of which is to develop the presence of δόξα vis-à-vis the σάρξ as the leading theme of the gospel (1968 [1966]). Is not, Käsemann asked rhetorically, the statement ὁ λόγος σάρξ ἐγένετο ("the Word became flesh") "totally overshadowed by the confession 'We beheld his glory,' so that it [the former] receives meaning from it [the latter]" (1968: 9-10). Jesus "belongs totally on the side of God even while he is on earth" (11). If, however, incarnation "does not mean complete, total entry into the earth, into human existence, but rather the encounter between the heavenly and the earthly" (65), and if Johannine christology is one of "naive" or "unreflected docetism" (26, 66), giving us a picture of "Jesus as God walking on the face of the earth" (73), and if in "the absence of a theology of the cross" (51) it is to be concluded that "the *praesentia Christi* is the centre of his [John's] proclamation" (15), then Bultmann's paradoxical concept of revelation and indeed "the use of the catchword 'paradox' becomes questionable..." (17).

Käsemann's thesis was in turn subjected to critical analysis by Bornkamm. From the latter's perspective, John has developed a genuine *theologia crucis*. To regard the passion narrative as an afterthought is hardly in accord with Johannine theology, for it is with growing intensity that the gospel story anticipates and prepares for the "hour" of Jesus' death (Bornkamm: 114). Käsemann's picture of "Jesus as God walking on the face of the earth" strongly resembles that of the pre-Johannine miracles, a tradition the gospel has subjected to criticism (115-16). Likewise, Jn 1.14, the formula of Jesus' incarnational commencement, already presupposes the existence of a gnostic worldview which the narrator of the prologue seeks to counteract (118). If, therefore, one interprets the gospel undialectically and in linear fashion as a story marked by docetism and voided of the cross, "one has at best arrived at the pre-Johannine tradition, but not at John" (117).

All three studies view the prologue's announcement of Jesus' incarnational commencement as a programmatic, theological thesis which the subsequent narrative undertakes to explicate or to resolve. Bultmann alone enlarges upon the inherently problematic nature of Jn 1.14, but he quickly converts the problem into a theological virtue. What further characterises these studies is the absence of a close narratological reading so as to demonstrate how John in fact did undertake to work out the problem of Jesus' earthly, but glorified mission. That the prologue could have posed a dilemma for the gospel which does not lend itself to a theological or narratological solution, however paradoxical a solution that might be, and that it lands the narrative into perplexing and inextricable dilemmas, is a thought not entertained with any degree of seriousness in Johannine studies.

A new generation of interpreters (Culpepper, Duke, O'Day) who are attuned to literary criticism has pursued more closely the narratological implications of the predicament announced in the prologue's third beginning. To reconcile the irreconcilable the narrative embarked upon the difficult and risky path of irony and metaphor, of *double entendre* and linguistic duplicity. A whole semiology of language is put to work blazing a trail from flesh to glory. It is this linguistic struggle over the relation of corporeality to transparency which accounts for a good deal of dramatic tension and conflict. "Those who were his own did not receive him" (Jn 1.11). With these words the prologue announces the tragic consequences of its own programme. The ones the gospel designates as "the Jews" will as a rule not be able to follow the signifying directionality of signs and words toward the transcendent signified. For them Jesus' autistic reference to his own zone of immaculate ideation is blasphemy provoking the charge that he is "making himself equal with God" (Jn 5.18). Caught in the dilemma of juxtaposing flesh and glory, they end up victims of the gospel's extravagantly ambitious project.

Others who receive the Λόγος are privileged to be called "children of God" (Jn 1.12). They are the ones "who believe in His name"...and are "born...of God" (Jn 1.12-13). And yet, many characters in the narrative, including the disciples, have difficulty in understanding, or believe in the protagonist for the wrong reasons. That the readers are in the better position is, of course, a hermeneutical commonplace. As a rule literary interpreters have suggested that for the readers John's figurative language serves the aim of revelation. O'Day's programmatic statement typifies the current literary, theological viewpoint: John's "irony is a mode of revelatory language" (31). On this view, the gospel's semiology of language is constructed primarily for the purpose of serving as a detour toward transparency, inviting readers "in an open search for solid ground" (Duke: 37). But if this is the aim of John's linguistic operations, how successful is his narrative in accomplishing its theological agenda? John's Bread of Life discourse (6.26-66) may serve as an example of the complications engendered by the explication of one of the gospel's central metaphors.

"Bread of life" (ὁ ἄρτος τῆς ζωῆς) in John 6 undergoes a series of ironic translations. Emanating from the feeding of the five thousand (Jn 6.1-13), a sign misunderstood by those who saw it (Jn 6.14-15), the metaphor is repeatedly transformed and its centre of meaning deferred in Jesus' famed bread of life discourse. At the outset he introduces a differentiation between perishable and imperishable food (Jn 6.27: τὴν βρῶσιν τὴν ἀπολλυμένην...τὴν βρῶσιν τὴν μένουσαν εἰς ζωὴν αἰώνιον ["the food which perishes...the food which endures to eternal life"]). He himself, the Son of Man, is the dispenser of the latter form of bread which conveys life in an abiding sense. The meaning of what constitutes genuine bread is thereby transferred from the material to the nonmaterial level. In response, the audience introduces the metaphor of the heavenly manna. Moses "gave them bread from heaven" (Jn 6.31: Ἄρτον ἐκ τοῦ οὐρανοῦ ἔδωκεν αὐτοῖς φαγεῖν). Jesus adopts the metaphor, but contests Moses as the originator of the heavenly bread. His father, not Moses, is the true giver of the heavenly bread (Jn 6.32: τὸν ἄρτον ἐκ τοῦ οὐρανοῦ τὸν ἀληθινόν ["the true bread from heaven"]) which gives life to the world. When the people request this kind of bread, Jesus identifies himself as the bread of life (Jn 6.35: Ἐγώ εἰμι ὁ ἄρτος τῆς ζωῆς ["I am the bread of life"]). The metaphor of the bread which had been translated from the material to the nonmaterial and on to the heavenly, is now attached to the person of Jesus himself. At this point the Jews raise objections (Jn 6.41: Ἐγόγγυζον οὖν οἱ Ἰουδαῖοι ["the Jews then murmured"]). They know his father and mother: he is the Son of Joseph, and not bread come down from heaven. The Jews, in other words, are scandalised by the ironic transference of the meaning of bread. They can go a long way with Jesus in the substitution of centres from the material to the nonmaterial, and on to the heavenly, but they cannot follow him in his move toward self-identification .

Far from accommodating the Jews, Jesus proceeds to radicalise the language of his self-identification with the bread. The bread he offers is his own flesh (Jn 6.51: ὁ ἄρτος δὲ ὃν ἐγὼ δώσω ἡ σάρξ μού ἐστιν ["the bread which I shall give...is my flesh"]). This triggers a heated dispute among the Jews (Jn 6.52: Ἐμάχοντο οὖν πρὸς ἀλλήλους οἱ Ἰουδαῖοι ["the Jews then disputed among themselves"]). If the transference of the meaning of bread upon Jesus was already objectionable to them, the identification of Jesus, the heavenly bread, with his own flesh is blasphemous. More than ever the Jews are marginalised.

As if to rub more salt into their wounds, Jesus elaborates the metaphor of flesh in starkly realistic, cannibalistic terms. "To eat" (φαγεῖν), indeed "to munch or chew" (τρώγειν), his flesh and to drink his blood will engender eternal life (Jn 6.53). With these words the course of ironic transformations has arrived at what it appears to have intended to attain all along: life in fullness and in the unity of the eucharistic flesh and blood. Upon hearing this message many of the disciples are puzzled and disoriented. They view this as a "difficult saying" (Jn 6.60: Σκληρός ἐστιν ὁ λόγος οὗτος), and they "grumble" (Jn 6.61: γογγύζουσιν). By the time, therefore, the ironic translations of bread (and wine) has attained the goal of sacramental presence, both Jews and many of the disciples are scandalised. The more irony is enforced, the more people are marginalised. In this process, marginalisation is a growing co-presence in the works of irony.

Marginalisation aside, the work of irony delivers benefits for the readers or hearers of the gospel. Or so we are confidently assured by literary critics of the gospel. Irony's repeated transpositions serve to usher us, the recipients of the narrative, from one deferral to the next with a view toward presence and transparency. But does John's irony reward us as readily as theories on irony and metaphor would have us believe?

Interspersed in the bread of life discourse are strong intimations of futurity. Four times Jesus assures his audience that he will raise up on the last day all those who eat the flesh and drink the blood (Jn 6.39, 40, 44, 54). Yet if "eternal life" pledged in the sacramental meal looks forward to the raising up on the last day, then presence is sapped of full strength, and what is accomplished by the ironic course of substitutions and deferrals is presence inhabited by absence or, strictly speaking, neither presence nor absence.

Still more problematic is one of Jesus' last words in the discourse: "It is the Spirit who gives life; the flesh profits nothing; the words that I have spoken to you are Spirit and life" (Jn 6.63). As a result, many of the disciples refused to stay with Jesus (Jn 6.66). This is a saying, which does, however, raise questions for the readers as well. The readers were subjected to metaphorical transformations which ushered them from the material to the nonmaterial, and on to the heavenly realm, and finally to Jesus himself and his sacramental flesh and blood. But no sooner were they united with the life-giving flesh and blood than they were strongly dissuaded from the flesh and redirected toward the Spirit. At this point Spirit is identified with Jesus's words, the very words which had sent them along the route of ironic transformations

In view of this, can it be said that the Johannine "bread of life" discourse has managed to reveal the ideal conditions, e.g., those of presence and life? Do the readers have clarity on matters relating to the

correlation and soteriological function of flesh and Spirit? Is the conflict
of corporeality versus transcendentality resolved for them? How much
advantage do they truly have over the characters in the narrative?

This one example suggests that metaphor and irony are not simply
reducible to revelatory language operating on behalf of the recipients of
the text. That view of irony's benevolence has failed to pursue more
rigorously the implications of its narrative involvements. Indeed, does not
this example exhibit irony more like "a figure dancing everywhere and
grasped nowhere" (Duke: 41)? For inasmuch as the Johannine narration
of irony delivers relief, it also confronts us with new conflicts. And
insofar as one commonly refers to Johannine irony, one might just as well
speak of "the failure of Johannine irony" (Moore: 159-63). In principle,
"irony is unsettling" (Marcus and Fischer: 13), and not always the most
expedient tool for arriving at transparency. To focus exclusively on its
revelatory aspects forecloses prematurely its narrative operations. In
short, readers do not entirely escape irony's victimisation.

In view of these all too brief deliberations on the work of Johannine
irony, call one view the programmatic statement of the prologue's third
beginning concerning Jesus' incarnational and epiphanic mission simply as
a programme to be delivered, or shall one not see it also, and perhaps
more appropriately, as the positing of a problem, e.g., of the central
dilemma, which will resist any clear narrative resolution? To deliver the
truth the Λόγος has to enter the realm of the flesh, but if he truly
"becomes flesh" (σὰρξ ἐγένετο), his revelation is concealed at best and
invalidated at worst. So he can either "become flesh" and forgo glory, or
reflect glory and forgo the flesh. The mediation of flesh and glory,
earthly and heavenly, literal and figural, a task entrusted to the signifying
character of John's narrative, is less successful than often claimed in
Johannine scholarship. For in the first place, signs, irony, and metaphor
operate less as a "mode of revelatory language," but more as a way of
suspending meaning. And secondly, once meaning is deferred, it can
become entangled in narratological and grammatological complications
without ever seeing the pure light of transparency. John's language, in all
its signifying striving after diaphanous purity, reserves a wide margin of
uncertainty for the characters in the story, and for the readers as well.

4. THE VISIO DEI

At the point of culmination the prologue returns to the beginning of
beginnings, the primordial ἀρχή of the Λόγος. In reaffirming
transcendental origin, the prologue once again upholds it vis-à-vis a
different authority which legitimated another beginning. But this time it is

not the authority of singularity which is affirmed versus the plurality of the λόγοι, but rather the authority of Jesus Christ which is played out against that of Moses. The prologue's culminating words, "For the Law was given through Moses, grace and truth were realised through Jesus Christ" (Jn 1.17), identifies the Λόγος and places him side by side with Moses. This juxtaposition articulates the authority of the Λόγος in relation to that of Moses who invokes yet another beginning, e.g., that of the Law at Sinai.

The prologue's final affirmation—"God no one has ever seen" and "this one has brought revelation" (Jn 1.18)—suggests that the Λόγος delivers what he had obtained by full sight. In the end, therefore, his authority is claimed to reside in the singular prestige of the *visio dei*. Following in the wake of the preceding Moses-Christ dichotomy, the polemical edge, "no one has ever seen God," is in part at least directed at Moses. But it is not Moses the lawgiver who is contrasted with the Logos, but Moses the visionary who on Sinai was in the presence of God (Exod 24.9-11; 33.18-23). Implied in these last verses is the understanding that Moses ascended and brought back the Law, without ever having seen, while the Logos who had "seen," descended and revealed what he had "seen ".

It deserves more than our parenthetical attention that the prologue culminates in the Christ-Moses antithesis. For Christ's *visio dei*, this unprecedented ontotheological beginning, once again sets thematic directives for the gospel's narrative agenda, but it sets them vis-à-vis a Mosaic ascent mysticism. In the narrative Jesus articulates the most direct polemic against an ascent tradition in the discourse with Nicodemus (Jn 3.1-21). Here he introduces himself as the visionary who has seen heavenly things (Jn 3.11a: ὁ ἑωράκαμεν μαρτυροῦμεν ["we bear witness to what we have seen"]; 3.12b: πῶς ἐὰν εἴπω ὑμῖν τὰ ἐπουράνια πιστεύσετε; ["how can you believe if I tell you heavenly things?"]; cf. 6.46) which he communicates to those on earth. Thus speaking as heavenly visionary who descended he asserts his authority vis-à-vis an opposite model. "And no one has ascended into heaven, but he who has descended from heaven, the Son of Man" (Jn 3.13). This statement has a polemical ring to it. There cannot be ascent unless there was antecedent descent. The authority which takes his beginning from above is set over against another one which arises from below.

Having subjected an ascent tradition to criticism by invoking the anteriority of descent, the subsequent verse (Jn 3.14) proceeds to redefine ascent. "And as Moses lifted up the serpent in the wilderness, so also must the Son of Man be lifted up" (Jn 314). In "lifting up" the bronze snake in the wilderness, Moses saved those Israelites who while afflicted with snake bites looked at the raised sign (Num 21.8-9). At this point Moses serves as an analogical model for Christ's ascent. But he can serve as typological model only after his ascent has undergone a drastic revision by way of John's christological motif of the "lifting up". In this sense the Nicodemus narration undertakes both a repudiation (Jn 3.13) and a revision (Jn 3.14) of the traditional Mosaic ascent mysticism.

If it is objected that one polemic against ascent and vision hardly proves a major concern for Moses and the traditions around him, it must be pointed out that a critical engagement in Mosaic themes and expectations is a central concern of the Johannine narrative (Glasson, Odeberg, Meeks, Dunn). The prologue's profoundly ontotheological culmination in the antithesis of the two visionaries, Christ and Moses, is thus hardly accidental. It enunciates a purpose which typifies the Johannine gospel in its entirety Christ's *visio dei* and his subsequent descent negate current beliefs in heavenly ascents, Mosaic and otherwise.

Creation of authority which legitimates the Λόγος at various stages of beginning—transcendentally versus the λόγοι, anteriorly vis-à-vis John the Baptiser, incarnationally against "his own" but on behalf of the "children of God," and ontotheologically in opposition to Mosaic ascent mysticism—is thus a central feature of the Johannine prologue.

THE PREFACE AS POSTFACE

Theobald theorised that the prologue to the fourth gospel belonged to the latest compositional stage in the production of the gospel (295, 398-99, 190). With this he confirmed a result of the 1982 symposium on "Das Evangelium und die Evangelien" at the University of Tübingen (Stuhlmacher: 426).

From the perspective of the psychodynamics of writing there is much to be said in support of this historical-critical observation. The writing of a preface to the gospel by creating a structure of three beginnings each of which legitimates the protagonist in a different ἀρχῇ is likely to be the product of what Theobald has termed a *Metareflection* (490). The prologue which carries readers back to transcendental originality and dislodges an emanation of beginnings displays a deeply retrospective gesture. But if the intense preoccupation with beginnings which marks this beginning of the gospel hinges on the consciousness of posteriority, then there is fictionality, pretence even, to the prologue as a project of writing. Then the preface can be viewed as encapsulating the consciousness of a postface.

BIBLIOGRAPHY

Baldensperger, Wilhelm. *Der Prolog des 4. Evangeliums. Sein polemischer und apologetischer Zweck.* (Freiburg i. Br. 1898).

Bornkamm, Gunther. "Zur Interpretation des Johannes-Evangeliums: Eine Auseinandersetzung mit Käsemann's Schrift 'Jesu letzter Wille nach Johannes 17'", (*EvTh* 28: 8-25 1968. Reprinted on pp. 104-21 in *Geschichte und Glaube. Gesammelte Aufsätze* 3, 1968).

Braun, F.-M. "La Réduction du pluriel au singulier dans l'Evangile et la Première Lettre de Jean." *NTS* 24: pp. 40-67 (1978).

Brown, Raymond E. *The Gospel according to John I-XII.* AB 29. (Garden City: Doubleday, 1966).

Bultmann, Rudolf "Die Bedeutung der neuerschlossenen mandäischen und manichäischen Quellen fur das Verständis des Johannesevangeliums." *ZNW* 24: 100-24 (1925. Reprinted on pp. 55-104 in *Exegetica.* Ed. E. Dinkler. Tübingen: Siebeck, 1967).

——, *The Gospel of John. A Commentary.* Trans. G.R. Beasley-Murray *et al.* (Philadelphia: Westminster, 1971).

Colpe, Carsten *Die religionsgeschichtliche Schule: Darstellung und Kritik ihres Bildes vom gnostischen Erlösermythus.* FRLANT NF 60. (Göttingen: Vandenhoeck & Ruprecht, 1961).

Cullmann, Oscar *The Johannine Circle.* Trans. J. Bowden. (Philadelphia: Westminster, 1976).

Culpepper, R. Alan *Anatomy of the Fourth Gospel. A Study in Literary Design.* (Philadelphia: Fortress, 1983).

Derrida, Jacques *Of Grammatology.* Trans. Gayatri Chakravorty Spivak. (Baltimore and London: Johns Hopkins University Press, 1976).

——, "Structure, Sign and Play in the Discourse of the Human Sciences." Pp. 278-93 in *Writing and Difference.* (1978) Trans. Alan Bass. Chicago: University of Chicago Press.

——, *Positions.* Trans. Alan Bass. (Chicago: University of Chicago Press, 1981).

Dewey, Kim "*Paroimiai* in the Gospel of John." *Semeia* 17: pp. 81-100 (1980).

Duke, Paul *Irony in the Fourth Gospel.* (Atlanta: John Knox, 1985).

Dunn, James D.G. "Let John be John—A Gospel for its Time." (1983) Pp. 309-39 in *Das Evangelium und die Evangelien.* Ed. Peter Stuhlmacher. WUNT 28. Tübingen: J.C.B. Mohr (Paul Siebeck).

Foster, Donald "John Come Lately: The Belated Evangelist." (1986) Pp. 113-31 in *The Bible and the Narrative Tradition.* Ed. Frank McConnell. New York: Oxford University Press

Glasson, T. Francis *Moses in the Fourth Gospel.* SBT 40. (London: SCM, 1963).

Johnson, Roger A. *The Origins of Demythologising. Philosophy and Historiography in the Theology of Rudolph Bultmann.* Studies in the History of Religions 28. (Leiden: E.J. Brill, 1974).

Käsemann, Ernst "The Structure and Purpose of the Prologue to John's Gospel." Pp. 138-67 in *New Testament Questions of Today.* Trans. W. J. Montague. (Philadelphia: Fortress, 1969).

——, *The Testament of Jesus. A Study of John in the Light of Ch 17.* Trans. Gerhard Krodel. (Philadelphia: Fortress, 1968).

Kee, Howard Clark *Christian Origins in Sociological Perspective: Methods and Resources.* (Philadelphia: Westminster, 1980).

Kermode, Frank "John." (1987) Pp. 440-66 in *The Literary Guide to the Bible.* Eds. Robert Alter and Frank Kermode. (Cambridge: Harvard University Press).

Kloppenborg, John S. *The Formation of Q: Trajectories in Ancient Wisdom Collections.* (Philadelphia: Fortress, 1987).

Koester, Helmut "Gnostic Writings as Witnesses for the Development of the Sayings Tradition." Pp. 238-61 in *The Rediscovery of Gnosticism*. Ed. B. Layton. (Leiden: E.J. Brill, 1980).

——,"Apocryphal and Canonical Gospels." *HTR* 73: pp. 105-30. (1980).

——, *Introduction to the New Testament*. Vol. 11. (Philadelphia: Fortress /Berlin and New York: Walter de Gruyter, 1982).

Lord, Albert B. *The Singer of Tales*. (Cambridge, MA: Harvard University Press, 1960).

Mack, Burton Lee *Logos und Sophia. Untersuchungen zur Weisheitstheologie im hellenistischen Judentum*. SUNT 10. (Göttingen: Vandenhoeck & Ruprecht, 1973).

Marcus, George E. and Michael M. J. Fischer *Anthropology as Cultural Critique: An Experimental Moment in the Human Sciences*. (Chicago and London: University of Chicago Press, 1986).

Martyn, J. Louis *History & Theology in the Fourth Gospel*. 2nd. ed., rev. (Nashville: Abingdon, 1979).

Meeks, Wayne A. *The Prophet-King. Moses Traditions and the Johannine Christology*. NovTSup XIV. (Leiden: E.J. Brill, 1967).

Moore, Stephen D. *Literary Criticism and the Gospels: The Theoretical Challenge*. (New Haven and London: Yale University Press, 1989).

O' Day, Gail R. *Revelation in the Fourth Gospel: Narrative Mode and Theological Claim*. (Philadelphia: Fortress, 1986).

Odeberg, Hugo *The Fourth Gospel Interpreted in Its Relation to Contemporaneous Religious Currents in Palestine and the Hellenistic-Oriental World*. (Uppsala, 1929. Reprint, Chicago: Argonaut, 1968).

Ong, Walter J. *The Presence of the Word. Some Prolegomena for Cultural and Religious History*. (New Haven and London: Yale University Press 1967. Reprint, Minneapolis: University of Minnesota Press, 1981).

Pannenberg, Wolfhart *Jesus—God and Man*. Trans. Lewis L. Wilkin and Duane A. Priebe. (Philadelphia: Westminster 1968).

Robinson, James M. "On the Gattung of Mark (and John)". (1970) Pp. 99-129 in vol. I of *Jesus and Man's Hope*. (Pittsburgh: Pittsburgh Theological Seminary). Reprinted on pp. 11-39 in *The Problem of History in Mark and other Marcan Studies*. (Philadelphia: Fortress, 1982).

Robinson, James M., ed. *The Nag Hammadi Library*. Rev. ed. (San Francisco: Harper & Row, 1988).

Said, Edward W. *Beginnings. Intention and Method*. (New York: Basic Books, 1975).

Smith, D. Moody *Johannine Christianity. Essays on Its Setting, Sources, and Theology*. (Columbia: University of South Carolina Press, 1984).

Sneller, Gary "The Word and the Words of Eternal Life." Unpublished Paper (1985).

Stulllmacher, Peter, ed. *Das Evangelium und die Evangelien. Vorträge vom Tübinger Symposium 1982*. WUNT 28 (Tübingen: J.C.B. Mohr, 1983) (Paul Siebeck).

Theobald, Michael *Die Fleischwerdung des Logos. Studien zum Verhältnis des Johannesprologs zum Corpus des Evangeliums und zu 1 John*. NTAbh NF 20. (Münster: Aschendorff, 1988).

THE ELUSIVE CHRIST:
A NEW READING OF THE FOURTH GOSPEL*†

M.W.G. STIBBE

1. THE THEME OF THE ELUSIVE CHRIST

One of the most significant works of New Testament scholarship in the 1980s was Gerd Theissen's novel, *The Shadow of the Galilean*,[1] subtitled "the quest for the historical Jesus in narrative form". After painstaking research into the first-century Palestine of the time of Jesus, Theissen reconstructs the world not in the form of a historical-critical introduction but in the form of a story. Instead of writing a descriptive overview of the Greek inheritance, the Roman world, the Jewish religion and Christians (such as we find in Sean Freyne's *The World of the New Testament*),[2] Theissen writes a novel which moves in the real world of Palestine but which also creates fictional characters from his own imagination. The primary fiction in Theissen's story is the narrator, a person coerced by Pilate into investigating the character and activities of the Galilean preacher, Jesus of Nazareth. The narrator tracks Jesus throughout the story. Indeed, the movement and suspense of the plot depend almost entirely upon this quest for Jesus. However, the quest is constantly frustrated: Jesus proves to be most secretive, always on the move, often evading those who would hunt him down. As the narrator reveals, "Although we asked about Jesus everywhere we never met him".[3] And, "he appeared in some places unexpectedly and then soon disappeared again".[4] And again, "I never met Jesus on my travels through Galilee. I just found traces of him everywhere...He remained himself everywhere intangible."[5]

Part of the success of Theissen's story must be attributed to this characterisation of Jesus as an elusive, itinerant preacher in the Galilee of

---

* This article was originally dedicated to Barnabas Lindars.
† This article appeared in *JSNT* 44 (1991) pp. 19-38.

[1] G. Theissen, *The Shadow of the Galilean* (London: SCM Press, 1987).
[2] S. Freyne, *The World of the New Testament* (Dublin: Veritas Publications, 1980).
[3] Theissen, *Galilean* p. 119.
[4] *Galilean* p. 119.
[5] *Galilean* p. 129.

the first century. Theissen's Jesus is an evasive Jesus, a Jesus with no definite contours, a Jesus who seems more like a shadow than a tangible human being. One of the attractive features of Theissen's novel is that this is a particularly Johannine presentation of Jesus. The fourth evangelist's characterisation of Jesus focuses primarily on his mysterious elusiveness. People constantly seek Jesus in John's narrative world. Some seek him for positive reasons: such include Nicodemus, who wishes to know more about him, or the official, who seeks Jesus for the healing of his son, or the Greeks in ch. 12, who seek Jesus for salvation. Others seek Jesus for more dubious reasons, such as the crowds in ch. 6, who seek Jesus because he gave them food. Most seek Jesus for negative reasons, notably the Jewish authorities, who, after ch. 5, attempt to arrest Jesus at a number of points because he appears to be breaking their law. Everywhere in John, as in *The Shadow of the Galilean,* people are seeking Jesus. However, again as in Theissen's story, Jesus is an elusive figure. Even when Nicodemus finds him, Jesus proves opaque to his understanding. When the crowds seek Jesus, he only allows them to find him when he is ready for them. And as for the Jewish authorities, I am reminded of Baroness Orczy's Scarlet Pimpernel: "they seek him here, they seek him there, those Jews they seek him everywhere!"

2. THE ELUSIVE PRESENCE OF JESUS IN JOHN

My argument in this essay is that the author's characterisation of Jesus depicts the latter as the *elusive Christ.* To demonstrate this, we need to appreciate John's portrait of Jesus' *elusive presence* in the Gospel. One of the things which John adds to the tradition is the narrative theme of hiding and seeking. There is, in the Fourth Gospel, a dynamic of hide-and-seek going on all the time. People seek Jesus, but often he hides from them. The verb "to seek", ζητεῖν, is used 34 times in John. One quarter of the usages of this verb in the New Testament are to be found in the Fourth Gospel. Clearly it is a key theme in the thinking of the evangelist. In Jn 1.38, Jesus turns to the two disciples of John the Baptist, and utters his first words: "What are you seeking?" (ζητεῖτε). In 6.24, after the feeding of the five thousand, the crowds get into the boats and set off for Capernaum, in search of (ζητοῦντες) Jesus. In 6.26, Jesus addresses them with the words, "you are searching for me" (ζητεῖτέ με). In 7.11, it is said that, at the Feast of Tabernacles, the Jews were seeking after (ἐζήτουν) Jesus. In 7.34, Jesus warns these Jews that there will come a time when they will seek for him (ζητήσετε) but they will not find him. Once again, in 8.21, Jesus says to the Jews, "I am going away and you will search for me" (ζητήσετε). In 11.56, the narrator writes that the crowds at the Passover kept searching (ἐζήτουν) for Jesus. In 13.33, in the farewell discourses, Jesus says to his disciples, "You will seek for me (ζητήσετέ με) but as I told the Jews, so I tell you now: Where I am going, you cannot come". In ch. 18, at the arrest scene in the garden, Jesus asks of Judas and the arresting party, "Whom are you seeking?" (ζητεῖτε). Jesus repeats the question in v. 7, τίνα ζητεῖτε; Then, in v. 8, he says, "if you are seeking after me (ζητεῖτε) let these disciples go!" Finally, in 20.15, the risen Jesus asks the same question of Mary at the tomb, "Whom are you seeking?" (ζητεῖς).

Alongside the theme of seeking is the theme of finding—a theme enforced by the recurrence of εὑρίσκειν, "to find". This verb is used 19 times in John's story. However, it is only used on three occasions to describe people finding Jesus—a fact which further indicates his elusive presence. First, in 1.41, Andrew tells his brother, "We have found (εὑρήκαμεν) the messiah!" Secondly, in Jn 1.45, Philip says to Nathaniel, "We have found (εὑρήκαμεν) the one Moses wrote about in the law!" Finally, in Jn 6.25, the crowds seeking Jesus after the multiplication miracle find (εὑρόντες) Jesus on the other side of the lake. By far the most frequent usage of εὑρίσκειν has Jesus as the subject—has Jesus as the one who does the finding, not those who seek him. Thus, in 1.43, Jesus finds (εὑρίσκει) Philip. In 2.14, Jesus finds (εὗρεν) men selling cattle, sheep and doves in the temple. In 5.14, Jesus finds (εὑρίσκει) the man who has been crippled for 38 years and whom he healed at the pool of Bethesda. In 9.35, Jesus goes in search of the man born blind, whom he has also healed earlier in the chapter, and is reported as having found (εὑρών) him. In 11.17, Jesus is said to find (εὑρών) a donkey. All these instances show how the author's use of the finding motif does not undermine the sense of Jesus' elusiveness. The cry of faith, εὕρηκα, is only given to Andrew and Philip during the whole of the Gospel. Everywhere else it is Jesus who does the finding. Indeed, the verb εὑρίσκειν is used to point out the difficulty of locating Jesus. In 7.34, Jesus says to the Jews, "You will look for me, but you will not find me" (εὑρήσετέ με).

Another motif which enhances the portrayal of Jesus' elusive presence is that of his withdrawals from places of hostility and unbelief. From ch. 5 onwards, there are many references to the Jews seeking Jesus in order to kill him: 5.18; 7.1, 19, 20, 25, 30; 8.37, 40; 10.39; 11.8. Typical of all these references is the negative use of the verb ζητεῖν, with the Jews as the subject, Jesus as the object, and Jesus' destruction as the purpose. It is because of this death-threat that Jesus is constantly seen to slip away from the Jews. The obvious connection between the attempts of the Jews to kill Jesus, and his ability to evade capture through his strategy of concealment, comes out at a number of points. In 4.3, Jesus hears that the Pharisees are disturbed at the number of his followers, so he leaves (ἀφῆκεν) Judaea and

234   M.W.G. STIBBE

returns to Galilee. In 5.13, we learn that Jesus has slipped away
(ἐξένευσεν) when the Pharisees arrive to interrogate the cripple at the pool.
In 6.15, after the feeding of the five thousand, Jesus withdraws
(ἀνεχώρησεν) to the hills by himself when he learns that the crowds wish
to make him king by force. In 8.59, the narrator says, "At this, the Jews
picked up stones to stone him, but Jesus hid himself (ἐκρύβη), slipping
away (ἐξῆλθεν) from the temple grounds". In 10.39, the Jews again try to
seize him but Jesus escapes from their grasp (ἐξῆλθεν ἐκ τῆς χειρὸς
αὐτῶν). Finally, in 11.54, the narrator tells us that, after the Sanhedrin had
decreed that Jesus must die, "therefore Jesus no longer moved about
publicly among the Jews. Instead he withdrew (ἀπῆλθεν) to a region near
the desert, to a village called Ephraim, where he stayed with his disciples."

There are other motifs which contribute to the evangelist's
characterisation of Jesus as the elusive Christ. There is, for example, the
motif of Jesus' escapes. The verb πιάζειν (to arrest, seize) is used a
number of times in the story and in most cases the evasiveness of Jesus is
stressed. In 7.30, we read: "at this the Jews tried to seize him (πιάσαι) but
no one laid a hand on him because his time had not yet come". In 10.39, we
hear that "again they tried to seize him (πιάσαι) but he escaped their
grasp". In most cases of the use of πιάζειν, the furtiveness of Jesus is
emphasised. The narrator takes the trouble to say that in spite of all the
attempts to arrest Jesus, no one laid hands on him (οὐδεὶς ἐξέβαλεν ἐπ'
αὐτὸν τὴν χεῖρα, 7.30, 44; 10.39). As for the practical means by which
Jesus actually evades arrest, this is all left a mystery to the reader. It is
enough for us to know that no one laid hands on Jesus because his
appointed time had not yet come. When his hour does come, Jesus allows
himself to be arrested and bound. Having eluded his captors for so long,
Jesus in 18.1-11 freely gives himself up to the arresting party. Their
reaction in 18.6 is most interesting: "when Jesus said 'I am he', they drew
back and fell to the ground". Of course, this is a stereotypical response to a
theophany and to Jesus' use of the divine name, *ego eimi*. But could it be
also that the response of the captors is one of amazement? That after so
many great escapes Jesus is at last in a place where he will not and does
not escape? Where he can be sought and *found*?

A further motif we should consider is that of Jesus' open and secret
movements. Jesus' brothers say to him in 7.4: "No one who wants to
become a public figure acts in secret. Since you are doing these things,
show yourself to the world!" There are two key words used in 7.4: first of
all, παρρησία (openly, in public); secondly ἐν κρυπτῷ (in secret).
παρρησία is used nine times and often of Jesus' geographical accessibility.
The brothers of Jesus encourage him to move around παρρησία, openly, in
public. They argue that Jesus should not move around ἐν κρυπτῷ, in an

undercover and elusive manner, but that he should openly demonstrate his authority and power to the Jews. Jesus' response in 7.10 is to go up to the feast after his brothers, not openly (φανερῶς this time) but ἐν κρυπτῷ. At the end of ch. 8, after two chapters in which Jesus has been speaking to the Jews παρρησία, publicly (7.26), Jesus is forced to go underground and move secretively again (8.59, ἐκρύβη). Finally, in 11.54, after the decision of the Sanhedrin to have Jesus put to death, the narrator informs us that Jesus "no longer moved about publicly (παρρησία) among the Jews". Throughout John's story there is a rhythm of public and secret movements in the ministry of Jesus. In chs. 1-4, Jesus moves about freely (apart from 4.1-3). In ch. 5, The healing of the man on the Sabbath precipitates opposition to Jesus. In chs. 6 and 7, Jesus' public teaching engenders further opposition so that he is forced to go underground at a number of points. These factors reinforce John's characterisation of Jesus as the elusive Christ.

Another characteristic of John's story which highlights the elusive presence of Jesus is the occasional uncertainty about where Jesus is geographically. John portrays Jesus as slipping out of geographical focus, both the focus of characters within the narrative world, and the focus of the readers interpreting the world. In the first instance, there are several occasions where Jesus slips out of geographical focus for a moment and minor characters are at a loss to know where he is. In ch. 5, where the healed cripple is confronted by the Pharisees about the identity of Jesus, he replies that he has no idea who he is because Jesus has slipped away just after the miracle. When the Pharisees ask the man, "Where is he?", the beggar replies, "I don't know!" These are moments in John's story when Jesus disappears for reasons which are not specified, which are not to do with death threats, and which seem to exist to strengthen the impression of Jesus' geographical elusiveness for the characters within the story.

John does the same thing to the reader. Just as characters within the story become uncertain about Jesus' geographical movements, so does the reader. The notorious difficulties in the geographical sequence of chs. 5-7 are one example. At the end of ch. 5 Jesus is still in Jerusalem, but ch. 6 begins with him crossing the sea of Galilee. H.E. Edwards comments as follows: "It is as if you were reading a letter from a friend in which he was telling you about salmon fishing in Scotland and then, when you turn the page, the letter went on :'After this I went over London Bridge'".[1] This sequence and the notorious problem with Jn 14.31 are deliberately designed to evoke in the reader a sense of Jesus' slippery evasiveness.

---

[1] H.E. Edwards, *The Disciple Who Wrote These Things* (London: Clarke, 1953), p. 41.

To sum up, the Jesus of John's Gospel is elusive in his physical presence. There is a game of hide-and-seek constantly being played out in the texture of John's narrative. People seek Jesus but, more often than not, they do not find him because he conceals himself. Four motifs in particular contribute to this theme of Jesus' elusive presence. First of all there is the motif of his withdrawal at times of danger. A good example of this is in 11.53-54:

> From that day on the Jews plotted to take Jesus' life. Therefore Jesus no longer moved about publicly among the Jews. Instead he withdrew to a region near the desert, to a village called Ephraim, where he stayed with his disciples.

Secondly, there is the motif of Jesus' escapes (e.g. 10.39). The third motif is that of Jesus' secret movements (e.g. 7.10: "after his brothers had left the feast, Jesus went also, not publicly but in secret"). Finally, there is the motif of the uncertainty of Jesus' geographical location. A good example of this is in 6.22-25:

> The next day the crowd that had stayed on the opposite shore of the lake realised that only one boat had been there, and that Jesus had not entered it with his disciples, but that they had gone away alone. Then some boats from Tiberias landed near the place where the people had eaten the bread after the Lord had given thanks. Once the crowd realised that neither Jesus nor his disciples were there, they got into the boats and went to Capernaum in search of Jesus. When they found him on the other side of the lake, they asked him, "Rabbi, when did you get here?"

These four motifs, withdrawals, escapes, secret movements and geographical confusions, create the sense of Jesus' elusive presence.

3. THE ELUSIVE LANGUAGE OF JESUS IN JOHN

Jesus is not only elusive in terms of physical presence, he is also elusive in his language. Just as Jesus conceals himself physically, so he conceals himself linguistically. The constant emphasis in Johannine scholarship on Jesus the revealer needs challenging precisely for this reason. The Jesus of John's story is just as much the concealer as the revealer; just as much the one who conceals the truth as the one who discloses it. One of the literary achievements of the fourth evangelist is his use on the lips of Jesus of a language which is rich in ambiguity and metaphor, a language worthy of a deity. Every student who has read *Paradise Lost* knows that this is precisely the area where Milton failed. When he came to Book VI, where God and Jesus converse in heaven, Milton—who elsewhere was capable of poetry in the 'Grand Style'—seemed to fail miserably. No doubt for the most pious reasons, Milton seemed unable to construct a sensible speech on the lips of God. Christopher Ricks speaks of "the staginess by which one member of the Trinity speaks to another", of "a wordiness that is meant to disguise the muddle", and of the pointlessness of God saying "and thou knowest" to Jesus when both parties are omniscient[1] (Paradise Lost, Bk VI, ll.684-703). As Ricks concludes, "It is at such moments when something goes wrong with Milton's style"; here the pomp comes down to mere noise.[2] Not so John's Jesus, who, to use Käsemann's description, is

> the one who, like a mystagogue, with long drawn-out monologues, symbolic speeches and cryptic intimations confronts the world, provokes its misunderstandings and precipitates its judgement.[3]

There are a number of literary strategies which highlight Jesus' linguistic elusiveness. The first is John's use of highly metaphorical language in the teaching of Jesus. Right from the beginning of the Gospel, Jesus' language proves opaque to the earthly mind because of its extravagant use of metaphor. In 2.19, Jesus says, "destroy this temple, and I will raise it again in three days". Jesus, says the narrator, was speaking of his body but the Jews understandably misunderstand what Jesus is saying because the conversation is taking place in the Temple in Jerusalem. In ch. 3, Jesus tells Nicodemus, "You must be born again/from above". Nicodemus completely misunderstands what Jesus is saying and asks, "How can a man be born when he is old?" In ch. 4, Jesus speaks of the living/running water that he offers. The Samaritan woman misunderstands what he is saying and says, "Sir, you have nothing to draw with and the well is deep". Towards the end of ch. 4 the disciples urge Jesus to have a lunch break, but Jesus tells them, "I have food to eat that you know nothing about!" The disciples' misunderstanding is made clear in their response: "Could someone have brought him food?" In each of these instances, Jesus speaks the heavenly language of metaphor. For him, the temple is both material and spiritual. The same is true of rebirth, running water and food. Jesus' language recreates, through metaphor, a unity of matter and spirit. That is why in Jn 3.8 he can speak of the wind of the desert and the Spirit of God in the same word, $\pi\nu\epsilon\hat{\upsilon}\mu\alpha$. Divine puns such as these emanate from an integrative consciousness which rejoices in metaphorical unions.

The second strategy which highlights the elusiveness of Jesus' language is his use of cryptic discourse, or what John calls the $\pi\alpha\rho\omega\mu\iota\alpha$. In 10.1-5, Jesus speaks of a sheep pen, a gate, a thief, a robber, some sheep, a shepherd, a watchman, a stranger, and various activities associated with

---

[1] C. Ricks, *Milton's Grand Style* (Oxford: Oxford University Press, 1963), p. 19.
[2] C. Ricks, *Milton's Grand Style*, p. 20.
[3] E. Käsemann, *The Testament of Jesus* (London: SCM Press, 1968), p. 8.

them. After painting this enigmatic picture, the narrator says, "Jesus used this figure of speech (παροιμία), but they did not understand what he was telling them". What then is a παροιμία? It is a cryptic word-picture which requires considerable expertise to unravel. One of the differences between John and the Synoptics is that the Jesus of Mark, Matthew and Luke speaks parables of the kingdom of God, while John's Jesus speaks enigmatic riddles which have nothing obvious to do with the kingdom. Indeed, the phrase "the kingdom of God" hardly occurs in John. John's Jesus is the deity who speaks a heavenly language consisting of demanding word-pictures and figurative riddles. The παροιμία in John 15 bears this out. Here Jesus speaks of himself as the true vine, of his Father as a gardener, and of branches which are either fruitful or destroyed. Again this is a cryptic word-picture requiring energetic interpretation. Even the disciples, the insiders of John's story, find such cryptic discourses elusive. They want Jesus to speak παρρησία, that is, plainly, without riddles. That is why they rejoice in 16.25 with the words, "now you are speaking plainly (παρρησία) and not in riddles" (ἐν παροιμίαις).

A third characteristic of Jesus' elusive language is his discontinuous dialogue.[1] In his book, *Overheard by God*, A.D. Nuttall examines the conversation between Jesus and Pilate in Jn 18.28-19.16a as "a work of literary art".[2] He describes Jn 18.33-38 as "a remarkably early specimen of what literary critics call discontinuous dialogue".[3] Nuttall explains:

> When Jesus is asked if he is the king of the Jews, he answers neither yes or no but instead asks a question of his own. When he is asked what he has done, he answers not that question but the earlier one with the mysterious, "My kingdom is not of this world". Even so, he skips one logical stage; to make the logic fully explicit he would presumably have had to say something like, "I am a king, yes, but not of the Jews nor of anything earthly". This logical ellipse seems to trouble Pilate and he asks, seeking confirmation, "Art thou a king, then?" and hears in answer the words "Thou sayest I am".[4]

What Nuttall is highlighting here is the systematic absence of logical fit between Pilate's questions and Jesus' answers. Nuttall suggests that this discontinuity is a "technique of deliberate transcendence".[5] "The gaps in Jesus' dialogue imply a transcending compliment, a super-nature."[6] As

---

[1] See D. Jasper's *The New Testament and the Literary Imagination* (London: Macmillan, 1986), pp. 45-46. Jasper takes Jn 18.33 for his example of discontinuous dialogue, as did A.D. Nuttall in his *Overheard by God: Fiction and Prayer in Herbert, Milton, Dante and St. John* (London: Methuen, 1980). Jasper does not mention Nuttal's work.

[2] Nuttall, *Overheard by God*, p. 128.

[3] *Overheard by God*, p. 129.

[4] *Overheard by God*, p. 129.

[5] *Overheard by God*, p. 131.

[6] *Overheard by God*, p. 133.

Nuttall eloquently continues, "all the while, amid the wreckage of his conventional legal defence, we sense an enormous mystery".[1] He concludes that Jesus' equivocal answers have three purposes:

> the first is merely evasive, the second obliquely adumbrates a universe of discourse which transcends the assumptions of the original question, and the third directs attention to a realm which is radically transcendent, so utterly Other as to resist any kind of specific illustration, in human terms.[2]

There are other literary qualities in Jesus' diction which we could study (irony, double entendre, etc.) but the three characteristics of Jesus' speech which I have described here, his metaphorical language, cryptic discourse and discontinuous dialogue, are the most potent linguistic strategies of evasion. How are we to explain these devices? We have been warned in John's prologue that Jesus is the Word of God, that he is the embodiment of the divine voice. The language that he speaks in the Gospel is therefore crucial, a reflection in speech of the mystery of his nature. The highly metaphorical language that he utters unites matter and spirit, as one would expect from a deity. The cryptic discourses he uses speak of his γνῶσις, his knowledge, of divine mysteries, shared with the Father before the creation of the world. The discontinuous dialogue in which he engages points to the higher plane of reality from which he derives, the realm of ἀλήθεια, truth. All three techniques speak of an elusiveness that is quite proper for one who "debates with men from the vantage point of the infinite difference between heaven and earth".[3]

What John has achieved in his characterisation of the divine protagonist is, therefore, something immensely subtle. At the level of both works and words, language and presence, Jesus refuses to operate παρρησία, openly, after ch. 5. From this moment on, the Jesus of John is the God who cannot be grasped either physically or intellectually. He is at the same time the one on whom people cannot lay their hands and the one to whom they cannot apply their minds. He is the God who ultimately cannot be apprehended or comprehended. This much is suggested in the prologue where the Word is described as the light shining in the darkness and which the darkness has not grasped. This points the reader in the direction of an elusive protagonist, the Word whose words will not be uttered παρρησία, and whose movements will not be made παρρησία. Thus, language is as important as presence in this respect. The profound diction of the protagonist is a far cry from the language of Milton's God.

---

[1] *Overheard by God*, p. 134.
[2] *Overheard by God*, pp. 137-38.
[3] Käsemann, *Testament of Jesus*, p. 9.

4. THE LITERARY BACKGROUND OF THIS THEME

The portrait of the elusive Christ is one of the most creative contributions of the author to his historical traditions. The theme of Jesus the concealer is *his* literary achievement. But it is important to remember that John's characterisation of Jesus as the elusive Christ is not a literary creation *de novo*; it is not original in the sense that it has no literary background. As T.S. Eliot has pointed out, there is always a relationship in literature between tradition and the individual talent,[1] and we need here to work out what literary traditions lie behind John's individualistic art. The following literary traditions may well be germane to John's storytelling.

a. The Elusiveness of Yahweh

The Old Testament literary tradition concerning the elusive character of Yahweh has almost certainly impacted the theme of the Johannine pimpernel. Whilst there is a sense of divine presence in the Old Testament, it also contains within it a tradition of the elusive transcendence of God. In the patriarchal narratives, the elusiveness of Yahweh is evident in the story of the three visitors in Genesis 18 and in the story of Jacob wrestling with the angel in Gen 32.22-32. Since Abraham and Jacob feature in Jn 1.51; 4.6; 8.31-59, we should not ignore these patriarchal stories of the elusiveness of Yahweh. Nor should we ignore the Mosaic traditions. The story of the burning bush, with the story of the elusiveness of Yahweh's self-revelation (I am who I am), has probably influenced John's characterisation of Jesus. The book of Isaiah is also significant. In Isaiah 8.17 the prophet says, "I will wait for the Lord, who is hiding his face from the house of Jacob. I will put my trust in him." While the exact nuance of the phrase "hiding his face" is not easy to discern, it may simply denote the concealment of God's presence. On many occasions in the Old Testament, the reason for Yahweh hiding from his people is clearly human sin. In Jer. 33.7, God says, "I will hide my face from this city because of all its wickedness". But Isa. 8.17 and other texts (e.g. Ps. 13.1) do not speak of sin overtly as the cause of God's elusive hiddenness. Isa. 45.15 simply says, "truly you are a God who hides himself, O God and Saviour of Israel". Since Deutero-Isaiah proves to be such a rich quarry for the evangelist in other matters, it is possible that his portrait of the elusive Christ stems from there also.

---

[1] T.S. Eliot, "Tradition and the Individual Talent", in *The Selected Prose of T.S. Eliot* (London: Faber and Faber, 1975), p. 38: "No poet, no artist of any art, has his complete meaning alone. His significance, his appreciation, is the appreciation of his relation to the dead poets and artists. You cannot value him alone; you must set him, for contrast and comparison, among the dead."

b. The Elusiveness of Wisdom

We must consider secondly the elusive character of the figure of Wisdom in the Old Testament and related literature, especially since Wisdom motifs are evident elsewhere in the Fourth Gospel (particularly, according to Raymond Brown, in the prologue).[1] Later Wisdom literature develops the idea that Wisdom searches for a place on earth in which to dwell (Sirach 24; Bar. 3.9-4.4). At the same time, a tradition evolves concerning the withdrawal of Wisdom from the earth. *1 Enoch* 42 depicts this graphically: 'Wisdom went out to dwell with the children of the people but she found no dwelling place. So Wisdom returned to her place and she settled permanently among the angels.' The theme reflected in these verses probably goes back to Prov. 1.28 in which Sophia/Wisdom says about her intended audience. "They will call upon me, but I will not answer; they will seek me diligently but will not find me". It recurs specifically in apocalyptic literature such as *4 Ezra* 5.9 where the seer is told about chaos everywhere: "Then shall reason hide itself, and Wisdom withdraw into her chamber, and it shall be sought by many but shall not be found". Likewise *2 Bar.* 48.36 records the words of many in the final days: "Where did the multitude of intelligence hide itself, and where did the multitude of Wisdom depart?" It is possible that this picture of people seeking diligently after Wisdom but not finding her has influenced John's characterisation of Jesus.

c. The Elusiveness of Dionysus

A third possible literary background may lie in the myth of Dionysus. There are some interesting parallels between Eurypides' version of the Dionysian myth and John's story of Jesus, as I have shown in my book, *John as Storyteller*.[2] Both Jesus and Dionysus are divine strangers who visit the city where they should be recognised and worshipped. Both are the offspring of a divine father and a human mother. Both are rejected by their capital city except, interestingly, by a group of women (the maenads in *The Bacchae* and the women disciples of John 4, 12 and 20), an elderly ruler (Cadmus in *The Bacchae* and Nicodemus in John) and one or two others. Other than these exceptions, the leaders of the formal, institutional religion in the respective cities of Thebes and Jerusalem reject the deities.

In both stories, wine plays a prominent part. In the Dionysian myth, Dionysus provides wine for humankind in order to relieve suffering. In

---

[1] R.E. Brown, *The Gospel according to John* (AB, 1: London: Chapman, 1966), pp. cxxii-cxxv.

[2] *John as Storyteller: Narrative Criticism and the Fourth Gospel* (Cambridge: Cambridge University Press, 1992). For a more detailed analysis of the elusiveness theme in John's story, see my *John: A Readings Commentary* (Sheffield: JSOT Press, 1993).

John 2, Jesus transforms six earthenware jars of water into precious wine—
a story which Bultmann and subsequent German scholars have seen as
Dionysian in character.[1] In both stories the deity is arrested and bound by
the rulers in the city. In both stories, above all, the deities appear to be
utterly elusive in their presence and their language. In the case of *The
Bacchae*, Dionysus constantly evades capture until he willingly allows
Pentheus to arrest him. He is truly the elusive god.[2] But Dionysus is also
elusive in his speech. His sharp exchanges with Pentheus are quite similar
to those between Jesus and Pilate. Both employ discontinuous dialogue. In
both cases, the statesman is outwitted and mystified by the deity. So it is
possible that John's portrait of Jesus is influenced by Dionysian
mythology.

d. The Elusiveness of Jesus

A fourth possible literary background for the Johannine story of the elusive
Jesus must be the Gospel of Mark. William Wrede's book, *The Messianic
Secret*, called attention to a group of facts which suggest parallels with
John's story.[3] These facts were related to the way in which Jesus constantly
silenced those who confessed him as messiah. The first group of facts
centres around the demoniacs who cry out and are rebuked to silence. Mk
1.25, 34 and 3.12 are the relevant texts. Mk 3.11-12 is not untypical:
"whenever the evil spirits saw Jesus, they fell down before him and cried
out, 'You are the Son of God!' But he gave them strict orders not to tell
who he was." A second group of facts concerns the miracle stories in which
Jesus gives orders that the person healed should not make him known: Mk
1.43-45; 5.43; 7.36; 8.26. When Jesus heals the man with leprosy in 1.40,
Jesus says in v. 43: "See that you don't tell anyone!" The third group of
facts concerns the occasions in Mark where Jesus retires from public view
as though to conceal himself: Mk 1.35-38; 7.24; 9.30-32. Mk 7.24 is not
untypical: "Jesus left that place and went to the vicinity of Tyre. He entered
a house and did not want anyone to know it; yet he could not keep his
presence a secret." The fourth group of facts concerns the passage in 4.11-
13, after the parable of the sower, where Jesus says to his disciples that the
secrets to the kingdom of God have been given to them. This implies an

---

[1] See Bultmann, *John*, pp. 118-19. Of Jn 2.1-11, he writes: "the motif of the story, the
changing of the water into wine, is a typical motif of the Dionysus legend."

[2] See C. Segal's *Dionysaic Poetics and Eurypides' Bacchae* (Princeton NJ: Princeton
University Press, 1982). Segal's excellent study focuses on the figure of Dionysus as the elusive
god.

[3] W. Wrede, *Das Messiasgeheimnis in den Evangelien* (Göttingen: Vanderhoeck &
Ruprecht, 3rd edn, 1963). In many ways my article represents the kind of analysis Wrede
himself might have provided on John had he been working in the present climate.

element of intentional obscurity in the language of Mark's Jesus with outsiders.

The elusiveness of the Markan Jesus may well have some influence on John's characterisation of Jesus. The same may be true of Matthew's portrait of Jesus. The elusive character of Jesus in the Matthean redaction has recently been discussed in Deidre Good's article, "The Verb ἀναχωρέω in Matthew's Gospel".[1] She argues that "the motif of 'withdrawal' is a feature of Matthew's Gospel that has been observed by scholars but never independently researched".[2] She detects seven occasions in Matthew where Jesus, or other characters are seen to withdraw from the public eye. In most of these cases the withdrawal is due to hostility on the part of the enemies of Jesus, and it is seen as the fulfilment of Old Testament Scripture. In every instance the verb ἀναχωρεῖν (withdrawal) is used. The instances which involve Jesus as the subject are: Mt. 4.12-18, where Jesus withdraws to Galilee after John is arrested, in fulfilment of Isaiah; 14.12-14, where Jesus withdraws after the body of John the Baptist is buried; 15.21-28, Where Jesus withdraws to Tyre and Sidon after controversy with the Pharisees. These narrative cameos of Jesus' withdrawals because of hostility may have influenced John's story.

Similarly, in the Lukan traditions, there is some suggestion of the elusiveness of Jesus. When Jesus is rejected at Nazareth after preaching in the synagogue, Luke tells us that Jesus was driven out of the town. The people took him to the brow of the hill on which the town was built in order to throw him down the cliff. However, "Jesus walked right through the crowd and went on his way" (4.30). Luke does not tell us how Jesus managed this, and it is this lacuna which creates the sense of Jesus' mystery. The mysterious dimension to Jesus' characterisation is further brought out in Lk. 24.13-35, where Jesus is very much the concealed God on the road to Emmaus. It is possible that these traditions, and possibly also the escape stories in Acts, have played their part in forming John's Jesus.[3]

Conclusion

Looking at these possible literary sources the reader is aware of a vast number of intertextual echoes between the Old Testament, other Jewish literature and Greek stories on one hand, and John's characterisation of Jesus on the other. However, there is some value in drawing a distinction between primary and secondary intertextuality here. The secondary, less

---

[1] D. Good, "The Verb ἀναχωρέω in Matthew's Gospel", *NovT* 32, (1990), pp. 1-12.

[2] Good, "ἀναχωρέω", p. 1.

[3] Notice the alternative readings of Jn 8.59, which depict Jesus passing through the midst of his enemies, in words reminiscent of Lk 4.30 (Kurt Aland, *Greek New Testament*, 3rd edition, p. 363).

probable intertextual echoes involve the Matthean and Lukan characterisation of Jesus and the Dionysan myth. Various arguments can be brought forward in each case to support this relegation of sources to the level of secondary intertextuality. To take one example, if John's story shows a direct literary dependence on Matthew's theme of the withdrawals of Jesus, then why does John only use ἀναχωρεῖν at 6.15 and not in any of the other allusions to Jesus' elusive movements? The great variety of John's words of withdrawal disproves the influence. In conclusion, then, I propose that we regard the Wisdom, Isaianic and Markan literary traditions as the primary sources for John's characterisation of Jesus as the elusive Christ. This is supported by the fact that the author uses material from Deutero-Isaiah, the Wisdom literature and Mark's Gospel elsewhere in his story.

5. A HISTORICAL EXPLANATION FOR THIS THEME IN JOHN

From the evidence above, it is clear that John may well have been affected by a whole cluster of literary traditions in his portrait of the elusive Christ. However, it is also likely that John was influenced by historical factors. Three factors suggest themselves.

a. The Elusiveness of the Historical Jesus

From a historical perspective, it is not unreasonable to suppose that the historical Jesus was himself an elusive figure as Theissen's novel suggests. It is not improbable that Jesus' attitude towards the Sabbath, towards purity law, towards the Temple, and so on, landed him in trouble with the authorities right from the start of his ministry (see Mk 2.23-28) and this forced him to be very circumspect about his movements. No doubt something of Jesus' elusive behaviour was preserved in the eyewitness tradition of the beloved disciple.

b. The Elusiveness of the Risen Jesus

Another important influence may well have been the charismatic experience of the Johannine community, by which I mean the experience of the Risen Jesus through the παράκλητος in the church(es) for whom the author was writing. We certainly get the impression from John 3.8 that the Spirit of God is an elusive presence. As Jesus himself puts it, "The Spirit-wind blows wherever it pleases. You hear its sound, but you cannot tell where it comes from or where it is going". The important thing about these words is the remarkable unity between the Spirit of God and Jesus, between the content of these words and the speaker of them. Both of them are elusive in the matter of their whence and whither. In both cases, people are unsure where they have come from or where they are going to.

We can justly assume, therefore, that Jesus' words in John 3.8 reflect something of the experience of the risen Jesus in the community of faith in the late first century. The real presence of the Spirit of God was certainly experienced in this community. The amount of space given to the ministries of the Spirit in the farewell discourses surely bears this out. But what John 3.8 seems to add is the idea that the experience of the Spirit cannot be either assumed or controlled. As Paul Tillich has put it:

> God is always infinitely near and infinitely far. We are fully aware of him only if we experience both of these aspects. But sometimes, when our awareness of him has become shallow, habitual—not warm and not cold—when he has become too familiar to be exciting, too near to be felt in his absolute distance, then he becomes the absent God. The Spirit has not ceased to be present. The Spiritual Presence can never end. But the Spirit of God hides from our sight.[1]

Maybe the Johannine community experienced the Spiritual Presence as a kind of ebb and flow. If so, the author of the fourth gospel—the story of the elusive Christ—was giving poetic voice not only to the elusiveness of the historical Jesus, but also to the elusiveness of the Risen Jesus.

c. The Elusiveness of the Johannine Community

Another historical factor which may have influenced the presentation was the community's own life-story. We need to remember that stories such as John's Gospel were originally written in order to establish a sense of social identity amongst the readership. The Gospels are, in a sense, legitimating narratives. They are narratives which vindicate the social identity of the community for which they were written. Redaction Criticism on John's Gospel has brought the social or community dimension of John's story into sharp focus. Scholars such as J.L. Martyn and R.E. Brown have demonstrated that John's story reflects a community in crisis, a community undergoing the painful process of asocialisation. Arguing in particular from the references to excommunication from the synagogues in 9.22, 12.42 and 16.2, scholars in this mould have cogently depicted the first readers of the gospel as, in the main, Jewish Christians who have been persecuted and pursued by non-Christian Jews. If there is any truth in this, then the story of Jesus' elusiveness in John may have been influenced by the experience of excommunicated Johannine Christians. The hiding of the Johannine Jews may reflect the strategies of concealment employed by the Johannine community. The secret movements of John's Jesus may reflect the secrecy

---

[1] P. Tillich, *The Eternal Now* (London: SCM Press, 1963), p. 73.

enforced upon Johannine Christians by the Jewish persecution. The geographical vagueness and dislocation of John's Jesus ("where is he?") may reflect the geographical mystery of the community's whereabouts after the excommunication ban came into operation, and so on.

6. A THEOLOGICAL EXPLANATION FOR THIS THEME IN JOHN

There are therefore literary, historical and sociohistorical reasons for John's striking portrait of the elusive Christ. In all of this, however, we must not forget the theological explanation for John's focus on the elusiveness of Christ. John's Gospel is a story which stresses that the invisible, eternal and transcendent God has made himself accessible to us in Jesus Christ. Jesus says in Jn 10.30, "I and the Father are one". Whether John intends us to think in terms of a functional oneness (a oneness of acts) or an ontological oneness (a oneness of being) is unclear. One thing is certain: that Yahweh, the Father, has become visible in Jesus. Consequently, John's Jesus takes on the characteristics of the Old Testament God. One of the characteristics of Yahweh, as we have seen, is his hiddenness and his transcendent elusiveness. John's portrait of God preserves these features; three times John stresses that "no one has ever seen the Father" except Jesus (1.18; 5.37; 6.46). John also omits any reference to an open heaven in the baptism of Jesus. In the light of these comments, a theological explanation for the theme of the elusive Christ seems in order. The portrait of the Christ who is *absconditus atque praesens*, the elusive discloser, is John's creative way of handling the paradox of the visibility of the invisible God in Jesus. In depicting Jesus as the concealed revealer, John has cleverly integrated the elusive transcendence of God, so precious to Judaism, with the accessible immanence of God, so precious to Christianity.

7. CONCLUSION

I have shown in this essay that the elusiveness of Jesus is one of the most striking facets of John's literary art. Indeed, it is this feature which accounts for the excitement of John's plot for the first-time readers. In chs. 1-5, Jesus proves evasive in his language with his mother (2.4), the Jews (2.19-21), Nicodemus (3.3-10), the Samaritan woman (4.10-15), his disciples (4.31-33) and the royal official (4.48). In John 5.1-10.42, Jesus' elusiveness is now focused on his movements more than on his language. It is in this section of the gospel that attempts are made to arrest and kill Jesus, and it is in this section that the theme of Jesus' mysterious escapes comes to the fore. In chs. 11 and 12, the tension mounts as Jesus openly returns to the place of maximum danger and as the Sanhedrin formally plot to have Jesus killed. Here Jesus' elusiveness is deliberately understated as the protagonist plays into the hands of the *theomachus*, the enemy of God (the Jewish antagonists). In chs. 13-17, Jesus' elusiveness is visible in the interpretative difficulties experienced by the disciples (until 16.29). Then in chs 18-19, Jesus gives himself up to those who have found him elusive since 5.16-18. Finally in chs 20-21, the theme returns in the context of the resurrection. Now it is the risen Jesus who proves elusive (see 13.33, 36; 16.16; then 20.2, 14; 21.4).

For the first-time readers of John's story, the elusiveness of Jesus is a key factor in the creation of suspense, movement and tension. John's Gospel, for such a reader, is very much a combination of an adventure story ("where is he?") and a mystery story ("who is he?"). However, this elusiveness is also a crucial device for encouraging rereadings of the Gospel. The obscurity of the protagonist is one of the major literary devices used by the author to create a narrative text which is inexhaustible in terms of its secrets and tantalising in terms of its elusiveness. In short, there is a mysterious, 'multi-story' character about John's narrative which is reflected in the characterisation of Jesus. That is why John's story has been compared to a magic pool in which children can paddle and in which elephants can swim. In many respects it is John's characterisation of Jesus as the elusive Christ which most contributes towards this hermeneutical seduction of the reader by the text. There is an elusiveness about Jesus, about the author, about the Gospel, and about the community, which means that people will continue to drink deep of John's mysteries long after their first encounter with the text is a forgotten memory.

LITERARY APPROACHES TO JOHN—
A BIBLIOGRAPHY

Balmforth, H. "The Structure of the Fourth Gospel", *Studia Evangelica* Vol.II (1961) pp. 25-33.

Bartholomew, G.L. "Feed my Lambs: John 21.15-19 as Oral Gospel", *Semeia* 39 (1987) pp. 69-96.

Beutler, J. "Zur Struktur von Johannes 6", *Studien zum Neuen Testament und seiner Umwelt* 16 (1991) pp. 89-104.

Black, D. "On the Style and Significance of John 17", *Criswell Theological Review* 3/1 (1988) pp. 141-59.

Boers, H. "Discourse Structure and Macro-structure in the Interpretation of Texts: Jn 4.1-42 as an Example", in Achtemeier, P.J. ed. *SBL 1980 Seminar Papers*, pp. 159-182. (Chico: Scholars Press 1980).

——, *Neither on this Mountain nor in Jerusalem. A study of John 4.* SBL Monograph Series no.35. (Atlanta: Scholars Press 1988).

Born, J.B. "Literary Features in the Gospel of John", *Direction* 17.2 (1988) pp. 3-17.

Botha, J.E. "John 14.16: A Difficult Text Speech Act Theoretically Revisited", *Scriptura* 35 (1990) pp. 1-9.

——, "Reader Entrapment as a Literary Device in John 4.1-42", *Neotestamentica* 24/1 (1990) pp. 37-47.

——, *Jesus & the Samaritan Woman. A Speech Act Reading of John 4.1-42.* Supplements to NovTest. Vol. LXV. (Leiden: E.J.Brill 1991).

——, "The Case of Johannine Irony Reopened I: The Problematic Current Situation", *Neotestamentica* 25/2 (1991) pp. 209-220.

——, "The Case of Johannine Irony Reopened II: Suggestions, Alternative Approaches", *Neotestamentica* 25/2 (1991) pp. 221-232.

Bowen, C. "The Fourth Gospel as Dramatic Material", *JBL* 49 (1930) pp. 292-305.

Braun, W. "Resisting John: Ambivalent Redactor and Defensive Reader of the Fourth Gospel", *Studies in Religion/Sciences Religieuses* 19 (1990) pp. 59-71.

Brown, R.E. *The Gospel According to John.* Vols I & II. (London: Geoffrey Chapman 1966, 1970).

——, "The Resurrection in John 20", *Worship* 64/3 (1990) pp. 194-206.

——, "The Resurrection in John 21", *Worship* 64/5 (1990) pp. 433-45.

Brown, S. "The Beloved Disciple: A Jungian View", in Fortna, R.T. & Gaventa, B.R. (eds) *The Conversation Continues: Studies in John and Paul in honour of J.L.Martyn.* (Nashville: Abingdon Press, 1990) pp. 366-77.

Bruns, J.E. "The Use of Time in the Fourth Gospel", *NTS* 13 (1967) pp. 285-90.

Burch, V. *The Structure and Message of St. John's Gospel.* (London: Hopkinson 1928).

Cahill, P.J. "Narrative Art in John IV", *Religious Studies Bulletin* 2 (1982) pp. 41-55.

Calloud, J. & Genuyt, F. *Le Discours d'adieu. Jean 13-17. Analyse Sémiotique.* (Lyon: Centre Thomas More 1985).

——, *L'Evangile de Jean (II), Lecture Sémiotique des chapitres 7 à 12* (L'Arbresle: Centre Thomas More 1987).

——, *L'Evangile de Jean (I), Lecture Sémiotique des chapitres 1 à 6* (L'Arbresle: Centre Thomas More 1989).

Cheetham, F.P. "The Unity of the Fourth Gospel", *Church Quarterly Review* (London, 1924) April, pp. 14-35.

Clavier, H. "La Structure du Quatrième Evangile", *Revue d'Histoire et de Philosophie Religieuses* 35 (1955) pp. 14-95.
——, "Ironie dans le Quatrième Evangile", in Aland.K. et al (eds) *Studia Evangelica, Berlin, Akademie* (1959) pp. 261-76.
Connick, C.M. "The Dramatic Character of the Fourth Gospel", *JBL* 67 (1948) pp. 159-69.
Cook, C. "'I gotta use words when I talk to you': A literary examination of John", *New Blackfriars* 72/852 (1991) pp. 365-376.
Cotterell, P. "The Nicodemus Conversation: A Fresh Appraisal" *ExpTimes* 96 (1984/5) pp. 237-42.
Crossan, J.D. "It is Written: A Structuralist Analysis of John 6", *Semeia* 26 (1983) pp. 3-21.
Culpepper, R.A. *Anatomy of the Fourth Gospel. A Study in Literary Design.* (Philadelphia, Pennsylvania: Fortress Press, 1983).
——, "The Gospel of John and the Jews", *Review and Expositor* 84 (1987) pp. 273-88.
——, "Un example de commentaire fondé sur la critique narrative: Jean 5.1-18", *La Communauté Johannique et son Histoire* (Geneva: Labor et Fides 1990) pp. 136-52.
——, "The Johannine *Hypodeigma*: A Reading of John 13", *Semeia* 53 (1991) pp. 133-52.
Deeks, D. "The Structure of the Fourth Gospel", *NTS* 15 (1968) pp. 107-29.
De Smidt, J.C. "A perspective on John 15.1-8", *Neotestamentica* 25/2 (1991) pp. 251-272.
Dockery, D.S. "Reading John 4.1-45. Some Diverse Hermeneutical Perspectives", *Criswell Theological Review* 3/1 (1988) pp. 127-40.
——, "John 9.1-41: A Narrative Discourse Study", *Occasional Papers in Translation and Textlinguistics* 2/2 (1988) pp.14-26.
Domeris, W.R. "The Johannine Drama", *Journal of Theology for Southern Africa* 42 (1983) pp. 29-35.
——, "The Paraclete as an Ideological Construct: A Study in the Farewell Discourses", *Journal of Theology for South Africa* 67 (1989) pp. 17-23.
Duke, P.D. *Irony in the Fourth Gospel.* (Atlanta: John Knox Press 1985).
Du Rand, J.A. *Die Struktuur van die christologie van die Evangelie van Johannes—metodologiese vorwegings.* (Bloemfontein: Universiteit van die Oranje-Yrystaat, 1982).
——, "Die Evangelie van Johannes as getuigende vertelling", *NGTT* 24 (1983) pp. 383-97.
——, "Die leser in die Evangelie volgens Johannes", *Fax Theologica* 4 (1984) pp. 45-53.
——, "The Characterisation of Jesus as Depicted in the Narrative of the Fourth Gospel", *Neotestamentica* 19 (1985) pp. 18-86.
——, "Plot and Point of View in the Gospel of John", in Petzer J.H. & Hartin P.J. (eds), *A South African Perspective on the New Testament,* (Leiden: E.J.Brill, 1986) pp. 149-69.
——, "Narratological Perspectives on John 13.1-38", *Hervormde Teologiese Studies* (Pretoria) 46/3 (1990) pp. 367-89.
——, "A Syntactical and Narratological Reading of John 10 in Coherence with Chapter 9", in Buetler, J & Fortna, R. (eds) *The Shepherd Discourse of John 10 and its Context.* (Cambridge: Cambridge University Press, 1991) pp. 94-115.
——, "Perspectives on Johannine discipleship according to the farewell discourses", *Neotestamentica* 25/2 (1991) pp. 311-325.
Ellis, P. *The Genius of John: A Composition-Critical Commentary on the Fourth Gospel.* (Collegeville, Minnesota: Liturgical Press, 1984).
Eslinger,L. "The Wooing of the Woman at the Well: Jesus, the Reader and Reader-Response Criticism", *Literature and Theology* 1/1 (1987) pp. 167-83.
Flanagan, N. "The Gospel of John as Drama", *Bible Today* 19 (1981) pp. 264-70.
Foster, D. "John Come Lately: The Belated Evangelist", in McConnell (ed) *The Bible and the Narrative Tradition.* (Oxford: Oxford University Press, 1986) pp. 113-31.
Giblin, C.H. "Suggestion, Negative Response and Positive Action in St. John's Portrayal of Jesus", *NTS* 26 (1980) pp. 197-211.
——, "The Miraculous Crossing of the Sea (John 6.16-21)", *NTS* 29 (1983) pp. 96-103.

——,"Confrontations in John 18.1-27", *Biblica* 65 (1984) pp. 210-31.

——,"John's Narration of the Hearing before Pilate", *Biblica* 67 (1986) pp. 221-39.

——,"The Tripartite Narrative Structure of John's Gospel", *Biblica* 72 (1991) pp. 449-68.

Girard, M. "L'Unité de composition de Jean 6, au regard de l'analyse structurel", *L'Eglise et Théologie* 13 (1982) pp. 79-110.

Hartman, L. "An Attempt at a Text-Centred Exegesis of John 21", *Studia Theologia* 38 (1984) pp. 29-45.

Harvey, A.E. *Jesus on Trial. A Study in the Fourth Gospel.* (London: SPCK, 1976).

Henaut, B.W. "John 4.43-54 and the Ambivalent Narrator", *Studies in Religion/Sciences Religieuses* 19, (1990) pp. 287-304 .

Hitchcock, F.R.M. *A Fresh Study of the Fourth Gospel.* (London: SPCK, 1911).

——,"Is the Fourth Gospel a Drama ?" *Theology* 7 (1923) pp. 307-17.

Jonge, de. M. *Jesus: Stranger from Heaven and Son of God.* (Missoula: Scholars Press, 1977).

Kelber, W. "In the Beginning were the Words: The Apotheosis and Narrative Displacements of the Logos", *JAAR* 58/1 (1990) pp. 69-98.

——, "The Birth of a Beginning: John 1.1-18", *Semeia* 52 (1991) pp. 120-44 .

Kennedy, G.A. *New Testament Interpretation through Rhetorical Criticism.* (Chapel Hill: University of North Carolina Press, 1984).

Kermode, F. *The Genesis of Secrecy.* (Cambridge, Mass: Harvard University Press, 1979).

——,"St. John as Poet" *JSNT* 28 (1986) pp. 3-16.

——,"John", in Kermode, F. & Alter. R (eds) *Literary Guide to the Bible.* (Collins: London, 1987) pp. 440-66 .

Kotzé, P.P.A. "John and Reader's Response", *Neotestamentica* 19 (1985) pp. 50-63.

——,"Ironie in die Johannesevangelie", *Hervormde Teologiese Studies* 43 (1985) pp. 431-47.

Kurz, W.S. *Farewell Addresses in the New Testament.* Zaccheus Studies. (Minnesota: Liturgical Press, 1990).

——, "The Beloved Disciple and Implied Readers", *Biblical Theological Bulletin* 19/3 (1989) pp. 100-107.

Kysar, R. *John's Story of Jesus.* (Philadelphia: Fortress, 1984).

——,"Johannine Metaphor—Meaning and Function: A Literary Case Study of John 10.1-18", *Semeia* 53 (1991) pp. 81-112.

Lee, E.K. "The Drama of the Fourth Gospel", *ExpTimes* 65 (1953) pp. 173-76.

Lemmer, H.R. "A possible understanding by the implied reader, of some of the coming-going-being sent pronouncements, in the Johannine farewell discourses", *Neotestamentica* 25/2 (1991) pp. 289-310.

Léon-Dufour, X. "Trois Chiasmes Johanniques", *NTS* 7 (1960) pp. 249-55.

Leroy, H. 1968a. *Rätsel und Misverständnis: Ein Beitrag zur Formgeschichte des Johhannese100vangeliums.* (Bonn: Peter Hanstein, 1968).

——, "Das Johanneische Misverständnis als Literarische Form", *Bibel und Leben* 9 (1968) pp. 196-207.

Liebert, E. "That you may Believe. The Fourth Gospel and Structural Developmental Theory", *BTB* 14 (1984) pp. 67-73.

Lombard, H.A. & Oliver, W.H. "A working supper in Jerusalem: John 13.1-38 introduces Jesus' farewell discourses", *Neotestamentica* 25/2 (1991) pp. 357-378.

MacGregor, G.H.C. & Morton, A.Q. *The Structure of the Fourth Gospel.* (London: Oliver & Boyd, 1961).

MacRae, G.W. "Theology and Irony in the Fourth Gospel", in Clifford. R.J. & MacRae G.W. (eds) *The Word in the World: Essays in honour of F.L. Moriarty.* (Cambridge, Mass.: Weston College, 1973) pp. 83-96.

Malina, B. "The Gospel of John in Sociolinguistic Perspective", in Waetjen H. (ed) *48th Colloquy of the Centre for Hermeneutical Studies.* (Berkeley, California: Centre for Hermeneutical Studies).

McDowell, E. "The Structural Integrity of the Fourth Gospel", *Baptist Review and*

Expositor 34 (1937) pp. 359-67.

McGann, D. *Journeying within Transcendence. A Jungian Perspective on the Fourth Gospel.* (New York: Paulist Press, 1988).

Moore, S.D. "Rifts in (a reading of) the Fourth Gospel, or: does Johannine irony still collapse in a reading that draws attention to itself", *Neotestamentica* 23/1 (1989) pp. 5-17.

Mlakuzhyil, G. *The Christocentric Literary Structure of the Fourth Gospel.* (Rome: Pontificio Instituto Biblico, 1987), Analecta Biblica 117.

Moloney, F.L. "The Structure and Message of John 13.1-38", *Australian Biblical Review* 34 (1986) pp. 1-16 .

——, "The Structure and Message of John 15.1-16.3", *Australian Biblical Review* 35 (1987) pp. 35-49

——, "Reading John 2.13-22: The Purification of the Temple", *Revue Biblique* 97 (1990) pp. 432-52.

——, "A Sacramental Reading of John 13.1-38", *CBQ* 53 (1991) pp. 237-56.

Moore, S. *Literary Criticism and the Gospels: The Theoretical Challenge.* (New Haven: Yale University Press, 1989).

Mourlon-Beernaet, P. "Nicodème et les Croyants. Trois Méthodes de Lecteur", *Telema* 42 (1987) pp. 11-20.

Muilenburg, J.L. "Literary Form in the Fourth Gospel", *JBL* 51 (1932) pp. 40-53.

Myers, D.E. "Irony and Humour in the The Gospel of John" *Occasional Papers in Translation and Textlinguistics* 2/2 (1988) pp. 1-13.

Newman, B.M. Some Observations Regarding the Argument, Structure and Literary Characteristics of the Gospel of John", *Bible Translator* 26 (1975) pp. 234-39.

Neyrey, J.H. "Jesus the Judge: Forensic Process in John 8.21-5" *Biblica* 71 (1990) pp. 509-41.

Nicholson, G.C. *Death as Departure.* (Chico, California: Scholars Press, 1983).

Nortje, S.J. "The Role of Women in the Fourth Gospel", *Neotestamentica* 20 (1986) pp. 21-33.

Nuttall, A.D. *Overheard by God: Fiction and Prayer in Herbert, Milton, Dante and St.John.* (London: Methuen, 1980).

O'Day, G. *Revelation in the Fourth Gospel: Narrative Mode and Theological Claim* (Philadelphia: Fortress 1986).

——, "Narrative Mode and Theological Claim: A Study in the Fourth Gospel" . *JBL* 105/4 (1986) pp. 657-68 .

——, *The Word Disclosed. John's Story and Narrative Preaching.* (St Louis, Missouri: CBP Press, 1988).

——, "'I have overcome the world' (John 16.33): Narrative Time in John 13-17", *Semeia* 53 (1991) pp. 153-66.

Okure, T. *The Johannine Approach to Mission. A Contextual Study af John 4.1-42.* (Tübingen: Mohr, 1988).

Olsson, B. *Structure and Meaning in the Fourth Gospel.* (Uppsala: Lund, 1974).

O'Rourke, J. "Asides in the Gospel of John", *NovTest* 21, (1979) pp. 210-19.

Ostenstad, G. "The Structure of the Fourth Gospel: Can it be Defined Objectively", *Studia Theologica* 45/1 (1991) pp. 33-55.

Pamment/Davies, M. "Focus in the Fourth Gospel", *ExpTimes* 97, (1985) pp. 71-75.

Pamment, M. *Rhetoric and Reference in the Gospel of John,* (Sheffield: Sheffield Academic Press, 1992).

Patte, D. "Narrative and Discourse in Structural Exegesis: John 6 and 1 Thessalonians", *Semeia* 26 (1983) pp. 85-106.

——, *Structural Exegesis for New Testament Critics.* (Minneapolis: Fortress Press, 1990).

Phillips, G.A. "'This is a Hard Saying. Who can be a Listener to it?': Creating a Reader in John 6" *Semeia* 26 (1983) pp. 23-56.

Pierce, E.L. 1960. "The Fourth Gospel as Drama", *Religion in Life* 29 (1960) pp. 453-55.

Reinhartz, A. "Great Expectations: A Reader-oriented Approach to Johannine Christology and Eschatology", *Literature & Theology* 3 (1989) pp. 61-76.

——, "Jesus as Prophet: Predictive Prolepses in the Fourth Gospel", *JSNT* 36 (1989) pp. 3-16.

Resseguie, J.L. "John 9: A Literary-Critical Analysis", in Gros Louis, K. (ed) *Literary Interpretations of Biblical Narratives*. Vol.II. (Nashville: Abindon Press, 1982).

Richard, E. "Expressions of Double Meaning and their Function in the Gospel of John", *NTS* 31 (1985) pp. 96-112 .

Rissi, M. "Der Aufbau des vierten Evangeliums", *NTS* 29 (1983) pp. 43-54.

Roth, W. "Scriptural Coding in the Fourth Gospel", *Biblical Research* 32 (1987) pp. 6-29.

Rudel, P. "Das Missverständnis im Johannesevangelium", *Neue Kirchliche Zeitschrift* 3 (1921) pp. 351-61.

Sands, P.C. *Literary Genius of the New Testament*. (Oxford: Oxford University Press, 1932).

Schneiders, S.M. "Women in the Fourth Gospel and the Role of Women in the Contemporary Church", *BTB* 122 (1982) pp. 35-45.

Schram, T. "The Logical Structure of John's Gospel", *Notes on Translation* 4/3 (1990) pp. 24-30.

Segovia, F.F. "The Structure, *Tendenz* and *Sitz im Leben* of John 13.31-14.31", *JBL* 104 (1985) pp. 471-93.

——, *The Farewell of the Word. The Johannine Call to Abide*. (Minneapolis: Fortress Press, 1991).

——, "The Journey(s) of the Word of God", *Semeia* 53 (1991) pp. 23-54.

——, "The Final Farewell of Jesus: A Reading of John 20.30-21.25", *Semeia* 53 (1991) pp. 167-190.

——, "Towards a New Direction in Johannine Scholarship: The Fourth Gospel from a Literary Perspective", *Semeia* 53 (1991) pp. 1-22.

——, *The Prayer of the Word: A Johannine Call to Unity*. (Minneapolis: Fortress Press, forthcoming).

Simoens, Y. *La Gloire D'Aimer: Structures Stylistiques et Interpretatives dans le Discours de Cène (Jn 13-17)*. AB 90. (Rome: Biblical Institute Press, 1981).

Staley, J. *The Print's First Kiss: A Rhetorical Investigation of the Implied Reader in the Fourth Gospel*. SBL Dissertation Series 82. (Atlanta: Scholars Press, 1986).

——, "The Structure of John's Prologue: its Implications for the Gospel's Narrative Structure", *CBQ* 48 (1986) pp. 241-64.

——, "Stumbling in the Dark, Reaching for the Light: Reading Character in John 5 and 9", *Semeia* 53 (1991) pp. 55-80.

Stibbe, M.W.G. "The Elusive Christ: A New Reading of the Fourth Gospel. *JSNT* 44 (1991) pp. 20-39.

——, *John as Storyteller: Narrative Criticism and the Fourth Gospel*. SNTS Monograph Series 73, (Cambridge: Cambridge University Press 1992).

——, "John 11.1-44: The Raising of Lazarus in Narrative-Critical Perspective", *NTS*, forthcoming (1993).

——, *John: A Readings Commentary*. Readings Series. (Sheffield: Sheffield Academic Press, 1993).

——, "Return to Sender: A Structural Analysis of John's Plot", *Biblical Interpretation*, (1993).

Talbert, C.H. "Artistry and Theology: An Analysis of the Architecture of John 1.19-5.47", *CBQ* 32 (1970) pp. 341-66.

Tenney, M.C. "The Footnotes of John's Gospel", *Bibliotheca Sacra* 117 (1970) pp. 350-64.

——, "The Symphonic Structure of John", *Bibliotheca Sacra* 120 (1963) pp. 117-25.

——, "The Imagery of John" *Bibliotheca Sacra* 121 (1964) pp. 13-21.

Theissen, K. "Jesus and Women in the Gospel of John", *Direction* 19/2 (1990) pp. 52-64.

Theron, S.W. "A Multi-Faceted Approach to an Important Thrust in the Prayer of Jesus in John 17", *Neotestamentica* 21/1 (1987) pp. 77-94.

Thompson, M. *The Humanity of Jesus in the Fourth Gospel*. (Philadelphia: Fortress Press,

1988).

Thyen, H. "Johannesbriefe", *Theologische Realenzyklopädie* 17 (1987) pp. 186-200 .

——, "Johannesevangelium", *Theologische Realenzyklopädie* 17 (1987) pp. 200-25.

Tolmie, D.F. "The function of focalisation in John 13-17", *Neotestamentica* 25/2 (1991) pp. 273-287.

Topel, L.J. "A Note on the Methodology of Structural Analysis in Jn 2.23-3.21", *CBQ* 33 (1971) pp. 211-20.

Upkong, J.S. "Jesus' Prayer for his Followers (Jn 17) in Mission Perspective", *Africa Theological Journal* 18/1 (1989) pp. 49-60.

Van Belle, G. *Les Parenthèses dans L'Evangile de Jean.* (Leuven: Peeters, 1985).

Van den Bussche, H. "De Structuur van het vierde evangelie", *Collationes Brugenses et Gandavenses.* Brugge (1956) pp. 182-99.

Van Tilborg, S. "The Gospel of John: Communicative Processes in a Narrative Text", *Neotestamentica* 23 (1989) pp. 19-27.

von Wahlde, U. "Literary Structure and Theological Argument in Three Discourses with the Jews in the Fourth Gospel", *JBL* 103 (1984) pp. 575-84.

Wead, D. *The Literary Devices in John's Gospel.* (Basel: Reinhardt, 1970).

——, "Johannine Irony as a Key to the Author-Audience Relationship in John's Gospel", in F.O. Francis (ed) American Academy of Religion, Biblical Literature: 1974. (Missoula: Scholars Press, 1974) pp. 33-50.

Webster, E.C. 1982. "Pattern in the Fourth Gospel", in Clines D. & Gunn. D. (eds) *Art and Meaning.* (Sheffield: JSOT Press, 1982) pp. 230-57.

Windisch, H. "Der Johanneische Erzählungsstil", in *Eucharisterion: Studien zur Religion und Literatur des Alten und Neuen Testaments, Festschrift für H. Gunkel,* Vol.II. (Göttingen: Vandenhoeck, 1923) pp. 174-213. [English Transtlation in the present volume.]

Wuellner, W. "Putting Life back into the Lazarus Story and its Reading: The Narrative Rhetoric of John 11 as the Narration of Faith", *Semeia* 54 (1991) pp. 113-131.

NEW TESTAMENT
TOOLS AND STUDIES

edited by

Bruce M. Metzger, Ph.D., D.D., L.H.D., D. Theol., D. Litt.

and

Bart D. Ehrman, Ph.D.